The Learning Revolution

The Learning Revolution

The Challenge of Information Technology in the Academy

Diana G. Oblinger
Sean C. Rush
Editors
IBM North America

Anker Publishing Company, Inc.
Bolton, MA

The Learning Revolution

The Challenge of Information Technology in the Academy

ISBN 1-882982-17-7

Composition by Deerfoot Studios
Cover design by Deerfoot Studios

Anker Publishing Company, Inc.
176 Ballville Road
P.O. Box 249
Bolton, MA 01740-0249

About the Authors

Robert E. Dunham. Dr. Dunham is Senior Vice President and Dean of the Commonwealth Education System of The Pennsylvania State University, responsible for the academic and administrative affairs for the 17 undergraduate campuses and one graduate center of Penn State. Dunham spearheaded the creation of Project Vision, an active and collaborative learning project.

Gregory C. Farrington. Dr. Farrington is Dean of the School of Engineering and Applied Science and Professor of Materials Science and Engineering at the University of Pennsylvania. He has served in a variety of university and government positions and committees and is the author or coauthor of more than 100 papers on the synthesis, structure, and transport characteristics of conductive ceramics and polymers. Farrington holds 27 patents. At the University of Pennsylvania he has been very active in leading the university in issues related to the new uses of information technology in education.

Thomas K. Hearn, Jr. Dr. Hearn has been President of Wake Forest University since 1986, during which time it has come to be recognized as one of the nation's outstanding private universities. Hearn is broadly involved in civic leadership activities and holds an appointed position on the North Carolina Education Standards and Accountability Commission. He currently chairs the state Transit 2001 Commission. The senior member of the Atlantic Coast Conference of university presidents, Hearn has been a leader in collegiate athletic reform.

Michael Hooker. Dr. Hooker is Chancellor at the University of North Carolina at Chapel Hill, and was previously President of Bennington College, President of the University of Maryland-Baltimore County, and President of the five-campus University of Massachusetts system. Hooker has been a national leader in educational organizations and serves on several corporate boards.

Michael O. Leavitt. The Honorable Michael O. Leavitt has been Governor of Utah since January of 1993. He has shown leadership on issues such as creating better schools and taking advantage of the tools of information technology through initiatives such as SmartStates which is focused on developing public-private partnerships to deliver state services through electronic commerce. The governor has held regional and national leadership roles among governors, such as the immediate past chair of the Republican Governors' Association and the Western Governors' Association as well as the president of the Council of State Governments.

William F. Massy. Dr. Massy is President of the Jackson Hole Higher Education Group, with 25 years prior experience as a university administrator, including 14 years as Stanford University's Vice President for Business and Finance and Chief Financial Officer, Vice Provost for Research, Acting Provost, and Director of the Doctoral Program and Associate Dean of the Graduate School of Business. In 1987 he founded the Stanford Institute for Higher Education Research (SIHER).

A. Frank Mayadas. Dr. Mayadas joined the Alfred P. Sloan Foundation in 1993 where he focuses on learning outside the classroom using computer and electronic communications-based education and training. Prior to joining the Sloan Foundation, Mayadas spent 27 years with IBM Corporation holding positions as Vice President, Research Division; Vice President, Technology and Solutions Development; and General Manager, University and College Systems. Mayadas has published more than 35 papers and holds several patents and awards from IBM.

Steve H. Nickles. Mr. Nickles is the Bess and Walter Williams Distinguished Professor of Law at Wake Forest University. Previously he taught at the University of Minnesota Law School where he worked with Lotus and West Publishing Company to put Lotus Notes to use in a law school course. Since then Nickles has worked with many other law schools helping law faculty use Notes for collaborative and distance learning as well as for publishing.

Terry O'Banion. Dr. O'Banion is the Executive Director of the League for Innovation in the Community College, an international consortium of leading community colleges in the United States and Canada dedicated to experimentation and innovation. In his 36 years in community college education, O'Banion has served in several faculty and administrative positions and has authored 12 books, and more than 100 articles, chapters, and monographs on community college education.

Diana G. Oblinger. Dr. Oblinger is Manager, Academic Programs and Strategy, IBM North America. She is known for her leadership in teaching and learning, including advancing the concept of student mobile computing and distributed instruction. Oblinger has also served as the program manager for the Institute for Academic Technology, a collaboration between IBM and the University of North Carolina at Chapel Hill. Prior to joining

IBM, Oblinger was responsible for managing the academic programs of 17 departments with 250 faculty and over 2,000 students at the University of Missouri-Columbia. She also spent several years on the faculty at the University of Missouri and at Michigan State University in teaching, advising, and research. Oblinger is the author of numerous papers on multimedia, enhancing instruction with technology, and academic advising. She has received three outstanding teaching awards, an outstanding research award, and was recently named Young Alumnus of the Year by Iowa State University. She has received several awards since joining IBM.

Craig Runde. Mr. Runde is Director of the Legal Education Division at the West Publishing Information Group, where he develops new technological tools for use in law schools, including the West Education Network. He has served on the research and development teams that created the WESTLAW on-line legal research service and the West CD-ROM legal libraries. Runde has served as an adjunct faculty member at the University of Minnesota Law School teaching computer applications in the law.

Sean C. Rush. Mr. Rush is General Manager of Higher Education, IBM North America, which includes the sales, consulting, and industry solutions teams dedicated to higher education issues. Mr. Rush has 25 years of professional experience working with service sector organizations. Prior to joining IBM in 1994, he spent 14 years as a consultant for Coopers & Lybrand, LLP in Boston where he served as chairman of the firm's National Higher Education and Not-for-Profit practice, which is responsible for more than 2,000 clients throughout the United States. He concurrently served as partner-in-charge of Coopers & Lybrand's Higher Education Consulting practice, providing financial, operational, and planning services to colleges, universities, and other nonprofit organizations. Throughout his career, Rush has worked with more than 75 public and private institutions in the areas of total quality management, business process reengineering, and operations management. Rush has published numerous books and articles in the area of higher education and is a member of several higher education organizations.

Donald Sargeant. Dr. Sargeant, Chancellor of the University of Minnesota at Crookston, is recognized for creating "ThinkPad University," a program where all students and faculty were provided with laptop computers beginning in 1993. His leadership of this program has attracted more than 100 institutions to visit the Crookston campus since its inception. He has worked with computers in teaching and learning for over 30 years.

Virginia D. Sorkin. Ms. Sorkin is the coordinator of the National Digital Library Visitors' Center of the Library of Congress which is responsible for the National Digital Library Program's public and staff outreach. She is active in Internet-related issues and activities and has managed projects in the Library of Congress automation office.

Suzanne E. Thorin. Ms. Thorin is Dean of University Libraries at Indiana University and formerly the associate librarian and chief of staff for the Library of Congress. She has played a key role in establishing and administering the National Digital Library Program as well as having served as the US Representative to the G-7 Bibliotheca Universalis (National Digital Library Working Group).

Charlie Tuller. Mr. Tuller is Technical Advisor to the IBM Senior Vice President and Group Executive of the Software group. Tuller has held a number of senior advisory positions in IBM involving strategy for both hardware and software.

Jack M. Wilson. Dr. Wilson is Dean of Undergraduate and Continuing Education and Professor of Physics at Rensselaer Polytechnic Institute. Known best for designing "studio" courses, Wilson has also served in various national offices in disciplinary societies for physics, computing, and higher education. He has authored two books, edited three, and published over 100 articles in physics research, science education, and computing.

Contents

Part 3: Looking to the Future

Preface

We have both spent our professional careers working with higher education. During those years there has been a gradual crescendo in the calls for reform. A 1983 report from the National Commission on Excellence in Education, *A Nation at Risk*, stimulated many to begin thinking about the future of education. Changes in our society and economic foundations have made education more important today than ever before and have increased the need to think about how higher education's future should be charted.

Another landmark report, *An American Imperative* (Wingspread, 1993), calls for the redesign of education. This is the first major report that placed learning at the center of the academic enterprise. The report poses such questions as

- In what ways have we organized our programs to develop and support a capacity for lifelong learning among our students?
- In what ways are we applying what is known about learning to the teaching practices of our faculty and graduate students? How do our pedagogical approaches enhance learning, and where do they fall short?
- How do we encourage and assist students to develop the basic values required for learning; e.g., self-discipline, perseverance, responsibility, hard work, intellectual openness?
- How have we tried to integrate curricular offerings for the benefit of students and faculty? Is "course sprawl" contributing to our budgetary problems and making it more difficult for students to register in courses required for graduation? What might be done?
- To what extent are our educational programs, class schedules, registration, and other administrative and support services organized around the needs of learners rather than the convenience of the institution? What improvements can we make?
- In what ways could we do a better job of helping our students to attain higher levels of both knowledge and skills?

As we work with colleges and universities across North America, we find exemplary programs which place learning and student needs at the center of the academic enterprise. In our opinion, these programs not only deserve honorable mention, but programs like them will be necessary for institutions to maintain their competitive position in the future. Why? Because there is a learning revolution underway.

There are fundamental changes occurring in higher education. For example, in working with one North American institution, its rationale for responding to change is articulated through four institutional issues. These issues are replicated with similar phrases across much of higher education.

Productivity

With declining budgets and increasing enrollments in higher education, there is a push to find new ways to accomplish its teaching mission while competing with other institutions for a limited pool of funds.

Quality

The institution takes pride in both its faculty and students and seeks to enhance quality rather than diminish it in the pursuit of productivity. Maintaining such high standards in the context of rapid change will require great attention to the institution's academic and social values. The commitment to both access and community are obvious and provide a foundation on which to strengthen the manifestation of quality.

Access

There is greater demand for the institution's educational services than the current infrastructure can provide. This demand is expected to continue. The commitment to students, both traditional and nontraditional, is causing the institution to look for more flexible ways of providing education to students.

Competitiveness

Other colleges challenge the institution's strategic position for funds and students. It is expected that competition with other institutions for high quality students will intensify. The institution will need to establish a competitive edge in a student-based market.

The purpose of this book is to share information on how a variety of institutions are using technology to respond to these types of challenges. A common theme from these colleges and universities is their focus on learning and on student needs and how technology can serve both.

Our first chapter lays the groundwork for many of the external variables in the learning revolution. From within higher education, Michael Hooker, Chancellor of the University of North Carolina at Chapel Hill, articulates some of the fundamental changes that are driving the transformation of higher education: the information revolution, the management revolution, and public scrutiny. He cautions us that we have been so expert at thinking and talking about the changes to come that we may have become numbed to what they will mean.

Change is the central theme of Charlie Tuller's chapter. As senior vice president and strategist for IBM, Tuller is a spokesperson for how information technology is a transformation agent that will affect everything: individuals, institutions, and society. Key themes of information empowerment, getting connected, and time compression help us understand why technology is having such a dramatic impact on our lifestyles and workstyles.

Providing us with a vision of what education will be like, Gregory Farrington, Dean of Engineering and Applied Science at the University of Pennsylvania, illustrates how the computer revolution has provided us with new educational tools that challenge us to not just preach change, but to practice it. As he notes, the new tools will open new markets for traditional educational institutions as well as expose them to vigorous competition.

Several chapters have been contributed by the practitioners of change. Don Sargeant, Chancellor of the University of Minnesota at Crookston, led the initiative to require laptop computers for all faculty and students. Although UMC may be best known for student mobile computing, Sargeant's chapter outlines the educational rationale that led to the program. To make it a success required much deeper institutional changes that involved faculty, curricula, financial creativity, and active teamwork across the institution.

Project Vision, a program designed to establish a more active and collaborative learning environment, was led by Bob Dunham, Senior Vice President of the Commonwealth Educational Systems at The Pennsylvania State University. Dunham's vision was to move the CES from a teaching environment to one where the emphasis was on students and faculty learning together. Project Vision was successful, not only in its stated goals, but in creating an environment for change that has spread across the 17 campus system.

Jack Wilson from Rensselaer Polytechnic Institute, traces the reengineering of the undergraduate curriculum at RPI. Wilson, a physicist, has been a leader in helping institutions understand the changes possible with the appropriate application of computing, communications, and collaboration.

Professional education is often regarded as different from the traditional undergraduate program. As an example of how professional education is changing, Steve Nickles and Craig Runde describe their work in collaborative legal education. They used a principle of maximizing learning by encouraging participation in the process of discovery. Discussion databases and guest participants (judges, lawyers, business people and faculty from other departments) provided considerable motivation and momentum to the first-year law class. As an indicator of the success of Nickles and Runde's work, their format for collaborative legal education expanded to over a dozen institutions in just its first year.

In a summary of the creativity community colleges have applied to technology in improving teaching and learning, Terry O'Banion, Executive Director of the League for Innovation in the Community College, provides compelling examples of change. The Community College of Denver, Lane Community College, Palomar College, the Maricopa Community Colleges, and Sinclair Community College form his case studies in tracing the development of "the learning college." In unique ways, each vignette illustrates how these institutions have made learners the most important people in the institution; everyone else is there to facilitate and support student learning.

President Thomas K. Hearn, Jr. of Wake Forest University traces this institution's efforts to balance tradition and change. Even with a strong sense of community, Wake Forest found it could not remain unaffected by the greater social and scholastic changes of the past half century. Their Plan for the Class of 2000 emphasizes that Wake Forest's academic advantage comes from providing education that is both personal and individual. The plan recognizes that the computer has become a basic tool of scholarship and a communications device suited to the nomadic lifestyle of students. The Plan for the Class of 2000 seeks to merge technology and Wake Forest's traditions to maximize the quality of student learning.

None of us can imagine education without access to the library. Libraries serve as collections of history, culture, and insight, offering access to information. However, the library of the future will be different than the site-specific facilities to which we are accustomed. Suzanne Thorin and Virginia Sorkin provide a view of the promise and problems surrounding the library of the future. Issues of content, cost, intellectual property rights, and competition are among the problems. The promise is clearly illustrated by examples of work at the Library of Congress.

A bold move by the Western Governors' Association has led to the development of a learning enterprise for the "CyberCentury:" The Western Governors University. The Honorable Michael O. Leavitt, Governor of Utah, captures the excitement and complexity of creating a new university for a new generation. With the country's economic success or failure dependent on how the learning needs of the 21st century are addressed, WGU seeks to increase access to lifelong learning and open the market for educational services to both public and private educational institutions. The challenges will be overcoming bureaucracy, tradition, regulation, and turf.

As the former chief financial officer of Stanford University and now President of the Jackson Hole Higher Education Group, Bill Massy begins by asking what colleges and universities will be like in the post-handicraft era. In contrast to the fear this image creates for some, Massy paints a picture of the opportunity ahead. His thesis is that information technology permits subject-matter and learning-process experts to project themselves across space and time. In addition to reaching locales and circumstances that better fit the needs of learners, he illustrates how learning can be accomplished at less cost without compromising quality.

Work supported by the Sloan Foundation on asynchronous learning networks is exploring the potential of ALNs to provide learning to anyone who wishes to learn, at a time and place of the learner's choice. Frank Mayadas of the Sloan Foundation provides an introduction to the concept of ALNs as well as case studies from several institutions. In addition to highlighting the conclusions of their research, Mayadas reviews work in progress that provides insight into issues of efficiency and scalability.

The final chapter summarizes many of the challenges identified by the various authors of this book. There will be resistance to change in higher education. Not only will individuals protect their territory, but education's traditional structures may limit change. Funding formulas, governance, culture, and curricular changes will need to be rethought. The fears of technology will need to be balanced by its potential.

We believe that there is a learning revolution underway. The chapters contributed by our colleagues illustrate how public and private institutions are providing leadership for this revolution. We hope they will provide insight, inspiration, and a compulsion for action.

Diana G. Oblinger

Sean C. Rush

ACKNOWLEDGEMENTS

Our thanks to a dedicated team of IBM personnel deployed throughout North America. Through close relationships with individuals in higher education, they have brought us in contact with the authors of this book. They recognized the insight and innovation these individuals and their institutions represented. These are not the only examples of innovation, to be sure, and we hope future books will share additional examples of commitment to learners and innovation.

We also thank the many others who have shared ideas and opinions with us. Even though they may not be represented in this work, they are here in spirit.

Diana G. Oblinger and Sean C. Rush

Over the past few years, IBM has provided me with a wonderful opportunity to experience my own learning revolution. I have been enriched by relationships with educators across North America who share a passion for learning. I must thank my family for the extra hours they've tolerated seeing me focused on a computer screen. Brian and Adam, you'll never know how much you helped with thoughtful words and small favors. Particular thanks go to my husband who has been supportive of my work, served as a sounding board for ideas, listened for countless hours, and been a consultant-without-pay.

Diana G. Oblinger

I would like to thank my good colleague and co-editor Diana Oblinger whose hard work, much more than mine, made this book a reality. In addition, my thanks to the many colleagues at IBM who have taught and tutored me enormously during my first two years with the company. My hat is off to them for the fabulous job they all do. Finally, I would like to thank my children, Alison and Christopher, for infusing me with their abundant energy; it buoys me each day.

Sean C. Rush

PART 1

UNDERSTANDING THE CHALLENGE

1

The Learning Revolution

Diana G. Oblinger and Sean C. Rush

"The Information Age is an epoch where 'higher education' could occupy the pivotal role in society."

Dolence & Norris, 1995

The American higher education system is the best in the world. It is, however, subject to the same dangers that have caused large corporations to falter. Those that lagged behind in anticipating customer trends were stifled by their own bureaucracy; those that adopted an "if it ain't broke, don't fix it" stance have seen their dominance eroded by smaller, more nimble competitors. Could this happen to higher education?

Dolence and Norris' statement is equivocal. Higher education is in quotation marks. Their view of the future is that higher education will become much broader than our traditional research, liberal arts, and community colleges, that the future will include commercial providers of higher education. They intentionally indicate that while higher education *could* occupy the pivotal role in society, such a position is not a certainty. When members of the academy are asked for their views, they indicate a firm belief that higher education has and will continue to play the pivotal role in society. However, many other people who look out over the next ten years are not so certain.

There is a learning revolution underway. The uncertainty about the future stature of higher education centers around whether these institutions are leaders of the learning revolution or bystanders.

What has changed so radically that higher education's traditions are inadequate? After all, few institutions have exhibited as much stability as higher education. "Many within the academy would argue that the critics do not understand how a college or university works. Those outside the academy would offer the counterpoint that the academy does not know how the 'real world' works" (Johnson & Rush, 1995).

The Real World

Society is being transformed by global competition and the power of technology. Futurists have coined a variety of phrases to describe our emerging world: "knowledge economy," "information age," or "digital economy" are only a few. Regardless of the term, change is the focus, with technology increasing the pace of transformation. What is happening in the "real world" that has such potential impact on higher education?

Indicators of Change

Volume of information. The volume of new information is increasing at such a rapid pace that the class of 2000 will be exposed to more new data in a year than their grandparents encountered in a lifetime. Knowledge doubles every seven years. Ten thousand scientific articles are published every day (Forman, 1995).

Technological competence. Technology is now a competency that is required in the workforce; it is becoming another basic skill. Sixty-five percent of all workers use some type of information technology in their jobs. By the year 2000, this number will increase to 95%.

Telecommuting. By the year 2000, 50% of the working population of the US will be employed in home-based business. In 1994, 39 million employees worked from a home office, 29 million in home-based businesses (National Home Business Association). Telecommuting is becoming a way of life.

Collaboration. The capacity for individuals to use technology independently and collaboratively in their work is increasingly required (Hall, 1995). No one person has all the competencies needed in today's high performance workplace.

Reskilling. It is estimated that the shelf life of a technical degree today is only five years. Although many of the critical skills required in the high performance workplace have not changed (e.g., science, engineering, finance, and law), the pace of knowledge advancement requires constant updating (Verville, 1995).

Reskilling is becoming a requirement for workers. Companies are reengineering themselves, revamping fundamental work processes, resulting in fewer people left to do more things (Forman, 1995). According to the American Society for Training and Development, by the year 2000, 75% of the current workforce will need to be retrained just to keep up.

Demographics. The changing demographics of higher education are placing new demands on institutions. Students are more diverse; they are older, must balance other life and career priorities, and prefer to attend college on a part-time basis. Individuals expect to have greater access to educational resources and alternatives, particularly from beyond the campus.

Five million working adults are currently enrolled part-time in American colleges and universities. This number masks an even larger adult population that would like to receive a college education but cannot attend a traditional college due to inconvenient class hours, campus inaccessibility, family responsibilities, business travel, or physical disabilities (Vigilante, 1994).

Selectivity. Students are using their purchasing power to be more selective about which institutions they attend. They expect to participate in a learning environment that fosters measurable improvement in their skill development, not just during college, but throughout their careers. Students are increasingly selecting curricula that enhance their chances of initial and sustained employment. "Today's learners are becoming increasingly impatient. Their dealing with world-class service providers in other settings have conditioned them to expect just-in-time and real-time services" (Dolence & Norris, 1995).

Government influence. Governors and other policy makers are pushing to make higher education more affordable and accessible to older, working students, and to make institutions more responsive to the changing workplace where many jobs now require continual retraining (Blumenstyk, 1995). In the western states, governors are discussing the creation of a regional virtual university. Accreditation is being criticized. Various boards and legislators are proposing that tenure be eliminated, or at the very least be reviewed periodically. There is a growing sense that government, not faculty senates, will dictate higher education policy.

Increasing demand. Looking slightly ahead to the year 2000, futurists estimate that just to keep even each individual in the workforce will need to accumulate learning equivalent to that currently associated with 30 credit hours of instruction, every seven years. This could equal over 20 million full-time equivalent (FTE) learners from the workforce. Using our existing educational model, these learners would require an additional 672 campuses with an enrollment of 30,000 students each. To meet the full potential demand by the year 2010, a campus would have to be opened every eight days (Dolence & Norris, 1995).

This is not merely an issue for American higher education. Dolence and Norris (1995) extrapolate the number of FTE learners from the workforce in the US and nine other industrialized countries. Even at a lower rate of retraining, the potential learning pool is over 100 million FTEs and 3,300 campuses. This does not even address the increasing demand for higher education in developing countries.

Transformation of the Workplace

American business has experienced a transformation in the past decade that dwarfs the changes brought about by the industrial revolution. Nearly all businesses are rethinking their strategies and operating structures. Reengineering has become a way of life. Competition is global. Incremental change is not enough. Knowing and anticipating your customers' wants and needs is essential. Organizations are lean, with less managerial direction and more employee empowerment. Teaming and group problem solving are critical skills. Technology and the power of information are key to a competitive edge.

Rapid change. In this business climate, there are significant implications for workers. Consider that more than 75% of the Fortune 1,000 companies are revamping fundamental work processes and undergoing radical change. Consider too the changes brought about by the move from mainframe to client/server applications. Reskilling such a worker calls for over 350 hours of training and an investment of $50,000 per person (Panepinto, 1994). Do the curricula in higher education reflect this rapid rate of change? Do faculty and their courses? Are institutions providing ongoing training for faculty?

Teamwork. The ability to work effectively in teams is an important characteristic of today's high performance workplace. In our current environment, no one person has all the competencies needed to create and deliver the kind of solutions our clients require. Whether in the lab or in the office, we value people who know how to work collaboratively; people who can work with colleagues on a problem or a new product, operating in cross-functional teams of engineers, marketers, lawyers, accountants, and other skilled professionals. These teams need to be increasingly diverse—in a global sense. People from all cultures and all countries will need to be able to effectively communicate as a team in the global market.

Teams are quite different than committees. Conversations and actions within a team focus on the objectives of the team, not on the personal objectives of the team members. Teams effectively organize themselves, efficiently determining roles and ground rules for working together. Teams constantly aim to improve their skill in working on a team (CMI, 1995). Does higher education teach students how to work with people with complementary skills who are committed to a common purpose for which they hold themselves mutually accountable? Is there the opportunity to teach teaming skills? Do faculty practice teaming skills in their own environment?

Decision-making. Increasingly, employees are empowered to make their own decisions. The days of a parent-child like relationship between management and employees are gone from business. In business' flattened organizations, employees are expected to make decisions and to make them quickly. Does higher education teach students the decision-making process? Are students allowed to practice these skills on complex, real world problems? Do faculty understand how decisions are made in business and industry? Are faculty skilled in this process themselves?

Building and applying competencies. The question "What competencies are needed here?" is constantly asked in the business environment. Employees are expected to engage in a constant quest to build their expertise, both in depth and breadth. Those with the greatest competence are expected to mentor others. The competencies of people are an important asset to business products and services (CMI, 1995), and lifelong learning is a requirement. Is this attitude fostered in higher education? Are students internalizing a process where they ask themselves questions such as: What are my competencies? What value have I created through applying these competencies? What skills/capabilities do I need to gain or deepen? This is an attitude and skill that is too important to be relegated to the senior year or to the career placement office. What role does the curriculum and student services play in helping students build and apply their competencies? Can students see this behavior modeled by faculty?

Many feel that there is a mismatch between what education provides and what society and our economy need. Forman (1995) presents a diminishing relationship between what is taught in schools and what is needed in the workplace.

TRADITIONAL EDUCATION	WORKPLACE REQUIREMENTS
Facts	Problem solving
Individual effort	Team skills
Passing a test	Learning how to learn
Achieving a grade	Continuous improvement
Individual courses	Interdisciplinary knowledge
Receiving information	Interacting and processing information
Technology separate from learning	Technology integral to learning

The perceived mismatch is revealed in how employers select new employees. Grades and recommendations from faculty are at the bottom of the list. "Employers say one-fifth of American workers are not fully proficient in their jobs, and they express a lack of confidence in the ability of schools and colleges to prepare young people for the workplace. When asked to rank on a scale of 1 to 5 the factors they use in making hiring decisions, employers ranked at the top applicants' attitudes, communication skills, and work experience. They rank near the bottom applicants' academic performance and the reputation of schools attended, and at the very bottom, recommendations from teachers" (Applebome, 1995).

FACTOR	RANK*
Attitude	4.6
Communication skills	4.2
Previous work experience	4.0
Recommendations from current employees	3.4
Recommendations from previous employer	3.4
Industry-based credentials certifying skills	3.2
Years of schooling completed	2.9
Score on tests administered as part of interview	2.5
Academic performance (grades)	2.5
Experience or reputation of applicant's school	2.4
Teacher recommendations	2.1

*(1=not important, 5=very important)

There is also a trend away from colleges and universities as business' first choice for new professional hires. They are cutting back on the number of new hires from higher education as well as the range of institutions from which they hire. The tendency is to raid the competition for 25 and 26 year olds with a few years of meaningful job experience and a track record of business potential (Geoghegan, 1996).

However, many in the academy argue that the purpose of a college or university education is not to prepare learners for careers. "That question is one of the fault lines running beneath higher education, with two great traditions pushing up against each other. One tradition argues that the pursuit of knowledge for its own sake creates fully-rounded men and women with sharp enough minds to succeed at anything they attempt. The other tradition contends that pursuit of practical knowledge, particularly the scientific, sharpens minds as effectively as the study of Greek or Latin, and addresses the broad needs of the people" (Wingspread Group, 1993).

Irrespective of which position is adopted, the prospect is that organizations other than higher education will fill the gap if traditional institutions do not prepare learners for the succession of careers that awaits them. Graduates now face retooling themselves every three to five years. By the early 21st century this could result in ten or more complete relearning cycles throughout a lifetime (Dolence & Norris, 1995). The pathway from the existing world, where colleges and universities substantially own the teaching franchise, leads to a world where the learning franchise is spread among many providers and new types of facilitators, learning agents, and intermediaries.

Technology Transformation

"Today we are witnessing the early, turbulent days of a revolution as significant as any other in human history. A new medium of human communications is emerging, one that may prove to surpass all previous revolutions—the printing press, the telephone, the television, the computer—in its impact on our economic and social life. Interactive multimedia and the so-called information highway are enabling a new economy based on the networking of human intelligence" (Tapscott, 1996). Whether you think it is a revolution or not, the changes are rapid and widespread.

Computers. The number of homes with PCs is growing at a phenomenal rate. In 1993, 21 million households had PCs; in 1994 the number reached 30 million, a 43% increase. By the end of 1995 there were 45 million households with PCs (Tapscott, 1996). Many of these PCs are multimedia enabled. In 1993, approximately 50% of all PCs shipped were multimedia capable. In 1994 the number rose to 75% with over 90% of the fourth quarter shipments multimedia enabled.

Networking. Networking is growing even faster than computers in the home. In 1994, about 5% of home PCs had modems. That number doubled in 1995 and is expected to double until 1998 when most homes will be connected to the Internet. Networking is the norm in the workplace (Tapscott, 1996).

The Internet carries our network traffic. Conservative estimates put the number of Internet users at around 10 million in 1993, approaching 50 million by the end of 1995. Predictions are for well over 1 billion before the end of the decade; network traffic will exceed telephone traffic (Tapscott, 1996). The average age of an Internet user is twenty-one and declining.

Interest in education. In a Bell Atlantic study, 82% of those polled expressed a residential interest in distance learning. Of commercial applications, the highest category was movies on demand at 84%, only slightly more desired by home users than education users. And the market for home education is drawing a great deal of interest from outside of higher education.

Technology in higher education. The fact that technology is becoming pervasive in homes is in stark contrast to the emphasis put on technology in higher education where access to information is an integral part of the educational process. A formal plan for integrating technology into the curriculum exists at only one-fourth of higher education institutions. The percentage of classes using information technology resources is less than 25%, nationally. Only 10% of classes use the Internet or World Wide Web.

Not only is usage low, but the availability of technology is inadequate. There are 22 students per institutionally owned computer (i.e., those available in public access labs). Fewer than 20% of colleges and universities recommend computer ownership for students, yet nearly 30% of students in US higher education own a computer (Green, 1995).

The Academy

Many question whether today's classrooms prepare students to be lifelong, adaptable learners. A majority of institutions construe teaching almost entirely in terms of lecturing (Barr & Tagg, 1995). Although lecture may be an effective instructional style for some students, it is not for all. Research on the effectiveness of lecture does not support it as the best method of developing learner competencies of critical thinking, problem solving, and lifelong learning.

The Status Quo

Dominance of lecture. Collaboration is an atypical style in higher education classrooms; approximately 80% of teaching is in the form of lecture. Unfortunately, the dominance of lectures does not indicate it is the most effective learning modality. "A major flaw in lecture-textbook courses is that students are mostly treated in the same way, with only minor individualization. The courses proceed in lock-step fashion, with no attempt to allow students who need more time to have it" (Bork, 1995).

Teaching emphasis. "Much of classroom teaching is based on faculty presentation of information to a group of students who are then responsible for demonstrating that they have accumulated it. The instructor is on center stage and determines the official agenda of the course. In the audience of lecture halls and classrooms, students are called on occasionally to demonstrate their comprehension and are tested periodically to determine their retention. The emphasis is clearly on teaching with the expectation that if it is done well, students with ability and ambition will learn" (Lemke, 1995).

Little interaction. Interaction—student-to-faculty, student-to-student, and student-to-information—is directly related to improved learning (Fletcher, 1991). However, significant interaction is lacking in most lectures. Research on classroom activity shows that, irrespective of class size, interactions between faculty and students are limited to a few individuals. In classes under 40 students, four or five students dominate the interactions. The remaining 35 are relatively passive; they abdicate in favor of a vocal few. For classes over 40 students, the number of students who interact is even smaller (Karp & Yoels, 1976). In a fifty-minute lecture period, questions and interaction comprises less than five minutes.

Whatever the reason, the existing lecture model lacks significant interaction among faculty and students. However, most students find peer interaction a powerful mode of learning. Eighty-five percent of the nation's first-year higher education students have already studied with other students and 40% have tutored their friends. Yet only 19% have asked a teacher for advice after class (Plater, 1995).

Inefficient learning experience. "The common assumption—that lecturing is an efficient way of transmitting information accurately—is wrong" (Johnstone & Su, 1994). In the average lecture, the instructor delivers about 5,000 spoken words, of which students record only about 500. In a study of chemistry lectures, students recorded about 90% of the blackboard information; they assumed that the blackboard information was sufficient. However, some parts of lectures went almost entirely unrecorded: demonstrations, examples of applications, detailed sequences of logical arguments, and the meanings of technical terms and symbols. Because of differences in student note-taking skills and in working memory, only one-third of students leave lecture with most of the information units recorded. Because lecture notes form the principle source of study material for students, the conclusion was that for two-thirds of the students, lecture was an inefficient medium. "At best, lectures are overviews or outlines of what has to be learned rather than learning experiences in themselves" (Johnstone & Su, 1994).

Re-creation of known results. Classroom experiences tend to be insular. According to Alpert (1991), "In an average classroom, students are persistently asked to produce work for which they can expect no audience other than their teacher. Furthermore, the work assigned to students often involves the re-creation of known results. Often students can assume that their teacher not only has little to learn from their work, but is knowledgeable enough to "fill in the gaps" if it is incomplete or ill-presented. This combination of factors makes many students' work grudging and perfunctory."

Factory model. The way we choose to spend our teaching/learning time conveys messages to students about what is valued and important. "If large amounts of time are devoted to listening to the teacher or working on independent tasks, we do not emphasize the skills needed in today's workplace where power is frequently shared, collaboration encouraged, and higher levels of thinking required. Long held educational models of teacher talk, textbook memorization, and moving people from box to box are poor examples for future workers and professionals" (Adams, Carlson, & Hamm, 1990). Even students who adapt to this model are finding that the skills they learned no longer count for much when they leave school. "The factory model, with its top-down organization, has been replaced in the world outside by new concerns about collective responsibility. This leaves today's students ill-served by the silent and frequently isolated teaching techniques formed in the days of factory assembly lines" (Adams, Carlson, & Hamm, 1990).

Place-based. Higher education today is place-based. The concept of a college or university centers around a physical location. Just as technology is replacing the "place" in workplace, it can replace the physical campus for higher education. For those wishing to look ahead, the question may not be about the campus of the future but the future of the campus (Graves, 1995).

Curricular changes. The educational system is also predicated on relatively inflexible degree programs. On many campuses, curriculum design is essentially a process of adding new courses to a historical base. True reassessment of needs, determination of competencies, and reevaluation of objectives is the exception. "Faculty and their interests dominate the teaching infrastructure. The infrastructure is based on the abilities and interests of faculty members who build individual courses, curricula, and requirements around those interests. Design all too frequently begins with the question "What do I want to teach?" rather than "What do students need to learn?" (Twigg, 1994). Note that skill requirements on the job changed at a rate four to five times faster than curriculum and organizational changes in our schools, leaving a gap between what students learn in the classroom and what is expected of them in the workplace (Daggett, 1992).

Financial structure. Problems arise from the existing financial structure of higher education, as well. "The higher education system as currently financed is not adequately serving the public interest. As long as payments are made to colleges and universities on the basis of intent and not results (for example, graduation rates or the demonstrated competence of graduates), inefficiency is built into the financial structure. As long as the higher education financial structure also includes a faculty reward system that encourages them to pay less attention to public need and more to professional demands, research will continue to be valued over teaching and teaching less over teaching more" (Eaton, 1993).

New Models

The historic stability of higher education may be laudable, but it simply may not be enough in the years ahead. A multibillion dollar learning industry is growing while higher education debates the issues. Although some institutions will survive virtually unchanged, the majority of higher education is facing challenges from students, legislators, parents, the public, and employers. Competitiveness is increasing. Calls for increased access, improved quality, and lower cost abound. There are fundamental shifts in learning needs.

Hundt (1994) suggests that education is about to experience an evolution and transformation of "punctuated equilibrium." According to this ecological doctrine (based on work by Stephen Jay Gould in *The Panda's Thumb*), a static ecosystem does not so much evolve gradually, but occasionally experiences jolts of change that cause entirely new species to emerge suddenly from the great pool of genes and to become dominant. For education, the current equilibrium has long consisted of a closed environment, relying on one-to-many communication as the core of teaching. The extension of networks into the classroom will cause radical change.

Dolence and Norris (1995) outline three questions that must be answered by the stakeholders contemplating the future of higher education:

- Is today's Industrial Age educational model appropriate to the learning needs of the Information Age—for either traditional learners or learners in the workplace?

- Is society willing to pay for a 20th century Industrial Age model in the 21st century Information Age?
- Can academe afford to miss the opportunity of reshaping itself to serve the emerging needs of the Information Age learner?

We believe that the answer to their questions is "no." New models are being developed which address this emerging environment. In fact, some see a future where students will receive their education on three "campuses:"

- A residential college community where—for a summer or for four years—students study and receive guidance, support, evaluation, and motivation
- A global electronic campus that they can enter via a computer, "commuting" from home, dormitory room, or community center
- The continuing education and training provided at their workplace by employers and community organizations (Rossman, 1992)

Student Centered View

Learners need to develop the capacity to search, select, and synthesize vast amounts of information to create knowledge (Dolence & Norris, 1995). Yet today's students are confronted with an array of seemingly independent entities which they must navigate. Courses stand alone. Faculty speak about "their courses." Although there are prerequisites, there is little integration or coordination of content within or among departments. Courses are combined to create a curriculum or degree program—a process which the faculty own. Students have minimal choices in customizing their programs of study. Career information pertinent to a particular degree is available in a separate location.

To complete a course, students go from place to place, acquiring the resources they need. Print materials are kept in the library. Advice from a faculty member is in another place and available only at certain times. The classroom, as a resource, is in a different location and time. Lectures are presented once but are not available for later review. Laboratories are open at specified hours, based on institutional convenience rather than student needs. Although computer labs allow access to the network and external resources, the student must arrive during open hours and hope for a free terminal. The students' learning resources are fragmented.

The model of the student environment is changing. The illustration on page 15 depicts the current model where an institutional organization or function is at the center; students must move from place-to-place or person-to-person. The emerging model places the student at the center, with more flexible access to people and information.

Not only are the locations of learning resources separate in the traditional model, but time is not flexible. Jobs, family commitments, and other activities must be scheduled around the campus timetable. Learning needs to occur at the time, place, and pace of the individual's choosing (Dolence & Norris, 1995). In the emerging student model, networked resources allow the student almost infinite flexibility in time, place, and pace.

"We are in the process of shifting what it means to be literate from the memory base of knowledge acquisition to knowing how to find and use channels of information. Knowing how to learn is more important than the facts accumulated" (Adams, Carlson, & Hamm, 1990). This shift carries with it technology implications.

Institutional Point of View

At an institution level, there are several possible scenarios for the future of higher education. One is that the academy does not need to change and won't.

A second scenario follows the historic model of higher education. A new type of institution will emerge to serve the future needs of learners. This, in fact, is the history of American higher education. When a more practical education was desired, the land grant institutions were created. In the mid-20th century, community colleges emerged as a means of bringing education closer to those who needed it for skill development with immediate application to jobs. "Over the past 300 years, much of the growth and innovation in higher education has come about through the addition of new institutions, not the adaptation of existing institutions" (Johnson & Rush, 1995).

In this scenario, a category of "perpetual learning institutions" would emerge to deliver certified education in a time-, location-independent fashion. Modeled along the lines of for-profit educational institutions, these institutions would bring together experts, via the network, to mentor, develop content, and certify learning. A new design model is essential to meet the needs of the Information Age. Barriers to learning must be replaced with mechanisms to facilitate 1) open access, to 2) a network of experts, in 3) both traditional and hybridized disciplines using 4) just-in-time learning, providing 5) perpetual learning, facilitated by 6) automated, "fused" learning systems, and 7) unbundled learning experiences based on learner needs (Dolence & Norris, 1995).

"In the Information Age, network scholarship will eliminate much of the advantage of vertical integration and the physical concentration of

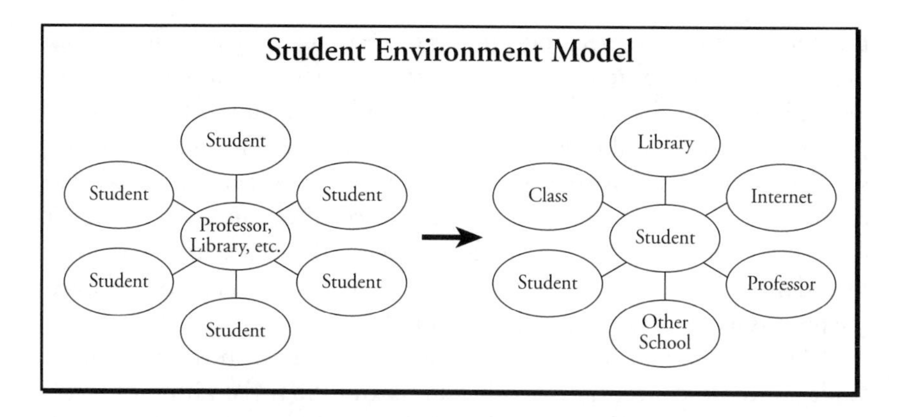

Alternative Educational Model

LECTURE MODEL	ALTERNATIVE MODEL	TECHNOLOGY IMPLICATIONS
Classroom lectures	Individual exploration	Networked PCs with access to information
Passive absorption	Apprenticeship	Requires skills development and simulations
Individual work	Team learning	Benefits from collaborative tools and e-mail
Omniscient teacher	Teacher as guide	Relies on access to experts over the network
Stable content	Fast-changing content	Requires networks and publishing tools
Homogeneity	Diversity	Requires a variety of access tools and methods

(Bourne, Broderson, Campbell, & Dawant, 1995)

scholarly resources. Not only can learners be anywhere, they can acquire learning and knowledge from sources in any location or mixture of locations. Owning the physical facility where faculty and other expertise reside will not be a critical differentiator in the eyes of many learners" (Dolence & Norris, 1995).

A third scenario is described by Tate (1996): New production, delivery, and certification organizations (PDCs) will invade distribution of higher education courses. These PDCs will operate on a national basis, using the most efficient and effective communications media available. Courses and programs will be designed and produced to commercial standards. These organizations will purchase subject matter expertise from many sources, depending upon the degree of expertise and the quality of the content preparation. PDCs will provide competence-based testing and certification services. Students may participate in interactive testing at any time and place of their choosing—and pay a fee to receive certification upon successful completion. At first, PDCs will "flow through" from the institution that provides the content. Later, independent accreditation agencies will assess the process, content, and certification of PDCs.

Tate sees the PDCs providing portable credits later in their evolution. Colleges would concentrate on liberal arts and the socialization of recent high school graduates. Specialized curricula would be purchased from the PDCs. Universities would concentrate on research and the development of new knowledge as well as training new subject matter experts and researchers. A university's revenues would partially depend upon its ability to sell its subject matter expertise to the PDCs.

What Will be Required?

"Realignment to the imperatives of the Information Age begins with an assessment of how the needs of one's stakeholders, clients, customers, and beneficiaries will change in the Information Age. Guided by this understanding, organizations can determine how they must change their structures, roles, and functions to serve those needs" (Dolence & Norris, 1995).

The advent of the learning revolution is facilitated by the availability of a reliable and ubiquitous network infrastructure as well as access to computers, any place and any time. Several institutions are exploring ways of improving access to education and the quality of the educational experience, while reducing cost. Some serve traditional, residential populations. Others are concerned with reaching new constituencies. Motivations range from financial crises to executive vision. This book details their explorations.

References

Adams, D., Carlson, H., & Hamm, M. (1990). *Cooperative learning in educational media: Collaborating with technology and each other.* Englewood Cliffs, NJ: Educational Technology Publications.

Alpert, B. (1991). Students in the classroom. *Anthropology in Education Quarterly,* 350-366.

Applebome, P. (1995, February 20). Employers wary of school system. *The New York Times.*

Barr, R. B., & Tagg, J. (1995). From teaching to learning: A new paradigm for undergraduate education. *Change, 27* (6), 12-25.

Blumenstyk, G. (1995). Campuses in cyberspace. *Chronicle of Higher Education, 42* (16), A19-A21.

Bork, A. (1995). *Rebuilding universities with highly interactive multimedia curricula.* Unpublished.

Bourne, J.R., Brodersen, A.J., Campbell, J.O., & Dawant, M.M. (1995). *Research on asynchronous learning networks for engineering education.* Memphis, TN: Vanderbilt University.

CMI. (1995). *Successful change strategies.* Cambridge, MA: Conflict Management, Inc.

Daggett, W. R. (1992). *Preparing students for the 1990s and beyond.* Unpublished.

Dolence, M. G., & Norris, D. M. (1995). *Transforming higher education: A vision for learning in the 21st century.* Society for College and University Planning.

Eaton, J. S. (1993). *The case for restructuring higher education finance.* New York, NY: Council for Aid to Education.

Fletcher, J. D. (1991). Effectiveness and cost of interactive videodisc instruction. *Machine Mediated Learning 3,* 361-385.

Forman, D. C. (1995). The use of multimedia technology for training in business and industry. *Multimedia Monitor, 13* (7), 22-27.

Geoghegan, W. (1996). *The high-tech workplace: What it needs from liberal arts graduates.* Washington, DC: American Association of Colleges and Universities.

Graves, W. (1995). The campus of the future or the future of the campus? *Edutech Report, 10* (12), 1, 4-5.

Green, K. C. (1995). *Campus computing survey.* Los Angeles, CA: University of Southern California.

Hall, J. W. (1995). Educational technology initiative: Greeting the dawn of a new millennium. Empire State College. *CLT News*, 1,1.

Hundt, R. (1994, February 28). The future of technology in the classroom. *First annual action for children's television lecture on media and children.* Cambridge, MA: Harvard Graduate School of Education.

Johnson, S. L., & Rush, S. C. (1995). *Reinventing the university.* New York, NY: John Wiley.

Johnstone, A.H., & Su, W.Y. (1994). Lectures: A learning experience? *Education in Chemistry, 31* (3), 75-79.

Karp, D. A., & Yoels, W. C. (1976). The college classroom: Some observations on the meaning of student participation. *Sociology and Social Research, 60* (4), 421-439.

Lemke, R. A. (1995). *Encouraging and supporting asynchronous learning networks.* Northern Virginia Community College.

Panepinto, J. (1994). Mainframes in transition. *Computerworld, 28* (11), 103.

Plater, W. M. (1995). Future work: Faculty time in the 21st century. *Change, 27* (3), 23-33.

Rossman, P. (1992). *The emerging worldwide electronic university.* Westport, CT: Greenwood.

Tapscott, D. (1996). *The digital economy.* New York, NY: McGraw-Hill.

Tate, R. G. (Winter, 1995). At the crossroad: Higher ed and technology development. *Technos, 4* (4), 26-30.

Twigg, C. (1994). The need for a national learning infrastructure. *EDUCOM Review, 29* (5), 16-20. Available electronically at URL http://www. educom.edu/educom.review.94/sept.oct/Twigg_Article

Verville, A. (1995). What business needs from higher education. *Educational Record, 76* (4), 46-50.

Vigilante, R. (1994). *The virtual college.* New York, NY: New York University Press.

Wingspread Group on Higher Education. (1993). *An American imperative: Higher expectations for higher education.* Racine, WI: The Johnson Foundation, Inc.

2

The Transformation of Higher Education

Michael Hooker

Higher education is on the brink of a revolution. For those who think regularly about the future of education, this proclamation will come as no surprise. We have become accustomed, even expert, at thinking and talking about the changes to come. Our familiarity with impending change, however, may have numbed us to what it will really mean. In ways not yet imagined, technology will change the way we order life. It has moved us toward a different kind of economy and modified ways of living. We are in the midst of changing from an energy-based to a knowledge-based economy which will alter the rules of international economic competition, thrusting universities into roles they have not traditionally played. Two of the greatest challenges our institutions face are those of harnessing the power of digital technology and responding to the information revolution. The opportunities and challenges technology presents are far greater than at any previous time in higher education's 750-year history.

There is still debate about exactly where higher education's history began. Irrespective of whether it was in Paris, Oxford, or Bologna, historians agree that it began at the start of the 13th century. It has not changed much since. Fundamentally, higher education is still a process of imparting knowledge by means of lectures to those who want to acquire it. This chapter describes the forces accelerating change in traditional modes of education, raises difficult questions that will help us determine what a transformed learning environment could be, and offers some thoughts on why it is important for higher education to take the lead in realizing that vision.

FORCES OF CHANGE

In oversimplified terms, there are two kinds of change in society: cyclical and structural. We accommodate cyclical change constantly, such as change in the weather, fashion, and interest rates. Structural change, on the other hand, is unidirectional and irreversible. Once a society, an economy, or an institution has undergone a structural change, it will never return to its former ways of doing or being. Examples abound: the Scientific Revolution, the Women's Revolution, the Industrial Revolution, etc. The way an organization responds to structural change can determine its future. For higher education, structural change is the result of the confluence of two forces. One force is the information revolution, which is driving the shift from an energy-based to a knowledge-based economy. The other is the management revolution, which itself is being driven partly by changes in our capacity to use information.

Information Revolution

In an energy-based economy, raw material is transformed by energy into a product. This service creates economic value. In a knowledge-based economy, information or knowledge creates economic value. Consider the process by which a new piece of software is developed. The process begins when an 18-year-old student sits down at her computer, hammers away at the keyboard for a few hours and—if she's clever and lucky—develops a new piece of software which can be of enormous economic value. The raw material—a polymer with a little paper attached—goes into the disk. But the disk is not the product; it's the package. While disks cost only a few cents to produce, software packages easily sell for $100. The value of the raw material is minimal relative to the total value of the product which itself is intangible—it is information organized in a novel way. The trend in every sector of the economy is that the relative contribution of energy to the total value of the final product is declining and the relative contribution of knowledge is increasing. Sometimes, as in the case of software, knowledge itself is the product.

As the millennium approaches, it is clear that knowledge will fuel prosperity and that those who can manage knowledge will enjoy a considerable advantage over those who cannot. As the primary facilitator of the process by which individuals learn to use knowledge, higher education will be even more essential to the economic success of regions, states, and nations. What has given competitive advantage to economies in the energy age—the availability of raw materials and indigenous sources of energy—will matter little. What will count more than anything is the way that an economy develops and deploys its brain power. Higher education will become more important than ever before. However, there is no guarantee that traditional universities will be the preferred providers of higher education. Unless colleges and universities embrace the management revolution, they will steadily lose ground to emerging competitors.

Management Revolution

The management revolution began before the information revolution, but took longer to become established. It was W. Edwards Deming who set the wheels in motion shortly after World War II when he said that a company would do better in the marketplace if it constantly asked itself this question: "How could we do our work or produce our product better, faster, and cheaper, that is, with higher quality, in less time, and with less cost?" No one in the United States listened, so he took his message to Japan.

As Japan began to rebuild its economy, the simple directive to do things better, faster, and cheaper led to sustained economic growth and eventually to Japan's market dominance in many sectors of the world economy. Decades later, the revolution moved to America. Over the past 15 years, the result is that American industry has undergone phenomenal change. The revolution has now spread to health care, where its impact is of unprecedented magnitude. Largely because of public anxiety about education's skyrocketing cost and legislators' misgivings regarding its efficiency, the management revolution has finally reached higher education, and it will never be the same again.

Cost Crisis and Productivity

The cost crisis in education must be viewed within the context of the shift from energy to knowledge as the basis for our economy. During the past 25 years, the shift has enabled productivity gains in virtually every economic sector except higher education. Higher education hasn't enjoyed the productivity gains of other industries because our costs—primarily labor costs—are growing disproportionately to the cost of living and we have not experienced offsetting growth in productivity. To raise salaries commensurate with the cost of living, colleges and universities have had to raise prices for the consumer. College costs, therefore, are growing out of proportion to the cost of living and out of proportion with other sectors of the economy. Although higher education has been slow to embrace Deming-style management initiatives on its own, outside forces, especially legislatures, are now prescribing change. There are currently 27 state legislatures that have commissions studying the question: "How can the public university do things better, faster, and cheaper?"

Public Scrutiny

Governors and legislators across the country are looking at their public university systems with increasingly critical eyes. They are acutely aware of the need to train labor to keep their economies competitive, and they are coming to recognize the value of universities as engines of economic development through their technology transfer activities. It is sometimes said that war is too important to be left to the generals. I fear that many are coming to believe that education is too important to be left to the educators. It is increasingly difficult to convince the public of the importance of a liberal arts education. We believe it cultivates intellectual traits and has intrinsic value. My fear is that if higher education does not respond by precipitating change and influencing its direction, legislators and lawmakers will take over the job. Unless we take the information and management revolutions seriously, quickly addressing the imperatives of those responsible for reallocating taxpayer dollars, many public universities will not survive, or at least their current levels of autonomy will not.

As it is now, lawmakers believe that higher education is unwilling to reallocate existing resources to priority areas such as technology. Their image of us is that we are often wasteful of taxpayer money. It is small consolation that this waste is not attributed to malice but to lax management, minimal accountability, and the inertia of doing things as we have always done them. We do not frivolously spend money on things that do not benefit our states. We do, however, spend money on things that benefit our states far less than others might. Corporations must maximize the value of their shareholders' investments. The public recognizes that responsibility. Similarly, public universities have a moral imperative to return the highest possible value to the taxpayers. That is our only justification for "confiscating money" from wage-earners to provide for the tax support of the university.

Impediments to Change

Adoption of the mandate to change higher education will require major cultural adjustments. A critic might say that the trend in higher education has been to take longer and spend more while working to do things better.

Our external constituencies will increasingly scrutinize the cost of education and measure it by the quality of our output, asking how much things have actually improved. They will challenge us to demonstrate that we are as good as we claim to be. We have avoided developing ways to measure our success. Yet, we cannot defend the university as providing something important for society if we cannot articulate what it is, explain why it is important, and demonstrate that we have, in fact, provided it to our students. We must respond aggressively to the public's suspicion that what we are doing is not worth the cost that taxpayers, students, and their parents, are having to bear.

While the demands of the external environment are for rapid and radical change in higher education, the internal environment has cultural textures that make change very difficult.

Consensus Governance

One problem that prevents higher education from progressing faster is our consensus form of internal governance. The cultural expectation within universities is that any major change will occur only after consensus is reached by the affected community. Because everyone understandably fears change, this culture works to retard the pace and magnitude of change. The culture also works to protect its weakest members; continued employment has come to be seen as a property right within the community of higher education. Rarely does anything get done that significantly inconveniences anyone. Once programs and positions have been created, they are rarely eliminated.

Reallocation

A necessary precondition for doing things better, faster, and cheaper in an organization is the reallocation of resources from low priority areas to areas of high priority. The cultural norms of higher education, however, hold that growth should come from addition rather than reallocation. New priorities must await the infusion of additional funds from the outside, either from tuition increases or from growth in state appropriations or philanthropy. As William Bowen has observed, institutions each raise all the money they can, spend all they get, and spend it in ways that relate closely to the way they spent the money the previous year (Bowen, 1980). Reallocation is not our *modus operandi.*

In the new atmosphere, we face the necessity of managing internal resources differently. The emerging expectation is that resources needed for new priorities will come from within through reallocation, achieved by closing, consolidating, or downsizing programs and activities of lower priority.

Although this may be a necessity, it is a dangerous move for any administrator seeking to maintain his or her position.

The search for new educational resources now focuses largely on technology. An emerging rule of thumb is that to stay current, an institution should spend five to ten percent of its budget on information technology. Few universities are doing that now. To do this effectively, universities must prioritize what they do and take the unfamiliar step of ceasing to do things of lower priority by reallocating resources from within. There is risk in reallocation. Without a vision of what the technology-enriched future could be, as well as consensus from the faculty and support from boards and legislators, it is unlikely that a significant number of campuses will reallocate significant funds from existing programs into technology.

Questions to Answer

Higher education has not developed the discipline of constantly looking for ways to maximize its value to those who support it. And this is where the two forces accelerating structural change join. Higher education managers—a category that includes faculty—must be no less compulsive in their efforts to maximize value to taxpayers than corporate managers are in trying to maximize their value to shareholders. Institutions should be flexible in their willingness to rethink how they provide education.

Learning Productivity

Rethinking education requires that we ask the right questions. I believe that one question we must ask is how to improve learner productivity.

In articles that are critical of higher education, you often see discussions of the need to increase faculty productivity. The main argument is that faculty should do less research and spend more time teaching. There is a fallacy in this argument (Johnstone, 1992). Certainly, faculty at our comprehensive research institutions could teach more. However, remember that these comprehensive research institutions employ about one-fourth of the nation's full-time faculty. These are the same faculty who are charged with leading the world in the production of research and the training of graduate students. If these faculty spent more time teaching or advising, it would not make them more productive, *per se*. It would simply assign them to different tasks. Those who deal with faculty issues on a daily basis are convinced, as I am, that the number of truly unproductive faculty is small. Increasing their teaching loads would not significantly improve higher education's productivity.

D. Bruce Johnstone has written a thoughtful treatise on learning productivity. His thesis is that significant and sustainable productivity increases must be achieved through greater attention to the learner. "Learning productivity relates the input of faculty and staff not to enrollments or to courses taught or to credit or classroom hours assigned, but to learning, i.e., to the demonstrated mastery of a defined body of knowledge or skills" (Johnstone, 1992).

One way to make learning more productive is for students to master a body of knowledge in less time. Learning that takes less time can cut the traditional costs carried by the institution, but also the opportunity costs (lost earnings) of the student. Another way to make learning more productive is to make it possible for students to get the courses they need when they need them. As Johnstone says, "There is inadequate learning when students are reduced to filling their course rosters according to what is available or convenient rather than what is needed or even wanted" (Johnstone, 1992).

The way we will achieve sustainable productivity gains in higher education is by facilitating more learning from students, not just increasing the workloads for faculty. If we are serious about learning, the learner should be our focus. How many would argue with the contention that the average student is not learning as much as he or she could? If we focused on the things that maximize learning—the best curriculum, the best pedagogy, the best learning environment, the most flexibility to adapt to learning styles—wouldn't all of us be more satisfied with higher education?

The Tough Questions

If we focus on learning, there are many traditions that we might question. Where is the proof that 120 credit hours makes an educated person? What does the baccalaureate degree certify? How did we come to believe that education parceled out in 50-minute increments, three times a week, was optimum for all of our students? What caused educators to decide that the length of the semester should be constant while student learning is allowed to vary? Why did we decide that mastery of the subject was less important than the time spent in the classroom?

The truth is that we don't have good reasons for some of these traditions. At some point in our past—during the agricultural age or perhaps the industrial age—this factory model might have been more efficient. We no longer need to accept that as true today. Technology allows us to customize education, to provide options, and to allow students to study for as long or as little as they need. Technology allows us to focus on learning productivity without an impossible increase in faculty numbers and facility costs. However, none of it will work unless we rethink what we want to achieve and how we go about it.

It's hard to break these habits. How many times do you hear faculty fret, "I have so much content to cover?" Why do we assume it is the faculty's responsibility to cover the material? First of all, it may be a false assumption that the material will even be relevant or correct by the time the student graduates. Second, why do we assume that it is the faculty member's responsibility to cover it? Why not set objectives for the students and let them explore and drive their own learning? The technology exists that will enable them to do so.

For whatever reason, we have many habits and traditions that make less and less sense in the information age. As educators and scholars, we in higher education should be in the lead to tear down these artificial barriers. If we don't, my prediction is that the public will lose more confidence in higher education and more control will be wrested from our institutions. This is not a prospect that any of us relishes, or that is in the interest of the public.

Paradigm Paralysis

Perhaps all of the stakeholders of higher education are caught in a paradigm paralysis: We have difficulty changing the way we think and the way we behave. What fundamental changes are we making in our educational system to handle the doubling of knowledge every seven years? Neither our courses, our curricula, our reward systems, or our funding models are changing at this rate.

To break this paradigm paralysis, we should consider asking ourselves some new questions. For example, should business bear some of the responsibility for the kind of education that is necessary for us to remain economically competitive? Higher education has been willing for business to fund educational projects. But why not incorporate business more intimately in the educational process? Would we benefit from business helping us establish curricula? How could business help us educate students? We all stand to lose or benefit from how we answer this question.

Are we asking ourselves how we are changing our methods and forms of delivery to shift from education defined as K–12 to K–80, or lifelong learning? If we were to define our market as lifelong learning, our major customers would be employees first and traditional students second. As Davis and Botkin (1995) articulate in *The Monster Under the Bed,* people have to increase their learning power to sustain their earning power. What should we do to reach our alumni and other adult learners who need our expertise? Davis and Botkin observe that colleges routinely say good-bye to their best customers at graduation rather than turn them into lifelong learners/customers. What benefit would society receive if our medical schools or colleges of public health were to reach out to consumers and help them understand the fundamentals of good nutrition or healthier lifestyles?

This paradigm paralysis does not exist just on campuses. In fact, it may exist because of the administrative structures we have inherited. If the accumulation of student credit hours is an insufficient measure of learning, why are we wedded to funding formulas that award dollars based on seat-time? If courses could effectively be shared among campuses—even within the same university system—why are there barriers to sharing the student credit hours? If students can learn anyplace at any time, what is the justification for residency requirements that mandate students enroll at a campus for their last two years of college? If education can be made available worldwide, thanks to technology, is there sufficient rationale to prohibit interstate sharing of courses?

Among our off-campus constituencies of parents and students, we may need to stimulate a paradigm shift. The scoring systems used to rank colleges and universities are based on measures such as volumes in the library, student/faculty ratios, numbers of full professors, etc. In the digital age, volumes in a campus library is less important than access to worldwide resources. A numeric score for student/faculty ratios is less meaningful than the quantity and quality of the interactions that occur. I contend that it is more important whether competency has been gained than how or from whom our students learn. We need to help our constituents define the true measures of quality so we can break away from ratings that reinforce the past instead of the future.

If technology competency is a competitive requirement for our graduates—and all indications are that this is true—are we willing to invest in it? There is hesitance to require that all students possess a computer, yet we have no difficulty requiring students to purchase textbooks. We require our faculty to have PhDs, but few institutions stipulate proof of technology competency or teaching excellence in their new hires.

These are difficult questions. They cause us to challenge our traditions. The point is not that our past has been wrong or bad. The point is that the future will be different. It is only by asking these difficult questions that higher education will retain the position of importance to society that it has enjoyed in the past.

Value of Traditional Education

As Robert Zemsky (1995) and others have pointed out, higher education's core values will be at severe risk if a larger share of the market for undergraduate education is secured by nontraditional providers. Proponents of the residential university experience will have to develop credible and persuasive arguments for the value of the programs they offer. The focus of the curriculum and other institutional priorities will necessarily shift from the simple transmission of information to the role of the undergraduate experience in developing capacities that are essential to success in the global knowledge-based economy. These capacities, which have been referred to as "executive virtues" (Macedo, 1990), include, among others: imagination, historical perspective, initiative, independence, resolve, perseverance, diligence, and patience. It may be difficult to convince the for-profit market of the immediate wisdom of investing in these qualities. However, as we redefine the strengths of the physical university, we must attempt to draw connections between the experience of an on-campus living/learning opportunity and the development of social and cultural characteristics that add significant value to the graduates universities produce (Noam, 1995). Extracurricular activities such as student government, the newspaper, and cultural events compound the value of the residential educational experience, and that experience will continue to be sought by those who can afford it.

Even so, there is significant risk that the current gold standard, the baccalaureate degree, will soon be devalued or will disappear altogether. Nontraditional providers of education will begin working with employers to define desirable skills and to design educational modules to provide them. As these partnerships emerge, the marketplace value of certificates validating the acquisition of specific skills will increase. They will signify exactly what abilities have been mastered by the holders of those certificates and what employers can expect of them. If higher education cannot defend the baccalaureate degree as certifying specific abilities, employers are increasingly likely to opt for the certainty of certificates which tell them exactly what curricula a student has mastered and exactly what knowledge base a student has. If we believe the baccalaureate degree has significant value, and I do, the challenge is ours to articulate that value and to provide mechanisms of accountability that will ensure that every degree awarded does certify what we contend it does.

We know that one of the most important functions of education is to mold the soul as well as to inform the intellect. I worry that, in focusing on the practical aspects of enabling our students to live productive lives in a knowledge-based economy, we risk paying too little attention to the challenge of enabling our students to live *meaningful* lives in the world of the future. There is no challenge more daunting or of greater urgency than providing our students the ability to contend with the moral ambiguities of a rapidly changing chaotic world. It is the traditional liberal arts disciplines, especially the humanities and the arts, that often enable students to understand the world. It is those disciplines that provide our best spiritual and psychological moorings and help us to define our place in an uncertain world.

The turbulence of contemporary change is best understood and dealt with against the background of history, literature, and those other timeless disciplines that connect us with the broader human experience. In a world of certificate-based education, we risk losing what may be of greatest value in traditional education. At risk is not just the quality of the lives of students whose education could be short-changed, but the ability of a democratic populous to make informed decisions. The Jeffersonian ideal of an educated democracy requires a breadth of education best provided by the classical liberal arts disciplines.

Toward a Transformed Learning Environment

Because of rising costs, insufficient accountability, and questionable productivity, public confidence in higher education has been declining steadily. Ironically, education will be vastly more important to society in the 21st century than it is today. National economies in the next century will find a competitive advantage in the way they develop, foster, nurture, cultivate, and deploy their brain power. Because of higher education's importance to the economy, questions related to college and university performance will be much more important; we will be scrutinized more closely than ever before and held to more stringent expectations. Education has always been important in enabling people to live meaningful lives, but it has not previously been so essential to a nation's economic productivity. The energy-based economy did not require as much of education as the knowledge-based economy will.

The structural changes precipitated by the information revolution will, therefore, transform what higher education does. For example, the role of the research library is shifting dramatically. The need for archives that make objects such as traditional texts available to scholars and students will increasingly be met through the use of digital technologies, both for storage and delivery. Libraries will become sites of information processing and dissemination as well as storage. In the future, instead of users coming to the library to access information, libraries will deliver information electronically to the user. This shift will require massive investments in technology and an equally great cultural change.

The information revolution is transforming research as well. We have already seen amazing benefits in scientific research through tools such as computer modeling and virtual reality. Emblematic of the breadth of effect that computers are having on scholarship is the burgeoning number of technology-based research applications in the humanities and the arts. Applications of digital technology in fields like history and literature are having stunning effects on the quantity and quality of pedagogical material available for the transmission of new knowledge. Software that links historical data with images, sounds, and text gives students and scholars the opportunity to engage subject matter in ways heretofore unthinkable.

Just as the digital revolution is changing libraries and research, it is also changing the way instruction takes place. For its 750-year history, the dominant mode of delivery has been the talking head (i.e., the lecturer standing in front of a group of students). That mode of information delivery makes two simplifying but incorrect assumptions. The first assumption is that every student comes to class with the same level of background preparation. We know, however, that no two students bring the same knowledge base to class, either in a specific field of study or in ancillary areas which provide a richer contextual understanding of the subject being studied. The second assumption is that all students have the same learning style and proceed at the same pace. We know that no two learning styles are exactly the same and that no two students learn at the same pace. In addition, we know that individual students will have varying levels of attention and different degrees of motivation from day to day. An appropriate fusion of technology and pedagogy offers us the opportunity to overcome the negative effects of both of these fallacious assumptions.

Many, including Gregory Farrington and Jack Wilson, have attempted to describe in greater detail than I have here the ways in which technology will change education and scholarship. While it is easy to think in terms of the tools and software available now, it is more difficult and would perhaps be more accurate to imagine the possibilities of our wildest imaginings. They will most likely come true sooner than we think. At the same time, the heart of the university's mission will not change fundamentally. Institutions will continue to manage the conversion of collections of facts and data into knowledge—information structured for innovative uses. What technology will do is transform exponentially the quality, speed, and breadth of our ability to effect that conversion and to convey it to our students and the public.

As it continues, the technological revolution will strengthen the mission of the university as it simultaneously promotes profound structural change. The economics of education may, for example, dictate that in the future we will need fewer full professors. There will be a tendency on the part of many faculty to resist technological change in order to protect their jobs, but market forces will have a stronger say. Proprietary institutions are likely to enter the marketplace first by contracting with the best professors to provide video-based courses with exclusive rights to their distribution and use. A vendor could easily afford to pay a professor an annual license fee of five times her university salary for the exclusive right to market her course. Economies of scale will make such partnerships possible.

Market realities and new pedagogical imperatives will have other far-reaching implications for the internal structure of colleges and universities. Technology will lead to increased research and teaching across disciplines. Traditional boundaries will break down. Technology will have a tremendous impact on criteria for tenure and promotion, workloads, copyright regulations, the research/teaching balance, physical/digital space, public/private partnerships, and assessment (Lanham, 1995). New university structures will also reflect demographic shifts in demand.

Changes in coming-of-age digital technology will, for example, enable the asynchronous delivery of courses at distributed or distant locations to students who could not heretofore travel to a site-specific program. One of the factors driving the rapid increases in the cost of education is the fact that students must present themselves at the same place and same time—repeatedly—for the process to occur. Once course content is digitized, it can be delivered anywhere at any time. E-mail and the Internet provide efficient means of communication and interaction between instructor and student, again asynchronously.

Once the above changes take place, educational institutions will be able to market their products virtually anywhere in the world. State and national boundaries will no longer define an institution's market area. In the United States alone, higher education represents a $175 billion/year market, so the emergence of new technologies will enable and encourage vendors to develop products for it. Other changes (such as in accreditation and a growing demographic-based demand that current universities will not be able to service) will enable alternative vendors to penetrate markets more quickly.

The thing that has kept competitors out of the higher education market to date has not been so much the capital cost of developing site-specific infrastructure, but the lockhold that accreditation has imposed on existing non-profit higher education institutions. In an action that had the effect of declaring that the emperor has no clothes, Roy Romer, Governor of Colorado, recently challenged the entire institution of accreditation. The governor's staff determined that the population of high school graduates in Colorado would grow by 30% between now and 2010. Alarmed that the state's future in a knowledge-based economy depended on having a well-educated workforce and recognizing that the state had neither time nor the capital necessary to erect new college campuses, Governor Romer convened a meeting of the eleven Western governors to tell them that they faced a similar predicament and to search for common solutions.

As a result of that meeting, the governors decided to create a "virtual university"—The Western Governors University—marrying the resources of their public institutions and linking them via telecommunications. Their intent is to deliver telecommunications-based baccalaureate and specialized training programs throughout their states. As the governors discussed the possibilities, the question was raised whether the program they were setting up would meet accreditation standards. The governors observed that the whole purpose of accreditation is to guarantee quality and that since the governors were concerned about adequately serving their citizens, they were more concerned than anyone about insuring quality. The governors declared that it should be the states, not a self-serving, self-appointed accreditation agency that should decide what was satisfactory for the states and their citizens.

I believe that the Western governors have issued a challenge that will have earth-shaking consequences in higher education. Once the stranglehold of accreditation is broken, the market will open up for alternative providers and will encourage the development of joint ventures between corporations who could conceivably create a global digital university. In any case, technology and telecommunications are gaining dominance. In addition to the governors of our Western states, the public higher education system in Maine has forged ahead with a telecommunications-based higher education curriculum. States will begin to contract with other states for courses and curricula, and very soon every university in the telecommunications business is going to realize that the market is not Colorado or Tennessee, nor is it the United States. It is, in fact, the world.

Conclusion

The challenge to educators is to preserve the essence of traditional education while changing with the times. Our highest obligation to society and to ourselves is to work within the context of change to ensure that it follows a trajectory of maximum benefit to society.

References

Bowen, H. R. (1980). *The costs of higher education: How much do colleges spend per student and how much should they spend?* San Francisco, CA: Jossey-Bass.

Davis, S., & Botkin, J. (1995). *The monster under the bed.* New York, NY: Simon & Schuster.

Ehrmann, S. C. (1995, March/April). Asking the right questions. *Change,* 20-28.

Hancock, L., & McCormick, J. (1996, April 29). What to chop? *Newsweek.*

Hooker, M. K. (1995). Restructuring a university. *Connection: New England's Journal of Higher Education and Economic Development, X* (1).

Johnstone, D. B. (1992). Learning productivity: A new imperative for American higher education. *Studies in Public Higher Education.* Albany, NY: SUNY.

Lanham, R. A. (1995). A commentary for the AAU provosts. *Vision 2010: Report to the Carnegie Foundation from the Commission on Preservation and Access and the University of Michigan.*

Macedo, S. (1990). *Liberal virtues.* Oxford, England: Clarendon Press.

Massy, W. F., & Zemsky, R. (1995). Using information technology to enhance classroom productivity. *Educomreg.1995*: Interuniversity Communications Council, Inc.

Noam, E. M. (1995, October 13). Electronics and the dim future of the university. *Science, V270.*

Wulf, W. A. (1995, Summer). Warning: Information technology will transform the university. *Issues in Science and Technology,* 50.

Zemsky, R. (1995). *Impediments to change: Comments on academic restructuring.* Proceedings of the Stanford Forum for Higher Education Futures Technology Roundtable.

3

ANOTHER PARADIGM SHIFT

Charlie Tuller

When you see the phrase, "paradigm shift," do you think, "Oh, great, another paradigm shift"? An overused term, perhaps, but "paradigm shift" is a realistic description of the effect technology is having on us, as individuals and as a society.

The essential process of higher education is the transformation of information into knowledge, and knowledge into insight. With technology catalyzing such massive changes in how we manage information, and with cognition, communication, and collaboration helping us transform information into knowledge and insight, the implications for higher education are immense. It constitutes another paradigm shift.

Our view of the future is that information technology is a transformation agent that will affect everything. Information technology is a defining force affecting all areas of society well into the next century, changing every institution, every business, and every individual in profound ways—causing a paradigm shift.

Technology itself has changed dramatically since the early 1980s. Anticipate even more rapid change in the future: changes that impact organizations and society. "Within 15 short years we have on the order of one thousand times better algorithms, five hundred thousand times more computing power per individual, and five hundred million times more mobility of information. We do not begin to understand the technical significance of all this, let alone the societal change it has unleashed or the institutional change it demands" (Hock, 1996).

Consider the term "local area network" (LAN). LANs are illustrative of the transformation (or paradigm shift) technology is catalyzing. Its initial meaning described a topology of wiring: Computers in a small, local area (e.g., a department) were connected by a network. The LAN connected us to information stored on a computer a few doors away. The current meaning is different: It describes a performance expectation. Today, we can connect client systems to servers, anywhere. From the office, most of us expect to be able to retrieve information from a distant server just as rapidly as we can retrieve information from the hard drive of our own computer. The term "LAN" has been transformed to meaning that everything should be local or accessible by us. Distance becomes irrelevant. Our expectation is that everything is connected to us, allowing every student to become the center of a vast universe. The technical meaning of a LAN is eclipsed by its social and educational implications.

During the next decade, a variety of enabling technologies will be important as well as advances in their form and function. More important, however, is how well these technologies enable organizations to function and compete.

A Paradigm Shift in Information

There are two major categories of information that are important to business and to higher education. Depending on the business of the specific college or university unit, different types of information may be important: structural or conversational.

The business of the cashier or bursar's office, for example, is to bill and receive payment for services. Students may enroll for different numbers of credits, with their fees varying accordingly. Student fees may be graduated for in-state and out-of-state students or for graduate versus undergraduate courses. Living in the residence hall will add to the fees assessed by the institution. A variety of meal plans are available for different amounts.

Most of the information used by the bursar's office is *structural* data, that is, data which has a specific structure. It is comprised of rows and columns of names, addresses, student numbers, residency, undergraduate or graduate status, residence hall contract, meal plan, unpaid parking tickets, overdue book fines, etc. It is the information required to run the business. Much of the data required to run admissions is structural data, as well. Many administrative functions use structural data. For example, admissions' structural data includes names, addresses, social security numbers, test scores, and other pertinent information.

Conversational data, on the other hand, is different. One place you would find conversational data is in academic disciplines. Conversational data is more contextual. The data could be a string of words, for example, where some words carry more emphasis than others. Or the context of the information carries additional meaning.

Research in the humanities has been aided by the availability of full-text search and retrieval techniques. How words and phrases are used can have great meaning. Take an example from Shakespeare. In *Romeo and Juliet*, there is a soliloquy by Romeo where the context of the words has great meaning (see Figure 3.1). Students studying this scene need multiple contexts to derive meaning. Notice the use of allusions to sin, for example.

FIGURE 3.1

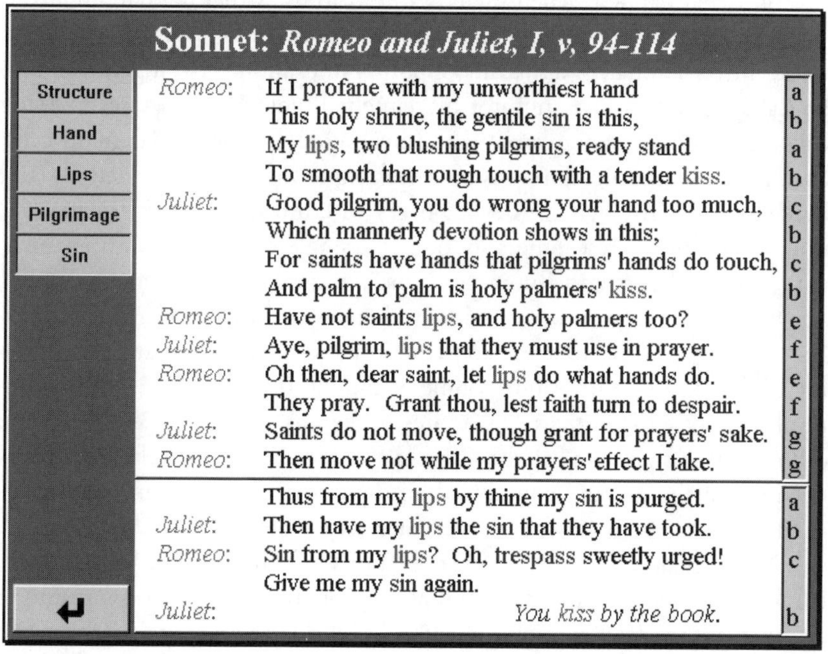

Sonnet: *Romeo and Juliet, I, v, 94-114*

Structure
Hand
Lips
Pilgrimage
Sin

Romeo:	If I profane with my unworthiest hand	a
	This holy shrine, the gentile sin is this,	b
	My lips, two blushing pilgrims, ready stand	a
	To smooth that rough touch with a tender kiss.	b
Juliet:	Good pilgrim, you do wrong your hand too much,	c
	Which mannerly devotion shows in this;	b
	For saints have hands that pilgrims' hands do touch,	c
	And palm to palm is holy palmers' kiss.	b
Romeo:	Have not saints lips, and holy palmers too?	e
Juliet:	Aye, pilgrim, lips that they must use in prayer.	f
Romeo:	Oh then, dear saint, let lips do what hands do.	e
	They pray. Grant thou, lest faith turn to despair.	f
Juliet:	Saints do not move, though grant for prayers' sake.	g
Romeo:	Then move not while my prayers' effect I take.	g
	Thus from my lips by thine my sin is purged.	a
Juliet:	Then have my lips the sin that they have took.	b
Romeo:	Sin from my lips? Oh, trespass sweetly urged!	c
	Give me my sin again.	
Juliet:	*You kiss by the book.*	b

Multimedia is a form of conversational data. There is no definable, predictable structure (e.g., the structure for rap music could not be used to define the structure for a reading of Shakespeare). The structures are transient and have meaning only in context. The multimedia information used in a music appreciation course has little in common with the structural data used by the registrar's office.

Different businesses within the college or university require different mixes of structural and conversational data for efficient operations. In relative terms, administrative functions use more structural data than academic disciplines. This has been manifested in administrative computing systems which have been mainframe-based, historically.

During the last ten years, campuses have found that not all their computing needs could be served by systems based on structural data. Conversations could not be handled by administrative systems. Campuses began to link PCs together to facilitate conversations. Client-server systems emerged. Academic computing centers evolved independent of administrative computing. The reason: Their data and information needs were different. The needs of data processing were largely structural; departmental needs were largely conversational (word processing, e-mail, etc.).

But what happens when there is a need to use structural data in a conversational mode? Consider research where information needs may be structural, conversational, or a mixture of both. For example, investigators of biological systems can now monitor fundamental biological processes in living cells—including metabolism, wound healing, behavior of malignant cells, and nerve communication—using a technique that shows the activity and behavior of living cells under a variety of conditions. Non-linear laser microscopy allows researchers to look at a single plane within a specimen, using pulsed lasers and fluorescent markers to detect and image cellular activity. This image reconstruction and analysis uses 10–50 megabytes of data to carry out 3D image reconstruction and quantitative analysis of the image data (Forefronts, 1996). Some of the information comes from structural data; other information is more contextual, e.g., the layer within the cell or stimulus provided to the nerve carries meaning. When the researchers need to collaborate and converse about what the results mean, both structural and conversational data must be accommodated.

Not only do different campus operations require a unique mix of structural and conversational data, but they probably have their own unique information technology requirements. Yet all these businesses comprise the university. How does the institution accommodate different information technology structures and data types without sacrificing efficiency and effective communications?

This challenge is exacerbated by the fact that a college or university may have 40 or 50 units making independent information technology decisions. This poses a significant challenge when an individual tries to access a student record, for example. Data on the student probably resides in different databases which may run on different hardware, under different operating systems, with different user interfaces and different levels of access. Instead of an information revolution where you imagine everyone has information at their fingertips, you can have chaos.

There is another form of chaos on campus: the desktop. No single desktop environment exists anymore. Different users "hang out" in different functional spaces. For example, two students might be sharing a white board—each from their own dorm room—working cooperatively on a design project with color, graphics, or even video. A staff member in purchasing might be "hanging out" in a monochrome business application with a rigid, character-based interface. Another staff member might be using personal productivity tools or e-mail. A faculty member might be surfing the web at his or her desktop. There is no single desktop. How does the campus integrate all these functions, provide straightforward, reliable access to information, and support its systems and people? Fortunately, over the next few years there will be significant changes in the desktop. The majority of emerging technologies will be focused on handling conversational data. The beginnings of this trend are already apparent in the interest in browsers, java applets, and multimedia, allowing the merger of structural and conversational data.

A Paradigm Shift in Relationships Due to Information Access

In spite of the growing dominance of technology in our lives, the world does not run on information; it runs on relationships. However, information enables us to have different relationships.

An everyday example may illustrate the concept. The relationship you have with your family and friends is much different than the relationship you have with someone you pass on the street. At least part of that difference is the result of the information you have about the person. There is great depth of information access about your family members. That information access allows you to develop a different relationship (one with much greater trust and confidence) than with someone you occasionally see on the sidewalk.

Consider the information a faculty advisor might have about a student (Figure 3.2). Having access to that information is important in establishing a relationship. The advisor can draw tentative conclusions based on that information, such as this student might be interested in majoring in computer science or electrical engineering. This could form the basis for their first meeting together.

FIGURE 3.2

Name: Brian Smith   Student Number: 523983

Permanent Address:
143 Handley Place
Carlson, GA 49833

Local Address:
1544 Davis Drive
Bolton, MA 02388

Social Security Number: 409-444-0023

SAT Score: Overall 1290 Verbal 480 Quantitative 670

Work Experience:
Computer support at Kinkos
Database programming
Grocery store

Interest Areas:
Computers
Cross Country

Academic Record:

Information is the currency of exchange in campus relationships. Information is exchanged in the classroom between faculty and students. Information is exchanged among research teams. Information is exchanged between the purchasing department and suppliers. Information is exchanged between college applicants and the admissions department. The potential quantities of information are staggering. But it is how the institution manages the information (both structural and conversational types of data) to form relationships that can yield competitive advantage.

Consider student recruitment. The institution seeks to recruit students from selected geographic areas, within a range of SAT/ACT scores, with a chosen grade point average and high school class rank, etc. Sorting information allows the institution to target selected individuals who are both more likely to be successful as well as more likely to be attracted to the institution.

For example, to build an applicant pool, colleges typically purchase names of high school sophomores and juniors from the College Board, which collects voluminous data about students who take the Scholastic Aptitude Test (SAT). Schools can purchase names by zip code, SAT performance level, race, etc. Once they have made their purchases, many schools use geodemographics. Geodemographics divides the nation's neighborhoods into 62 geodemographic clusters based on economics and lifestyle. The theory is that schools tend to attract students from similar geodemographic backgrounds. The process helps institutions target markets in which they are likely to be successful. It also helps schools reduce as many as 30,000 names from lists of 100,000 or more. That can translate into saving over $30,000 in mailing costs (Sanoff, 1995).

Volume of information is not the issue for higher education. How the information is aggregated and used to solidify relationships is. For example, imagine the possibilities if my *alma mater* could aggregate information from the registrar's office and alumni affairs. The institution would know that I graduated in 1972 with a degree in science, yet I'm currently employed as a manager in a business. From my records, they know that I have taken no business or management courses. They also know from alumni records that I have two children. The continuing education division aggregates the data and sends me information on business courses I can complete from a distance. They invite my younger child to a summer camp on environmental sciences and offer my eldest an opportunity to join a network of high school students interested in engineering. My *alma mater* has the opportunity to forge a stronger and more lasting relationship with me by mining their information.

In a sense, computing may also displace physical relationships. People will be able to do things with computing that used to be done in a much more laborious, time-consuming, and costly way. Computing will take the place of many physical processes, including automobile and architectural design, pharmaceutical research, as well as chemical and physical simulations. It will, for example, enable virtual laboratories that will replace time-consuming and costly physical mock-ups for research.

A Paradigm Shift in Effectiveness through Data Mining

There are three informational characteristics common to highly effective organizations.

1. The business has full information instrumentation, that is, it has the information it needs. This is exemplified by the recruitment office that has a complete profile on prospective students. Not only do they have the information, but it resides in databases that can be manipulated to suit the needs of the recruiters. If a recruiter is traveling to Montgomery County for a college fair, he/she can pull the names of prospects from Montgomery County, sort the names for those whose parents are

alumni, select those with the highest SAT scores, refine the list by intended major, etc.

2. More information is collected than is needed for the specific transaction. If the recruitment office was only responding to a request for a catalog, then name, address, and zip code might suffice. Some institutions collect additional information when receiving the prospect's request (e.g., interest areas, what attracted the prospect to the institution, etc.). But if you collect more data, what do you do with it?

3. Institutions who are enhancing their competitiveness—taking away other's market share—are collecting more information than they need for a simple transaction; they warehouse it and use it to see relationships within the information after the transaction.

For example, DePauw University uses geodemography for target marketing to pinpoint prospective students whose economic and lifestyle characteristics are similar to those of its approximately 2,000 already enrolled undergraduates. Those prospects are then targeted through direct mail.

DePauw also relies on a sophisticated computer system to track all of the nearly 2,200 students who apply each year. Once students indicate an interest in DePauw, everything from their test scores to their Internet address is entered in the system. Each time there is a contact with a student that, too, is put into the computer. Faculty, coaches, and the admissions staff can tap into the system at any time to check on the status of an applicant. The system allows DePauw to focus more effectively on students who are a high recruiting priority and, at the end of the admissions cycle, to evaluate the process to see what worked and what did not (Glastris, 1995).

Take another example: smart cards. A smart card allows the owner to buy sodas from a vending machine, to check books out of the library, to purchase football tickets, to call home, and to get meals in the residence hall. If that smart card stores information on the student's transactions, the data can be mined. For example, if a student has been an avid sports fan during college, the athletic department may target him/her as an alumni booster.

Perhaps more familiar is an experience from everyday life. We have all been the recipients of data warehousing and data mining by the telephone companies. How does Company X know that you make $50 worth of long distance calls each month and that their service would save you 30%? They use the data from their transaction systems to see relationships among data.

Applying this data mining technique has allowed MCI to gain several points of market share each year over their competition. That growth has been worth millions of dollars. The conclusion is that some organizations are using computers well enough to take market share away from their competitors. The same potential exists within higher education.

A Paradigm Shift in Organizations

Information empowerment is allowing organizations to move from static, functional organizations to dynamic ones. This trend is not yet apparent in higher education but will become important if higher education enters new ventures such as the virtual university.

In business, we have seen several trends that are the result of competitive pressures and information empowerment. The intended result is to allow the organization to be more flexible and dynamic:

- More decisions are made at lower levels.
- Business process reengineering and transformation are more prevalent.
- Competitive pressures in the global marketplace are intense.
- Changes in the size, skills mix, and source of the workforce are allowing the creation of virtual organizations.

Access to information allows decisions to be made at lower levels. Those closest to the problem have the ability to solve it.

Through business process reengineering, organizations are transforming themselves. Information technology is a key enabler in reengineering, but the fundamental rethinking of the enterprise is what leads to more dynamic organizations. For example, the typical steps in an admission process require between 45 and 60 days for processing (see Figure 3.3). Through redesign the process can be shortened to five days or less.

Competitive pressures are gaining in intensity in all sectors, including higher education. Competition is no longer local or regional; it is worldwide. Staying ahead of your competition requires anticipation of customer or market trends and a rapid response. Institutions are rethinking how they reorganize dynamically. One approach is to assemble teams as needed. If you are reorganizing to seize a new opportunity, where will you find the necessary skilled personnel?

FIGURE 3.3

TYPICAL STEPS IN AN ADMISSION PROCESS

Open Mail

Date Stamp

Sort Documents by Type

Correspondence

- Send requested materials
- Answer questions
- Route supplemental information
- Etc.
- File

Application

- Examine for completeness or errors
- If incomplete or unsigned, return to applicant
- Search files for other documents
- Evaluate residency
- Update computer
- Etc.
- File

HS Transcripts

- If not applied, put in holding file
- If applied, flag "in office"
- Categorize classes
- Etc.
- Update computer
- File

College Transcripts

- If not applied, put in holding file
- If applied, flag "in office"
- Summarize
- Evaluate
- Update computer
- Determine equivalents from catalogs
- Update computer
- Etc.
- File

Essays

- If not applied, put in holding file
- If applied, flag "in office"
- Read and rate
- Update computer
- File

Letters of Recommendation

- If not applied, put in holding file
- If applied, flag "in office"
- Read and rate
- Update computer
- File

International Documents

- If not applied, put in holding file
- If applied, flag "in office"
- Etc.
- File

As a part of the dynamic team building process, organizations are asking themselves what skills they must own as well as what skills should be acquired. Decisions on which skills should be in-house compared to which should be outsourced depends on whether the skill is essential to the organization's core competency and how rapidly the need will change.

Consider how the British Open University is organized. Their core business is education. Their resources are not organized just as a physical business (i.e., a campus), but as a logical or virtual business. Their 200,000 students are spread around the world. Their network of 7,000 tutors and counselors operate through regional centers. Teaching material is made available worldwide through partnerships with other countries (e.g., Russia, Romania, Singapore, Hong Kong). They do not necessarily own the delivery channel; many courses are available via the BBC. Our traditional campuses own the delivery channel, i.e., faculty and classrooms.

A long-term trend in business and industry is for nonessential elements of the enterprise to be outsourced. Higher education has begun this trend by outsourcing operations such as food service and bookstore operations. Some futurists predict that higher education will eventually contract with technology and telecommunications companies to provide the distribution of content created on campuses.

Universities share some of the attributes of other industries. They manufacture information (scholarship), reprocess it into knowledge, they warehouse it (libraries), they distribute it (articles and books), and they retail it (classroom teaching). Information technology has already changed each of these processes. These changes make it feasible for higher education to become a more dynamic organization (Wulf, 1995).

Three Paradigm Shifts in Computing

We have seen three major waves of computing: *host-centric*, *client-server*, and *network-centric*.

Host-centric or top down computing dominated the environment for the past twenty years. The focus was on the physical enterprise, with a specific behavior pattern:

- Buy a computer system
- Write applications
- Define the reports needed; develop fixed screens to display the results
- Operate over a private, wire network

We still see a dominance of host-centric computing among administrative applications in higher education. Many institutions operate their institutional research or registration offices with a specific computer, using applications written in-house. Creation of reports are fixed by the application: A new program must be written to generate a new report.

Today a distributed *client-server* model dominates. The focus is the distributed enterprise with a different behavior pattern:

- Buy individual client units
- Purchase applications
- Use windowing to view information
- Operate over private wire LANs or mixed private and public switched networks

The client-server architecture has enabled organizations to do a great deal of mixing and matching to suit individual needs. An example of this pattern is in purchasing client machines. People are buying CPUs separate from memory. Specific hard drive sizes are ordered. Memory modules may be different. Connectivity is a mix. Customization is the rule rather than the exception.

Applications are no longer written in-house; they are purchased. Information is viewed through a windowing system, whether Windows, OS/2, Mac operating system or something else. Users tile their windows to view what they need.

The next step is *network centric* computing. The behavior pattern changes, again:

- Multi-source hardware platforms
- Subscriptions for software rather than purchase
- Human-centered, multi-form factors
- Public switched infrastructure, both wired and wireless

Hardware comes from many sources. The network contains your applications as well as the data. The network is, in fact, your application. Software need no longer be purchased and installed on your computer. When you connect to the network, you access the latest version of the software for which you have a subscription.

The ubiquity of information technology will change how we perceive it. What if information technology was as ubiquitous as telephone service?

When you place a phone call from your office, you might be using AT&T. When you call from your home, the carrier may be Sprint. From your car, the signals travel to a satellite. From the hotel in Raleigh, it may be Bell-South. It is not important to you whether your voice is carried over copper wire or fiber optic cable. What is of importance is that you are able to communicate with the person you are calling.

The world of network centric computing will be similar. The network's technical characteristics will be of little concern to its users. Its presence will be assumed. The vendors and the technologies which enable service will be in the background. It will not matter what the topology is, where the server is located, or whether the connection is facilitated by wire or wireless technology. From your computer, you will have access to the resources you want and need.

In spite of its importance, the network is dumb: It is unaware of individual computing needs and preferences. It is merely a transport vehicle. Yet one individual's computing needs are different than another person's. The personalization of your computing interface will reside in the software.

Advances in computing technologies, such as high-resolution displays, 3D graphics and animation, handwriting and speech input, and natural language understanding, will be used to improve the end-user interface, to facilitate personal interaction and customization with computers.

This will enable new interaction models, including

- Intuitive, task-tailored interfaces
- Virtual reality environments
- Mobile, hands-free, and eyes-free use
- Intelligent agents that will isolate users from the details of the infrastructure but will carry out tasks tailored by the user
- Easier searching techniques

Speech recognition technologies, an example of hands-free computing, can recognize over 30,000 words at a rate of 70 words per minute. In addition, researchers are currently developing a large vocabulary, speaker-independent, continuous speech recognition system for multiple languages.

These paradigm shifts in computing are not restricted to hardware platforms and networks (mainframe, client-server, or network-centric). As technology matures, there is an evolution in its use. As a new technology is introduced, its early uses are likely to be found in niche areas. For example, when CPUs were introduced, they were first incorporated into accounting functions. Calendaring and mail functions were promoted with the introduction of laptops. The early applications of voice-recognition showcase the use of voice, but do not reach everyday activities.

The second phase of technology introduction is characterized by a migration to general purpose uses. Personal computers are in this phase today. PCs are used for many purposes: word processing, electronic communications, spreadsheets, graphics, multimedia, etc. The PC, itself, is highly adaptable because of the range of applications used to tailor its functionality. Yet to obtain this functionality, users are required to purchase specific software packages as well as upgrade hardware, operating systems, and keep up with new versions of the applications. Over the next few years, the PC will move into the third phase of evolution, that of being an appliance.

This move will be motivated by a growing frustration with the fundamental limitation of general purpose use: constant upgrading. Today's general purpose computer use can be described as a fat client model. The client machine must have increasing memory and processing capacity, more and more software with a seemingly endless procession of upgrades. As computers and software improve, fatter and fatter clients will be required. From an individual user perspective, this can be a frustrating experience. Installing and integrating new versions of software, reconfiguring hardware, and ensuring compatibility require time and skill that the average user may not possess.

The appliance phase is characterized by a thin client, fat server model. In this scenario, code does not permanently reside on the client; it resides on a server. When the user needs an application, it is accessed through the network, executed on the client machine, but does not reside on the client. The network becomes the application. There is no requirement for an individual user to reconfigure, install, or update.

For large organizations with hundreds or thousands of users, the fat client model is becoming insupportable. Many in higher education experience the inherent limitations of the fat client model for even simple activities. Have you used one version of a word processor at home, only to find you cannot print that version at the office? Has a colleague sent you a file that you must spend hours converting into a format you can read or use? A much more efficient model is that of the thin client, fat server. An organization would invest its resources in ensuring that the network is up-to-date and that its users have information appliances. Changes would be made to the network, not to individual client machines. Actually, the evolution is underway. Java, Internet plug-ins, and compound documents are the emergence of the appliance model.

PERCEIVED PARADIGM SHIFT IN TIME

Microprocessor performance has been increasing at a relatively constant rate, doubling approximately every 18 months. This trend is expected to continue. Its impact, however, is a perceived time compression which will cause a change in the business model of computing.

As an example, we have had word processors since the 1980s. Initially, it did not seem that word processing changed much as we moved to new generations of technology. The word processor used on an 8088 machine was not radically different than the one used with a 286 machine. By the time 386 machines became common, the major impact users saw was a point-and-click interface instead of keystroke commands. Microprocessor performance was doubling every 18 months to two years: The rate of change was the same as it is today. The base was relatively low so the increment of change remained small, and function did not appear to change radically or quickly.

With today's technology (Pentium), it is possible to type using voice dictation as well as opening and closing applications through voice commands. This is a sizable change from a manual interface. The next generation of technology will double the capacity of a 200 mHz Pentium chip. What functionality will we have available after the next doubling of microprocessor capacity? The pace of change, as we have moved from keystrokes to a point-and-click interface to voice commands, seems to be increasing. It is not. The rate of change is still 2x. Our perception, however, is that the increasing capacity of technology seems to be occurring in a shorter and shorter time frame. Imagine extrapolating processor performance for four years; it will have doubled twice. Will word processing have migrated from voice recognition to mind reading?

The result is that we sense a breathless pace of change. The impact is felt on organizations, as well. Asset volatility is high. Neither organizations or individuals can purchase the right machine. As soon as it is bought, it is out of date. No one can keep up with the current version of the software. Organizations are spending enormous energy, time, and money churning hardware and software in an attempt to stay current. In spite of large investments, institutions find themselves with two or three levels of technology that are now obsolete, but which they cannot afford to discard.

The increment of change between generations of technology is becoming too large for this purchase-based model to survive. The emerging model is that of network station management: a subscription model. For both individuals and organizations, it makes better business sense to pay a subscription or rental fee (e.g., $20 per month) for access to an information appliance as well as the software and storage needed on the network rather than to continue the upgrade cycle. The perceived compression of time will lead to a different business model for providing computing and networking resources.

PARADIGM SHIFT IN SOCIETY

In addition to the exponential changes in technology, two social forces will drive change:

1. The increase in the value of time
2. The recognition that information technology is a competitive differentiator

Information is being digitized. This causes another paradigm shift. The significance is that the conversion of text, graphics, images, and video into bits gives information a digital passport to travel across global networks. Powerful new communications technologies are giving networks the bandwidth needed to handle rich but space-consuming content like video, MRI scans, or great works of art. Networks are developing the speed to support interaction, enabling two-way communication and collaboration. Together, digital content and high-speed networks make the once-improbable entirely possible.

In this decade, we will move beyond client-server computing and packet-based Internet connections to global connectivity, which will be embodied in a worldwide, highly distributed computing *infostructure.* Connectivity enabled by the *infostructure* will profoundly change access to content, services, and communications. Consider the explosive growth of the Internet in just the past few years. Today, there are approximately 30 million Internet users. This number is expected to grow to 200 million users by the year 2000. The Internet enables individuals to get connected and stay connected.

There are likely to be three paradigm shifts that result from the *infostructure.*

1. Everyone will become a technology user because costs will be low enough and compatibility will be high. New software will allow the broader population of users to easily deal with ever more complex systems.
2. Inter-enterprise integration will become pervasive. We already see this in the form of electronic links among suppliers, distributors, and customers.

3. We will process and transport bits, instead of things and people; information will displace the physical. Working this way will be faster and less costly, as well as less harmful to the environment.

Technology enables the transmission of information. But fundamentally, the critical process is people interacting with other people. Technology enables us to develop a much more participatory and collaborative society.

The societal implications of participation and collaboration could be immensely powerful. Drawing on research in collaborative learning, there are significant cognitive and non-cognitive effects of collaboration. For example, delivery of education through a collaborative, computer-mediated environment alters the relationship of the instructor, the students, and the course content. The many-to-many, asynchronous nature of the medium democratizes access and encourages student input (Harasim, 1991). In fact, studies are showing that teaching on-line fosters a sense of closeness between the student and instructor.

The basis of the non-cognitive benefits appear to be that cooperative learning is a social method where learners work together as equals to accomplish something of importance to all of them (Slavin, 1990). There are positive effects on students' self-esteem, social relations, cross-cultural relationships, and attitudes (Hamm & Adams, 1992). Retention is improved (Adams, Carlson, & Hamm, 1990). If the power of technology can be harnessed to bring such benefits to society, as a whole, it may engender a new era.

CONCLUSION

Technology is a transformation agent. We have seen paradigm shifts in the types of information used and the types of computing (host-centric, client-server, and network-centric). Information access can determine relationships. In fact, institutions can enhance their competitiveness by finding relationships in the information they collect. The results are paradigm shifts for individuals, institutions, and society through information empowerment, getting connected, and the apparent compression of time.

Information Empowerment

Information content will dramatically increase in scope. There will be digital newsstands, where one can browse a variety of periodicals, electronic catalogues, and vast digitized video libraries, including everything from today's news programs and sporting events to your favorite movies, television reruns, and educational courses. Dramatically easier and more effective access to enormously large information resources will fundamentally change how we work, how we learn, how we obtain information, and how we interact with each other.

Getting Connected

A new computing paradigm, enabled by the emergence of global connectivity, will allow access to information and services from anywhere, at any time. This will enable access to content, services, and communications from the campus, from the workplace, from the home—from virtually anywhere. Connectivity will become an essential part of the real world; we will expect continuous availability of services and applications. Users will be able to access the same information whether in the classroom, at home, at work, or while traveling.

Time Compression

Not only have the changes in technology allowed us to do more, but they give the appearance of accelerating the rate of change. Time seems compressed. Technology has enabled us to do more, at a pace that will lead to a new business model.

Imagine this scenario. From your computer you are sending and receiving e-mail and faxes while you monitor the changes in the futures market for your research. Later, you conduct a videoconference with a colleague on another continent. In the background, your personal information agent is searching the Internet for new topics of interest on the World Wide Web. Your calendar is being queried for a committee meeting time. Students are sending you messages to clarify concepts in preparation for an exam. Assignments are being submitted and logged for your review later. A program you submitted to the supercomputer is generating results that are being downloaded to you. Time seems compressed in comparison to the pace of work a decade ago.

Within the next decade, information technology and its effects as a transformation agent will have dramatic impact on our lifestyles and workstyles. Technology will become ubiquitous. Its presence and power will be taken for granted. We will have an increasing capacity to integrate structural and conversational data, allowing us to enhance a variety of relationships because we derive meaning from information. Relationships will be strengthened. We will transform data to information and knowledge. Knowledge will lead to insight. Our world will be transformed by information technology—the insight we gain will lead to a world of enormous opportunity.

References

Adams, D., Carlson, H., & Hamm, M. (1990). *Cooperative learning in educational media: Collaborating with technology and each other.* Englewood Cliffs, NJ: Educational Technology Publications.

Glastris, K. (1995, September 19). DePauw uses all the new tools. *US News and World Report,* 122.

Hamm, M., & Adams, D. (1992). *The collaborative dimensions of learning.* Norwood, NJ: Eblex Publishing Corporation.

Harasim, L. (1991, June). *Teaching online: Computer conferencing as an educational environment.* Proceedings of the International Symposium on Computer Conferencing, The Ohio State University.

Hock, D. (1996, March 11). *The birth of the chaotic century: Out of control and into order.* Presented at the Extension National Leadership Conference, Washington, DC.

Sanoff, A. P. (1995, September 19). The consulting game: Schools turn to outside help to target and select students. *US News and World Report,* 119-122.

Slavin, R. (1990). *Cooperative learning: Theory, research and practice.* Needham, MA: Allyn and Bacon.

Wulf, W. A. (1995, Summer). Warning: Information technology will transform the university. *Issues in Science and Technology,* 46-53.

Yarrish, E. (1991, June 13-15). *The fully electronic university.* Paper presented at Applications of Computer Conferencing, Ohio State University.

__________. (1996, Spring). New biological imaging techniques developed at Cornell. *Forefronts, 11* (2), 1-2.

4

Higher Education in the Information Age

Gregory C. Farrington

Introduction

Almost 400 years passed from the invention of moveable type to the development of the rotary press, the key technological advance that made printed materials inexpensive. Inexpensive printing fueled one of the great information revolutions, as books and newspapers brought literacy and knowledge to millions and transformed education, society, governments, and economies.

With computer technology, an equal or greater revolution has been compressed into a few decades. Modern computers were born only 50 years ago, with ENIAC at the University of Pennsylvania. ENIAC weighed 30 tons, entirely occupied a large room, cost millions in today's dollars, yet could compute no better than today's pocket calculators. From ENIAC grew the computer industry, and now the new age of information in which we will be connected and able to receive and transmit text, data, sound, and pictures, virtually instantaneously, all over the world. We are living at the start of this technological revolution and just beginning to understand its impact on our lives.

Because of these dramatic technological advances, education, particularly higher education, is entering one of the most challenging and potentially creative periods in its history. Education is partly about information: its creation, storage, organization, validation, and transmission. It is also about practice: thinking, writing, speaking, and experimenting; and human interaction: challenging, critiquing, debating, and motivating. The computer revolution has created entirely new educational tools that can be used not only to transmit information but also to enrich human interaction. These new tools challenge the educational establishment to rethink itself and education as well. They challenge people and institutions that have long been good at preaching change to practice it themselves.

There are two technologies driving these changes. The first involves storage of information. It is now possible to capture the entire works of Shakespeare on one CD-ROM disk. Within a year or two, that same disk will store even more, up to two to three hours of full-motion video and sound, and that is only the beginning. A second revolution has been in the transmission of information. Now, "books" can move around the world in seconds. In addition, dramatic increases in computational speed have produced computers that are capable of powerful visualization, simulation, and interactivity. Information can be displayed more creatively and clearly than ever before. Finally, individuals have been liberated, not only to receive information faster than ever before, but to transmit their ideas as well. The individual has become a self-publisher and can project his or her thoughts to the world without the intervention of a gatekeeper. What is truly remarkable is that all these capabilities become less expensive each year.

Of course, the computer revolution is just one of several information revolutions that have taken place over the past two centuries. First came inexpensive printing, followed by the telegraph, telephone, radio, and then television. Print, radio, and television all allow an individual to receive information at a distance. Each technology has transformed education and society, though not always in ways educators would have hoped. However, for the most part, these technologies are not interactive; it is hard to talk back. The greatest technological advance for interaction at a distance was the telephone, but it has been limited to sound and also requires that the sender and receiver be synchronized, that is, they must talk and listen at the same time.

The new information/interaction tools combine many of the most powerful capabilities of print, the telephone, radio, and television. They simply work faster, are truly interactive, and also are asynchronous; senders and receivers do not need to be on-line at the same time.

What then will happen in the future? A good starting point is to assume that within a few years virtually everyone in developed nations will be able to connect to each other through inexpensive desktop and laptop machines that can access and exchange information, store and manipulate it, as well as simulate and display it, anywhere in the world. This revolution is underway; it will not be held back.

How will the new information tools change the structure of the university and the process of education and learning? Several changes seem inevitable. One is that learning and education will become more informal, accessible, and learner-centered. Another is that the demand for education, particularly life-long education, will grow significantly, as will competition in the education market. The new tools will open new markets for traditional educational institutions and also expose them to vigorous competition. Those universities and colleges that can change, innovate, and lead are likely to thrive; those that cannot will be at risk. Surely some will disappear.

The Changing Scholarly Community

What we currently consider the traditional structure of universities and colleges has been determined in large part by the information technology of the book. For centuries, information has been stored in books and books in libraries. Professors have had to work within a short distance of the books, and students have clustered around the books and the professors. As a result, universities have been physical locations to which students have come to live for several years after secondary school. This residential character of universities has required dormitories, dining halls, admissions selectivity, and has even produced the college football team.

Universities and colleges have developed into highly independent and self-contained organizations. Institutions several miles apart duplicate books, journals, and faculties, in large part because of the inconvenience of transporting books and people over even short distances. Faculty have been largely limited to professional scholars who live near and are employed by a university or college. By necessity, programs of study have been divided into courses that are delivered largely by the lecture method in semester-long units. As a result, universities and colleges have been restricted to serving students for only a small fraction of their lives, the time when it is convenient for them to live at the university, but have been largely cut off from educational interaction with them later.

The new tools of information storage, simulation, and interaction liberate education from many of the constraints that have been imposed by the book. They make it possible to rethink how faculty will create, organize, sort, and validate information and engage in the intense intellectual interaction that lies at the heart of education, but do so with fewer constraints of time and distance.

One major change already happening is in the form of the scholarly community. Scholarship has always been undertaken in local communities in which scholars live and work alongside each other and are close enough to be in regular personal contact. These scholarly communities have been linked by various means of communication, which for centuries have principally been variations on the letter, either from person to person or to the community in the form of a scholarly paper printed in a journal. Unfortunately, communication by letter and the printed page is quite slow; scholarly papers generally take 6-18 months to appear after they have been written.

Today, linked by the Internet, scholars and students can be anywhere and still be part of whatever community they choose to join or establish. Once a scholar or student is on-line, his or her data, pictures, and text travel as easily around the world as down the hall. Communities can form and dissolve with the screen as intermediary. As a result, the pace of research and scholarship is already accelerating as the exchange of observations and ideas takes place faster and faster. It is also becoming easier for new researchers and those in distant or isolated locations to interact and present their work to the community worldwide.

These changes are also having an impact on the lives of students, who now have unprecedented access to each other and to scholars from around the world. The idea of the international university takes on an entirely new meaning when students from around the world can study and learn in a virtual classroom mediated by communication on the Internet. In the same way, students can now interact with a university without having to live at it, which opens up major new opportunities for universities and colleges to create educational programs that are delivered via telecommunications to students wherever they may be.

One result of these changes will be an increased globalization of the scholarly community. Good brains are not a monopoly of those born in developed countries. When talented people anywhere can have access to information and education and are able to create and interact, wherever they may live physically, then the pool of researchers, thinkers, and scholars will surely grow, as scholars in previously-isolated regions join the mainstream. Inevitably, scholarship and research will move at a faster pace, and new competition will develop for the already scarce resources that support advanced research and scholarship.

These changes may affect jobs as well, particularly those in areas of high commercial value such as research and development in engineering, technology, and science. The new communications tools make it possible for very smart people in low wage economies to be fully engaged and interactive with those whose thoughts come at much higher cost. As a result, software development that might have occurred in Silicon Valley now can thrive in New Delhi and Beijing. Multi-national corporations will find it possible to shop for the best ideas and most attractive development costs wherever they can find them, not just at the high-priced university in the neighborhood or at their in-house research laboratory.

It is clear that what started as a large and cumbersome collection of relays and tubes has evolved into one of the great tools of personal communication. Society is just beginning to comprehend and exploit the power of the new technologies.

Learner-Centered Education

One of the most demanding challenges posed by the new technologies for the educational establishment is that of refocusing on its core mission and exploring how the new information tools can be used to create education that is more effective and more truly learner-centered.

Of course, education involves far more than just information. Essential to learning is practice and integration as well. To learn how to write, a student must write; to understand previous knowledge, a student must attempt to create new knowledge. This is true from the study of chemical engineering to that of poetry. The new communications tools provide powerful new ways to approach the learning of theory as well as practice, and new means to stimulate intellectual interaction as well as deliver information.

Regardless how familiar, the traditional patterns and styles of education are not absolute. Courses do not have to be taught by the lecture method nor subjects in semester-long units. Students do not have to gather in a classroom to interact and learn. The goal of educators, having been presented with the most interesting set of educational tools in decades, should be to choose those most appropriate to each task and not to cling to old methods and notes, pretending that they are best simply because they are familiar. The new tools should be used for what they do best so that humans can be liberated to do what they do best.

Take the study of poetry, for example. A good course in poetry must go far beyond reading; it must engage students and faculty in discussion, debate, and the sharing of personal reactions and thoughts. Pretending that a discussion of this sort can always be orchestrated—on schedule—in a class meeting from 10:00 AM until 10:50 AM on Tuesdays and Thursdays for fourteen weeks is a creative exercise in itself. Insights, large and small, come at all hours; they do not follow schedules. Not everyone is ready to be inspired or inspirational at the same time. Some students arrive at class with something to say and say it. Some are reluctant to say anything for fear their thoughts could not possibly be important. Others have no such fear but should. Some students do not come to class at all.

Recent experiments have shown that the simple use of network-based discussion groups can expand classroom discussions and liberate students, and faculty as well, from having to be their best—on schedule. Students can talk in class and then continue to talk with each other on-line, whenever inspiration might strike. The shy can speak, and often do when the medium is the screen. Those who drone on can be deleted with a keystroke. Discussions can surge and ebb on the schedules of students, which do not always overlap the hours of faculty. Even alumni can join in, contributing their different perspectives. The experience can be far richer and more intense than it would ever be if confined to the traditional classroom.

The potential for the use of simple tools like e-mail discussion groups to enrich the study of the humanities is vast. Contrary to what many might believe, these products of chips and liquid crystals humanize rather than dehumanize learning and make participants more eager to meet for real discussions rather than less. They also change the definition of faculty/student contact hours. When a telecomm-mediated discussion catches fire at 11:00 at night, a faculty member may be tempted to join in. Class and life merge.

Then there is the study of language. Most Americans grow up speaking only English, and they are notoriously reluctant to attempt any other language. One reason is that no one really likes to advertise his ignorance, and, while it may be possible to bluff and pretend to know American history, it is impossible to do the same with French, at least for long. Given the situation, Americans retreat into English, but just speak it more loudly.

Of course, the key to learning a new language is practice, and, in the beginning, getting enough practice can be difficult, especially in a formal class of several dozen students and one teacher who, regardless how dedicated, cannot give each student enough personal attention. It is also intimidating for students to attempt to speak a new language and in doing so instantly demonstrate their inexperience.

Innovative software provides a powerful new method for learning languages. The simulation ability of desktop computers has made it possible to create interactive programs that help students learn how to speak and even correct their pronunciation, all without becoming tired or forcing them to display their difficulties publicly. In the future, these tools will become more interactive, more lifelike, and more effective. They can be used to liberate human teachers to do what they do best, which is to conduct normal conversations, challenge students to listen, comprehend, and speak as they would have to do in everyday life, but after they have mastered the basics with the help of their indefatigable and non-judgmental computers.

Sound is also critical to the study of music, and a number of engaging approaches have been developed that use the computer to present musical compositions so that the underlying structure and creative rationale are much easier to comprehend.

The challenges are similar and just as interesting in the teaching of mathematics, engineering, science, and art history. In these subjects, a key challenge is in visualization. The fact that even relatively inexpensive laptop and desktop computers can perform feats of calculation and visualization has the potential to revolutionize the teaching of these subjects. Mathematics is a good specific example. Many people find grappling with mathematical equations and deriving meaning from them to be difficult at best. Often after struggling with a course or two in mathematics, students conclude what they suspected all along, that math is not for them.

In fact, the ability of the computer to quickly display visual representations of equations on-screen and to allow a student to change the values of key variables, manipulate the functions, and see the effects on the visual representation, can transform the learning of mathematics. After all, humans are visual creatures: We derive a great deal of information about the world through sight. The computer, with its powerful ability to calculate quickly, can now translate the abstract code of mathematics into forms more easily assimilated.

Similarly, many areas of engineering are visual. One particular example is in the study of materials science, which deals with the structure and properties of solids. It has always been difficult to illustrate dynamic, three-dimensional processes occurring in crystals and other solids using static, two-dimensional professional drawings. Mentally reconstructing a three-dimensional reality from a line drawing is difficult. Today, the calculation and visualization power of the computer makes it possible to create dynamic, three-dimensional representations of critical solid state concepts and distribute them to students, either on-line or via CD-ROM.

Another example is in the teaching of art and art history. Studying painting and sculpture involves a great deal of learning by seeing and learning how to see. The ability of the computer to store and display images and to create self-paced tutorials makes it ideal for helping students in the study of art.

Studies in archeology, ancient art, and architecture also are suited to the computer age. Already, scholars have exploited the powerful simulation ability of the computer to recreate ancient buildings and monuments as they once existed and thus make it possible to walk through ancient temples that have long-since collapsed, and see the Parthenon as it was in the time of the ancient Greeks and the statue of Athena in all its bright colors as it appeared thousands of years ago.

Computer simulation is also making it possible to illustrate, on-screen, key technical principles that could only be observed previously in the laboratory. Whereas once the teaching of science and engineering was rather rigidly divided into lecture sessions, recitations, and laboratory exercises, some colleges and universities are now combining all three experiences into a unified, studio-style approach. (See Chapter 7 by Jack Wilson.) In the studio method, students work in groups of two or three and make use of computer-based teaching modules that incorporate theory, problems, and associated real and simulated experiments. The professor acts as a coach, interacting with the groups as they work their way through the learning process. In this way, learning and doing are intertwined and thus reinforce each other more effectively. Initial evaluations indicate that students remain more interested with this approach and learn more quickly. Faculty also are more satisfied with the depth of student learning and with their more personal and informal interactions with students. Perhaps the only students who might prefer the old style of lecturing are those who never came to class anyway; their absence becomes more obvious when they are expected to be contributing members of small teams!

Courses that involve laboratory study also are prime targets for experiments with the new teaching method. In a conventional laboratory session, students must learn a great deal in a very short time, much of it not necessarily central to the intellectual concepts being explored. A major challenge is in learning how to use the instruments needed for the experiment and in developing a sense of how the experiment should proceed. Time pressures often distract students from the real purpose of the experiment toward a focus on getting the right result.

Experiments are underway at many universities and colleges to use computers to present preparatory material important for a real laboratory session, including the equipment that will be used, video clips of its operation, and tutorials about the experiment, so that students can develop an understanding of the mechanics of an exercise and be freer in the real experiment to explore the physical principles that are the point. These new approaches have proven to be effective additions to traditional laboratory exercises. They do not replace reality; they just help a student appreciate it more quickly.

Examples of this sort could fill page after page. The message is simple: We are living in an exceptionally fertile time for educational creativity across the curriculum. Virtually every college and university has faculty and staff who are experimenting with and developing new teaching methods similar to those just described. The impact on curriculum, learning, and faculty-student interaction is just beginning to be felt.

Of course, the new freedom that allows students to access information as powerful images brings with it the risk of confusing information with insight and pictures with understanding. Anyone who has strolled through an art gallery knows that seeing is not the same as perceiving. The same is true for mathematics, science, and engineering. Converting mathematical formulas into pictures and difficult scientific concepts into moving images may tempt students to confuse fascination with learning. For all that computers can help, learning involves practice as well as theory. Practice takes many forms: writing, speaking, debating, composing, and experimenting are just a few. In the end, humans have to create in order to understand. Computers can access information, display images, cavort with mathematics, repeat Italian verbs, present music and art in digestible snatches, and connect us into more human communities, but they cannot learn for us. We must still do that.

In all of the confusion of creativity, it is important to focus on the goal, which is to make learning more effective, accessible, affordable, and personal. The new tools can be so captivating that the issues of whether they actually work and are affordable sometimes get lost in the sparkle. Assessment is critical, and will be done, if not by the creator then by the marketplace. Dazzle does not always deliver, and many creative ideas will wither as educational Darwinism weeds out those that do not represent genuine progress. Ultimately the learner will decide what works best.

What is certain is that the new technologies will give learners greater personal control over the process of education. Students will be able to access information in many different ways—text, speech, visualization, and simulation—and then choose the combination that works best for them. They will also be able to interact with each other more closely, to work together as well as alone, and to work in learning communities that include participants, both faculty and students, from around the world. Learners will be more in control of their options, which is to say that learning will become more learner-centered and less under the control of the traditional providers of teaching.

CHALLENGES FOR HIGHER EDUCATION

It is too early to understand the long-term impact of the new technologies on higher education. Some of the more extreme seers have predicted the demise of the university. Fortunately, university and college faculty are actually quite good at innovating, once the opportunities, or pressure, become compelling. So rumors of the death of the university will surely prove premature. However, change is already underway in several key areas. They involve issues such as the sharing of facilities and faculties, the use of real estate, the emergence of new markets and new competition, and the need to reaffirm the importance and ensure the strength of the residential undergraduate experience.

Real or Virtual Colleges and Universities?

Virtually all colleges and universities are physical institutions that involve land and buildings. At the functional center of most campuses, and often the literal center as well, has always been the library, both as storehouse of information and gathering place for the academic community. Perhaps no other academic function will be transformed so much by the new information technologies as the library. This makes the library a good place to begin considering how the new information technologies may change the physical structures of the university.

In the future, newly published works will increasingly be made available in digital form, and older books and journals will gradually be converted to allow on-line access. Of course, books will not disappear, but the size of the book and journal collection will become an anachronistic measure of university or college excellence. What will matter is not where information is stored, whether ten feet or half a continent away, but how fast it can be accessed, which will be more a function of network bandwidth than bookshelves and corridors. All colleges, regardless of size or stature, will be able to access comparable banks of information.

All this is not to say that libraries as physical locations with specialized staff will disappear. Just because people can access information on-screen in the privacy of their office or residence hall does not mean that they will want to remain closeted with their glowing screens all the time. Students have gone to libraries to check out each other as much as books. In addition, just because a user has the world of information a keystroke away does not mean that he or she can find the right piece among all the spinning disks.

These issues have major implications for the physical design of libraries and for their staffing. As an architecture, libraries will surely continue to be meeting places for students and faculty even as their role as principal information repositories diminishes. Library staffing, on the other hand, is likely to change as the need for specialists to select books and journals (bibliographers), purchase them (business staff), catalog and process them (technical services), shelve, check-out, borrow them from other libraries, is gradually made obsolete by electronic access.

It seems inevitable that two organizations that typically are separate on today's campus, the library and computer/information technology services, will merge into one whose mission will be to educate new users in the use of information technologies and to support them technically and intellectually wherever they might be physically. Library staff will increasingly focus on being information access specialists whose job it is to help extract the information that users want from the flood that is available.

Elsewhere on campus, fast telecommunications will make it possible for universities and colleges to share faculty as well as books. Small schools will be able to access leading faculty and provide course offerings previously only available at large universities. All colleges and universities will be able to project themselves far beyond their physical locations, which is likely to change the nature of competition in higher education. For example, specialized graduate and professional schools of Big Private U. might become truly international through telecommunications. In this way, universities and colleges, particularly those with high quality and well-recognized brand names, might expand services to new markets and extend their national and global reach.

On campus, high bandwidth networks will allow the fast transmission and receipt of information, services, and each other through portable computers that are able to dock virtually anywhere on campus, ultimately through wireless connections. Along with these changes will come a redefinition of the physical classroom. Lectures will not disappear, but spaces that allow for more informal interaction among faculty and students, for discussion rather than lecture, will grow in importance.

The definition of faculty may also change. Traditionally, in order to interact with students and each other, faculty had to live and be physically present as part of an educational community. Faculty have been a distinct class of professionals who have devoted their lives to teaching and scholarship. However, using telecommunications, it will be technically possible for experts, wherever they might work, to interact with students, wherever they study. No longer does formal teaching have to be the exclusive domain of professional faculty. In concept, the pool of professionals who are able to share their experiences, knowledge, and expertise with students can be greatly expanded.

For example, in areas of research that are of direct economic importance, such as pharmaceuticals and telecommunications, to name just two, the leading scientists and engineers are as likely to be found in industry as in universities. Institutions like the Smithsonian are full of experts with interesting stories to tell and knowledge to share. Formal educational involvement of guest faculty may come from outside academe. Telecommunications faculty who make their living primarily in what academia calls the real world, whether in the humanities, the fine arts, music, public policy, or business may contribute. Of course, the use of experts from outside the educational establishment as guest faculty will pose significant economic, legal, and organizational challenges.

However, despite the likely changes, it seems certain that universities and colleges, as physical scholarly communities of faculty and students, will continue to thrive. Video networks, despite their power, cannot replace the laboratories needed for engineering, science, and medicine. The practice studios that are at the heart of fine arts, architecture, and music, or late night impassioned discussions of literature and ideas will not go away because we now have fiber optic cable. Universities and colleges ultimately are communities. CD-ROMs are no substitute for genuine human interaction. People want to be with people, and scholars who interact with each other via the Internet will still want to have lunch together. But the physical university will be connected to the world more powerfully than ever before. It will be as much a transmitter and receiver of information and interaction, a node on the network, as a physical community of students and scholars.

The Pool of Students: New Markets for Education

The existence of universities and colleges as physical locations to which students must come to study has meant that formal higher education has been compressed into the four to eight year period after students complete secondary school and before they become economically independent. The need for education, of course, is not so neatly scheduled. Interest in formal learning and the need for it are lifelong, even if they become difficult to indulge after traditional college age.

Various schemes have been designed to bring education from the university to the home and make it possible for students to interact with the university without being at it. The open university model in operation in a number of countries is one example. It uses books, specially-designed tutorials, and student exercises exchanged through the mail to deliver education directly to students wherever they might be. The challenge is not simply to provide information, which is relatively easy, but to make the educational experience interactive and stimulating. Unfortunately, interaction via the postal service is slow and hardly allows for lively discussion, brainstorming, and all the other interactions that occur when real people are present in the same place at the same time.

Today, the new information tools make it possible for students who are scattered over large distances to interact with much of the spontaneity of a live meeting, and sometimes more. Already courses are being delivered to remote locations through videoconferencing technology, although this is still in its infancy.

Soon, personal videoconferencing will become possible as even more powerful personal computers and faster communication networks support the transmission of sound and video, so that students and faculty will be able to see and hear each other as well as exchange text. The addition of sound and video will make personal and informal videoconferencing feasible for ordinary people with relatively inexpensive equipment.

When communications technology of this sort becomes widely available, the opportunities for universities and colleges to market programs of continuing education will increase dramatically. The most attractive market initially will likely be for high-end, expensive education in fields in which the need exists and the economics can support the cost. Already, several virtual universities have been established to deliver continuing education courses in high-margin subjects, such as business, engineering, law, and medicine.

Another potential market is that of lifelong recreational learning. Interest in learning hardly ends at graduation, and even increases as people grow older. Well-designed courses in topics such as history, literature, music, and art would surely attract considerable interest, particularly among a university's alumni, if they could be delivered through a medium like the Internet and were relatively low in cost. For recreational learners, the opportunity to be part of a virtual community—interacting and discussing with others around the world without leaving their homes—might well prove to be the most engaging feature of distance learning. The charges for courses of this sort could not be as high as for high-end continuing professional education. However, this recreational learning market allows colleges and universities to serve and stay in contact with alumni throughout their lives and to do so in a way that provides new revenues.

New Competition

The possibility that universities can soon deliver programs of high-level professional and executive education by means of telecommunications suggests that other organizations or corporations might do the same. Universities that connect with their students by means of telecommunications do not need a traditional campus or full-time faculty and departments. Instead, a professional staff would design individual courses and programs of study on the basis of systematic market analysis to determine the kind of educational products needed by potential customers, and then contract with effective teachers in a particular field, whoever and wherever they might be, to present courses for delivery to students via telecommunications. The standard of success for each faculty member would be the quality of student learning. In this type of university, excellent teaching would be well-rewarded with prestige and money; poor teaching would not last long.

Some faculty at traditional universities might feel that this model cannot work, or should not be allowed to work. Universities and colleges today control the credentialing process by which the university name on a diploma imparts much of its value. Ultimately, however, the market will be ruled by excellence, and Internet U, if it can deliver excellent education for the right cost, can become a premier brand name in itself, much the way that CNN evolved quickly from an upstart to the television channel of choice for high quality and timely news. The important point for traditional universities to realize is that the new telecommunications tools pose much greater threats to their monopolies than they have ever faced before, particularly in the high-prestige and lucrative markets for advanced professional education.

A creative entrepreneurial university, however, might consider this situation to be an opportunity rather than a threat. In a marketplace open to many competitors, prospective students may have a hard time identifying quality. Inevitably, the market will be segmented according to factors such as type of customer, level of study, quality of teaching, and cost. Brand names will become important indicators of quality. The challenge is for those institutions with established brand names to be among the most innovative; for Old Ivy U to create Internet Ivy U.

The institutions that will face the greatest threat are likely to be less prestigious colleges and universities that have served local populations. Their markets can be invaded by competitors with better faculty and more prestigious brand names. Some weaker institutions will surely lose in the competition.

The Future of Residential Undergraduate Education

Traditionally, undergraduates have been the core constituency of higher education, and the residential undergraduate experience in America has become the rite of passage that bridges secondary school and economic independence. However, on-campus, residential undergraduate education is expensive, both in tuition and living costs and in terms of the time students must devote to it. At leading private universities and colleges, undergraduate education takes four to five years and costs upwards of $30,000 per year in the mid-1990s.

Can an educational program delivered on-line or based on an interactive CD-ROM presentation, perhaps delivered and overseen by a professional corporation whose mission is purely education, provide a successful alternative to the residential undergraduate experience? Might students move directly from secondary school into the work force and then pursue the equivalent of undergraduate education while employed? Can a modern version of the correspondence school serve a larger fraction of the educational market than have traditional, book and mail-based programs?

The answer to each of these questions is most certainly yes, but by no means does that imply that the residential undergraduate experience will disappear. It is more likely that the new tools will provide alternative pathways for learning and expand the opportunities for students who are highly motivated yet unable to pursue higher education because of its cost or problems of access. Residential undergraduate education will thrive so long as it delivers more than a CD-ROM ever can.

At its best, undergraduate education should be about much more than information. The most effective undergraduate experience produces graduates who have mastered the processes of how to learn, to think, and to continually renew themselves. Successful students are prepared for a life rather than a job, and for a future rather than the next year. Education of this sort must go far beyond information and be concerned with structure, integration, motivation, creativity, and the kind of intellectual interaction not possible with a computer program. Ultimately, the best education is about people and the creative interactions that occur when they debate each other, discuss and argue, and struggle with the challenge not only of understanding existing knowledge but also of creating new knowledge. People do these things. Silver disks do not.

What then is the future of the undergraduate experience? It is fair to say that those colleges and universities that are lulled by their lecture notes into confusing the delivery of information with the creation of educated students might be threatened by spinning silver disks. Ideally, the new tools will help students master the informational aspects of education more quickly, more effectively, and at a rate better matched to the pace at which each student learns. Faculty will then be free to do what only they can, which is to discuss, challenge, experiment, create, and involve students in the kind of intellectual ferment that integrates and transforms information into education.

Those colleges and universities that recognize the new technologies as powerful tools that can help them serve what has been, or should have been, their mission all along are likely to flourish and to remain deserving of their cost. Those that do not will be at more risk than ever before. The ironic conclusion is that the new digital technologies will force residential undergraduate education to be more human, more interactive, and more learner-centered—the very characteristics considered its strength long before computers ever appeared.

Who Will Create the New Learning Tools?

The traditional lecture style of education involves relatively little cost other than the salary of the faculty member and the investment in the lecture hall. Creating textbooks has not been a particularly capital intensive enterprise either. For centuries, scholars have written textbooks with the equivalent of pencil and paper. Some have made fortunes from their output, but rather few.

The future will be different. Advanced teaching materials, such as CD-ROM or Internet-based versions of texts, cannot be created in an attic. Their production costs typically are quite high, driven by their level of visual and graphical sophistication. Creating texts of the new sort involves teams of contributors and resembles more closely the production of a film than the writing of a novel. Faculty will be the central intellectual leaders of the process, but they will work more as members of teams than alone.

Telecommunications will make it possible for faculty to be individual entrepreneurs in other ways as well. In the past, it has been difficult for faculty to take their lecture notes and compete directly with their employer by offering their star course in "Economics 101" or "Telecommunications Today" to non-matriculated students, outside the academy for direct payment. Now, faculty are being approached by independent resellers to deliver their courses to a new audience, outside of their university or college structure. Executed well and marketed with skill, the outcome can be very lucrative for the professor.

These changes will express themselves in terms of money, either as new opportunities to earn it or threats to divert it. Colleges and universities will inevitably have to rethink who owns the intellectual output of faculty, particularly as it relates to teaching.

Fortunately, universities and colleges are fundamentally well-positioned to thrive in the information age. Their strength is in owning content. Certainly, computers and telecommunications channels will be very important in the future, and a lot of money will be made in these technologies. But computer equipment and communications lines are becoming commodities. The real economic growth and value will be in content, whether in software programs or in on-line teaching.

To take advantage of these opportunities, colleges and universities will be challenged to find capital, since entering the new markets for their products will be far more capital intensive than traditional teaching has been. Institutions of higher education also will be challenged to rethink how they govern themselves, how faculty are rewarded, and how their products are marketed. Unusual partnerships will likely be formed. Might an old-line university that is expert in content combine with a leading Hollywood studio that is superb at effective presentation to create completely new educational tools and share in the revenues? These opportunities will challenge higher education to be faithful to its core values while finding new ways to thrive and share in the creation of new wealth.

Looking to the Future

We are, without question, entering a time of major change in education. Whether existing universities and colleges will be able to innovate fast enough to take advantage of the new opportunities and lead the pace of change is less apparent. High quality teaching has seldom received the emphasis it deserves on campuses, and educational innovation has been rewarded far less than research and scholarship. Can faculties trained to be research specialists find fascination in developing new teaching methods? Can existing academic, political, and governance structures adapt to the need for rapid curricular change and a new market mentality? Will educators expand their vision and embrace the intellectual challenge of leading all of our institutions into the information age? It is not clear that the answers are yes, which is why the development of new educational models may proceed most quickly at small institutions that have long placed a major emphasis on teaching, and also in new educational corporations.

In the 21st century, education will become even more important for success in life. The political and economic battles that swirl around the highly uneven state of American education, particularly that at the pre-college level, are likely to intensify. Issues of the "have's" and "have-not's" will be even more important than they have been before. There can be little doubt that the most critical period for education is when a student is very young, long before he or she reaches even junior high school let alone college. The new tools have the potential to be powerful adjuncts for teaching basic skills and many other subjects as well. How they will be used will depend, more than anything else, on the political structures of education. The most important issue dividing the "have's" and "have-not's" will not be the availability of a computer but the motivation to learn and the energy, guidance, and inspiration needed to convert motivation into action. Computers cannot instill motivation, only channel and reinforce it. The biggest problems with education will remain the difficult human ones.

Finally, traditional colleges and universities will certainly face new threats to their markets from nontraditional competitors, earliest in areas of high-value professional and continuing education, such as in business, medicine, engineering, and law. The delivery of learner-centered education to students wherever they live and work, throughout their lives, without requiring them to live on campus to access it, is likely to become a lucrative opportunity for entrepreneurs and a liberation for many students.

The information revolution is well underway. The existing educational establishment is being challenged to innovate, reinvent itself, and take advantage of the new information tools to create more affordable and learner-centered programs of education. If it can respond quickly enough, it will maintain its historic position of leadership in guiding educational change. If it cannot, others will.

PART 2

MEETING THE CHALLENGE

5

Moving Toward a Mobile Teaching and Learning Environment: Using Notebook Computers

Donald Sargeant

Introduction

About thirty-five years ago, I—like most students—attended college full-time and lived in on-campus residence halls. The computing world featured a tightly regulated mainframe in a central location with 'dumb' terminals. My learning involved using static equipment at a fixed location.

Today, fewer than 25% of the full-time students at the University of Minnesota, Crookston (UMC) reside on campus and only half are attending full-time. Full-time students are provided notebook computers which are connected by networks to many independent computers. Learning to use computer networks and software occurs everywhere.

Most colleges and universities realize that there has been a paradigm shift. Previously, institutions served primarily full-time students, with minimal connection to society, and with institution-controlled stand-alone courses which *might* use computers. The shift is toward colleges which serve a broad range of students in collaboration with other educational institutions and businesses, as well as shared courses which rely heavily on the use of technology (computers, software, and networks). In addition to the changing demographics of our students, the life cycle of most technology is less than a year, and the body of knowledge is doubling every four years. This acceleration of technological and knowledge advancements along with expanding expectations of students, faculty, employers, and society at large present a growing challenge throughout higher education as institutions strive to enhance learning environments.

In response, colleges and universities are striving to provide enhanced technology for faculty and students. The University of Minnesota, Crookston solution was to provide faculty and students with mobile notebook computers beginning in the Fall of 1993.

Institutional Strategic Plan

Colleges must develop strategic plans as a means of responding to change and surviving in an increasingly competitive educational environment. At UMC in 1992, the strategic planning process focused on the goal of developing exemplary technical baccalaureate programs. A key underlying assumption was that this must be done with limited incremental funds from the federal or state government. As part of developing the strategic plan, over 2,000 prospective students, parents, employers, legislators, alumni, and faculty from within the university and from other educational institutions were surveyed. They were asked what they saw as important in developing technical baccalaureate programs for the future. Their responses included the following:

- Students and employers wanted more applied projects in courses and programs.
- Students and employers wanted a connection between the workplace and the programs.
- Employers wanted more management, supervision, and technology courses.
- Employers sought access to education in their places of business.
- Employers wanted more short-term, module-oriented courses.

The overall conclusion was that the UMC curriculum would be redesigned with more emphasis on self-directed and interactive learning, courses would have modules, and would use technology. That meant that all courses, programs, and services would need to be revised.

As an outcome of the survey and upon review of the changing demographics, *UMC 2002: A Strategic Plan* was developed which contains the following five strategies:

- Focus on students and employers' needs and meet or exceed their expectations
- Actively seek and establish partnerships with other educational institutions and employers
- Incorporate the use of technology and telecommunications throughout the institution
- Develop quality programs and services
- Be accountable by establishing critical measures and benchmarks for all strategies

This strategic plan has been the focal point of planning and budgeting for every unit on campus. Nearly every student, faculty and staff member, employer, and legislator who visits campus would say that the teaching and the services at UMC are more effective today than they were three years ago. They also believe it will be even more effective two years from now. Two institutional strategies seem to capture everyone's attention: collaboration and technology.

The focal point is the notebook computer. Over 100 colleges and universities have visited UMC in the first two years of the initiative to observe and visit with students, faculty, and administrators about the notebook computer environment. Nearly every day someone at the institution is answering questions about the technology strategy by telephone or by e-mail. The remainder of this chapter describes how UMC first provided notebook computers to students and faculty and how it continues to revise its technology strategy to match the mission and resources of the institution.

Barriers in the Traditional Computer Laboratory Setting

Historically, UMC's approach to meeting student computer needs had been one of placing computers in specialized classrooms, laboratories, the library, and in dormitories. Some students owned computers, which in some cases were not compatible with those in the campus facilities. There were significant barriers to continuing to support this multi-platform environment:

- Students were tied to a specific location, and the hours which this space was available were restricted. The doors were locked throughout the night.
- Faculty also competed for access to the limited computer laboratory time. This limited the use of computers and technology as an education-enabling tool for enhancing teaching and learning.
- Most of the computers and software in the laboratories were outdated. Funds were used to purchase new technology, but we continued to keep the older computers.
- There were usually a few empty seats in all classrooms each hour of the day. Computers were in classrooms, but they were unavailable for general student use during class hours.
- There was a growing need for student use of computers outside the classroom.
- There were not enough funds in the budget to address the growing technology needs.

Solution: The Mobile Computer

The solution chosen by UMC was to purchase mobile notebook computers and provide them to all full-time students as part of their tuition and fees. This solution addressed each of the above barriers, and provided additional benefits:

- Nearly all faculty incorporated technology into their courses and began to rethink teaching and learning.
- Current technology was significantly advanced.
- Out-of-classroom learning was enhanced by 24-hour student access to technology, software, and networks.
- Financial resources were available to purchase current technology.

The outcome of this solution is that each student has a personal computer to use whenever they want. By providing the computer and software as part of the tuition and fees, the technology fee qualifies as a financial aid expense because it is a mandatory fee. Dollars that had been spent on computer replacements in laboratories are now spent on building the campus networking infrastructure. Since all students and faculty have mobile notebook computers, they bring their personal computers to the classroom, which assures that the desired software and files are present. Every classroom essentially becomes a computer laboratory. Providing standardized computer hardware and software helps define academic expectations and provides for cost effectiveness. The notebook computer is becoming the classroom of the future.

BUILDING THE MOBILE ENVIRONMENT

UMC has used the following framework to continue to adjust its mobile computing environment. It consists of nine components. Each and every component is both important and constantly changing.

Technology Plan

The first step in the technology planning process involved describing our vision for the use of computers and technology ten years into the future. Consensus was that notebook computers would be commonplace and that the notebook computer would be used in every academic course and program and all college services. No one would be excluded from being involved with technology. Thus, the institutional technology plan to accommodate this vision was that

- Everyone would have a notebook computer.
- Everyone would be connected to everybody.
- Everyone would have 24-hour access to their computer and the network.

This plan is very simple and easy to understand.

Project Management

The first year could have been called crisis or survival management at UMC. The risk was obvious and there were no models to follow. There were numerous activities that needed to be done and areas that needed improvement. A list of nearly 1,000 projects was developed.

Work teams were established and assigned projects. They were to gather broader input and to move quickly. Teams were composed of faculty, administrators, and students. Examples of the work team titles and their activities were technology (reconfiguring classrooms, developing the local area network), curriculum (developing core components, defining new degree requirements), finance (computer purchase or lease, technology fees for full- and part-time students), faculty and staff development (identifying training needs, review of courseware), policy development (e-mail, notebook computer inventory), and publications (developing notebook computer flyer, revising all flyers and publications). A similar process has been followed each year. It begins each summer with a planning retreat focused on the strategic plan.

Curriculum Revision

Undertaking a drastic change such as converting to mobile computing provides an opportunity to revisit each and every course, service, and activity. Curriculum revision is the most important part of the transition. College wide core components were defined for integration into all courses and programs. Critical measures were developed for each core component. These components are to be implemented into the courses and programs within five years. UMC's educational mission as an applied technical institution has been strengthened, and program assessment, measurable learner outcomes, and active learning have become an integral part of the institution.

Faculty and Staff Training

The initial training focused on basic productivity software such as Microsoft Windows, Word, Excel, PowerPoint, Pegasus e-mail, and Gopher. It was important to have all faculty, staff, and students communicating using a standardized core package of software. There is a required course for all new students with proficiency modules for the productivity software. At this time, very few students enter with proficiency abilities. Upgrade training as well as training on new software is a continual process. Most of the faculty and student training continues through a colleague-to-colleague pyramiding or a one-on-one process. An instructional technology center was established for review of new software and hardware and to coordinate technology skill building.

The identification and support of early adopters and innovators are key in the adoption and advancement of the technology strategy. Additional instructional development funds were provided in two grant programs to aid faculty in course redesign. A mini-grant fund was established whereby faculty could receive funding for salary, equipment, software, and/or travel projects/activities which enhance student learning by incorporating the use of technology into a course. A second grant program was created to provide funds for faculty to employ students to enhance the student's education and work experience while assisting faculty to integrate multimedia and technology based instructional materials into the curriculum. Examples of faculty course redesign this year were course delivery on the Internet, analysis and development of student home pages, replacement of traditional textbook with LAN delivery of course pack, and web access to view plant materials. There is an increasing interest by faculty in redesigning courses for student projects, course conference centers, and other interactive learning tools.

Financial Creativity

UMC entered into the mobile computer environment with no new state funds and no grants to support the initiative. Therefore, early in the planning it became apparent that UMC would not have the resources within the existing budget to purchase a computer for each student. The most viable solution was to increase student fees to purchase the computers. No one wants their fees increased unless it is demonstrated that there will be an increase in the value of the service being provided. Therefore, dialogue with students was initiated focusing on the possibility of implementing a technology access fee which would provide each full-time student with a personal notebook computer. Nearly all students liked the idea of having their own computer. Reviews of position announcements and employment surveys were indications to students that nearly every baccalaureate career required computer literacy. The use of technology to enhance their educational experience and, in turn, to enhance their career opportunities became the most important value added factor to students.

It was concluded that the computers would be needed by all students since most classes had a mix of students by major and by grade level. It would not be acceptable to have some students in class with mobile computers and not others. Most important, in order for the university to manage the rapid changes in hardware and software as they relate to teaching and learning, it was imperative for the university to own the technology. It would be very difficult to change hardware and software if it were owned by the student. The constantly changing technology, software, and courseware were key factors in the rationale for the university to own computers.

The most recent computer is the IBM 701 CS notebook with color monitor, modem, sound, and Ethernet card. The notebooks are pre-loaded with Microsoft Windows 95 and Office 95, Pegasus Mail, and Netscape. The 1996–97 technology access fee is $300 per quarter which finances the computer equipment and software, an on-site help desk, access to local information resources including the library, Internet access, e-mail, and free printing. The computers are financed by the IBM Credit Corporation with a monthly lease payment. The student technology access fee budget also includes expenditures for the pre-bundled software, insurance, and bad debt loss.

Investments in the institution budget have been redirected to provide all faculty with notebook computers, additional faculty development funds, an instructional technology center, reconfiguration of classrooms to accommodate network activity at each student seat, upgrades in the local area network, and additional dial-in access. The transition is viewed as a five-year project, and great strides have been made in the first three years. The redirection of funds continues because no additional new funds appear to be forthcoming. Before initiating the notebook computer strategy, the annual computer services budget was $170,000. Additional funds have been reallocated as shown in Table 5.1.

TABLE 5.1

UNIVERSITY OF MINNESOTA, CROOKSTON
Summary of Expenditures

	FY94	*FY95*	*FY96*	*FY97 (Est.)*
Student Investment				
(Hardware/Software/ LAN Access/Printing)				
Technology Access Fee	$705	$750	$780	$900
TOTAL	**$705**	**$750**	**$780**	**$900**
Institution Investment - Reallocations				
Faculty Notebook Computers (lease)	N/A	$75,000	$107,000	$110,000
Classroom Remodeling (No. and Cost)	2 $40,000	6 $120,000	6 $120,000	5 $75,000
Faculty/Staff Development				
Training	$20,000	$25,000	$30,000	$30,000
Mini-Grants	N/A	N/A	$20,000	$20,000
Instructional Development-Student Employment	N/A	N/A	N/A	$20,000
Support Services (FTE and SEE)				
Help Desk	1 $22,000	1.5 $33,000	2 $49,000	2 $50,000
Instructional Development Center	N/A	N/A	1 $55,000	1 $65,000
WEB Master	N/A	N/A	$6,000	1 $50,000
Telephone (Additional lines and costs)	N/A	8 $8,000	16 $12,000	$16,000
Infrastructure				
Servers, Routers, Software	$46,000	$74,000	$43,000	$68,000
TOTAL	**$128,000**	**$335,000**	**$442,000**	**$504,000**
Outcomes-Critical Measures				
FTE Enrollment	1,036	1,043	1,181	1,375
Institutional Technology Investment per FTE	$123	$321	$374	$367
Average Class Size	19.2	20.4	22.6	23.0
Credits per Faculty	42	50	54	57

Facility and Local Area Network Redesign

The campus local area network (LAN) is a combination of multiple small networks. It is managed with Novell 3.12 and 4.1, and Windows NT operating systems. All faculty, staff, and students have e-mail addresses and have access to the LAN. About one-third of the general purpose classrooms have been remodeled to include Ethernet and electrical connections at each student seat, a digital overhead camera and projection unit in the teaching station to connect the faculty notebook into the server system and a printer. More classrooms and laboratories continue to be remodeled to provide Internet access. Every residential life student has an Ethernet connection in their room. The common areas on campus have similar connections. Students are seen carrying and working with their notebook computers everywhere.

Faculty and student expectations of the technology strategy continue to rise. Success was attained when everyone could send and receive documents both on and off campus and everyone could access the web on the first attempt. Now, everyone expects faster, easier to use, and more powerful hardware and software at least on an annual basis. When something is changed on the LAN or the LAN is slow, it doesn't go unnoticed. Even if one explains to students and faculty in Minnesota that freezing and thawing have an effect on telephone lines which in turn can effect a particular location on Netscape; they want this corrected now.

Computer Standardization

It was agreed early in the project that UMC would not be able to support more than one computing platform. The DOS platform was common on campus and in the business world. The advantages of standardizing on one platform are many. It provides for cost effectiveness in purchasing and in service. The big advantage was that nearly everyone could help everybody. Students in particular could help other students and, in some cases, faculty. Standardizing is very important at the help desk for it simplifies the product line that staff and students must be familiar with in addressing warranty, hardware, and software questions.

UMC has changed notebooks every year for the first three consecutive years. The initial computer in Fall 1993 was the IBM 350 monochrome, equipped with four megabytes of RAM but without a modem or Ethernet card. Since over 50% of UMC students live off-campus, the need for modem access quickly became very apparent. Also the need for Ethernet cards to enable each computer to connect to the campus network became a high priority. Therefore, in the second year the IBM 350 was traded for the

IBM 340 monochrome with modem and a PC Ethernet card. In Fall 1995 students were interested in color screens and Windows 95 software so the IBM 340 was traded for the IBM 701 CS with color display, 8 megabytes of RAM, and a 14,400 baud fax/modem, in addition to the PC Ethernet cards. The interest of students in having new notebooks and software was best exhibited at the end of Fall 1995. Eight-hundred fifty students had the 340 IBM notebook computer, and they were asked to turn in their computers when they finished fall final exams. They would then be issued a new IBM 701 notebook computer. Within 10 days, all 850 of the IBM 340 notebook computers were turned in for the new computer.

In Fall 1996 students continued to use the IBM 701 notebook computer. Faculty use the IBM 365 ED with 24 megabytes of RAM, 28.8 baud modem, and built in CD-ROM.

Software—Adjusting to Trends

Discussions concerning software occur nearly every day. The pre-bundled Microsoft software package which is used campus wide has been upgraded each year. The Microsoft Office 95 Professional applications of Word, Excel, PowerPoint, and Access, with Pegasus e-mail and Netscape Navigator serve as the core software. Faculty also use assorted off-the-shelf software unique to their courses. Some faculty have developed their own software applications. Although software can be accessed on the LAN, the most reliably available software is that which is loaded into the notebooks. The addition of Lotus Notes as part of the core software for every computer is being evaluated.

Technology Support Service Additions

The first support service added was a help desk. It is staffed from early morning to late night and serves as the distribution and service center, provides warranty service, checks out notebooks for part-time students, and is a place for everyone to go for problem assistance. It is the busiest place on campus.

The second year, a campus instructional technology center was added. The center is staffed by an instructional designer and is equipped with evaluation hardware including video capture and editing equipment, scanners, color printers, writeable CD-ROM, and numerous software packages including authoring applications. Its purpose is to aid faculty in the review of various software and technology related equipment and to provide some training programs. Often students work on faculty projects using the specialized equipment in the center. It is the focal point for faculty and staff to work and share in the redesign of courses and curriculum.

A Webmaster position was added to direct, manage, and maintain the campus Web site. The Webmaster provides technical support to faculty and staff in the integration of instructional and informational materials on the Web. The Web has become the first reference source for many in the Information Age.

Technology support services that enhance user friendliness are critical to the incorporation of technology in improving teaching and learning.

ASSESSING THE STUDENT EXPERIENCE

In December 1995, UMC students were surveyed to evaluate the progress of the adoption of the notebook computer as part of the teaching and learning environment. The survey was administered to all students enrolled in second period classes. They were surveyed about the benefits they have gained, about the extent of their use, and about their perceptions of the overall impact on their education and career preparation. The following graphs illustrate the results.

Student Rating of the Benefits of Notebook Computers

FIGURE 5.1

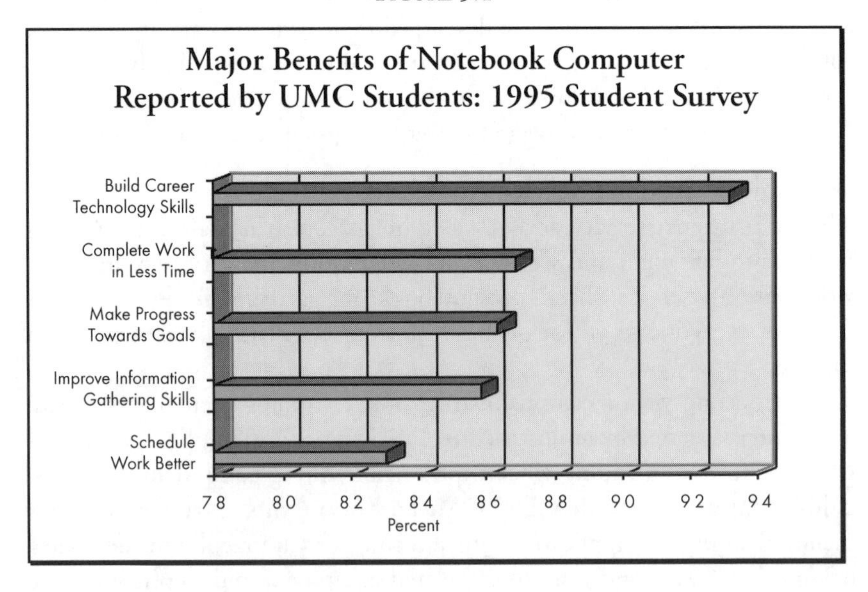

The large majority of UMC students indicated that they receive major benefits from the technology commitment. Almost 9 out of 10 students reported benefits. The strongest perceived benefits come from building technology skills that students associate with career preparation. They also perceived gains in efficiency of their learning experiences as 87% of students indicated that they are able to schedule and complete their work more quickly. The perception of increased quality was noted as 75% reported an increase in the amount and quality of learning.

Student Use of the Notebook Computer

FIGURE 5.2

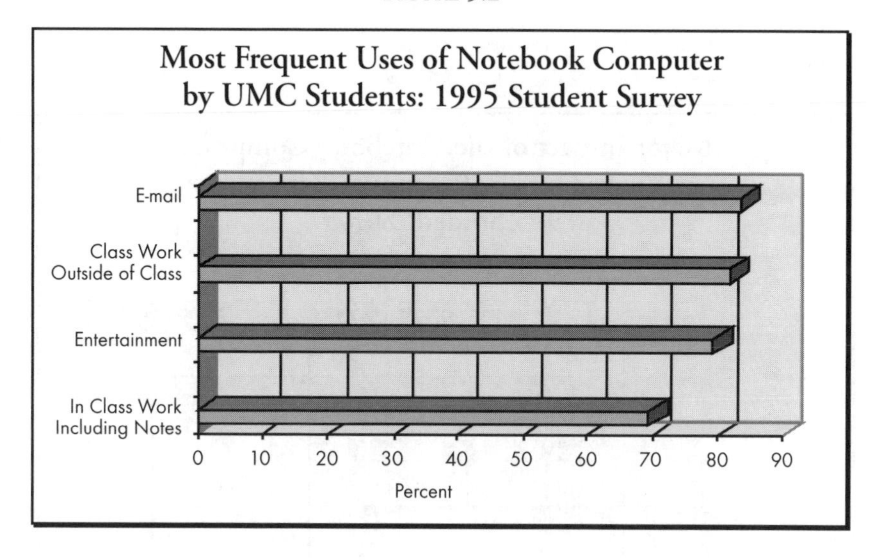

The use of computers and networking reflects the diversity of students and programs at UMC. The most popular applications are writing papers, completing assignments, sending e-mail, and entertainment. Note taking, information searches on the Internet, self-directed learning, and communicating with faculty and other students, also ranked high in frequency of use. UMC students illustrate a growing level of sophistication with approximately 50% of the students using spreadsheets, presentation graphics, and problem solving applications.

Student View of the Impact of the Notebook Computer Technology Strategy

Students are also validating several of the key assumptions behind the UMC technology strategy. For example, two out of three students stated they believe their prospects for getting the job they want after graduation are enhanced by their UMC experience. Four out of five students indicated that they have gained in ability to continue learning after graduation as a result of exposure to technology. One out of two students indicated that the technology commitment of UMC was a factor in their decision to enroll, and an equal number said that it influenced them to stay at UMC to pursue a degree once they were enrolled. The lower percentage for each of these questions is influenced by the fact that half of the students surveyed were already enrolled at UMC before the technology strategy was implemented.

FIGURE 5.3

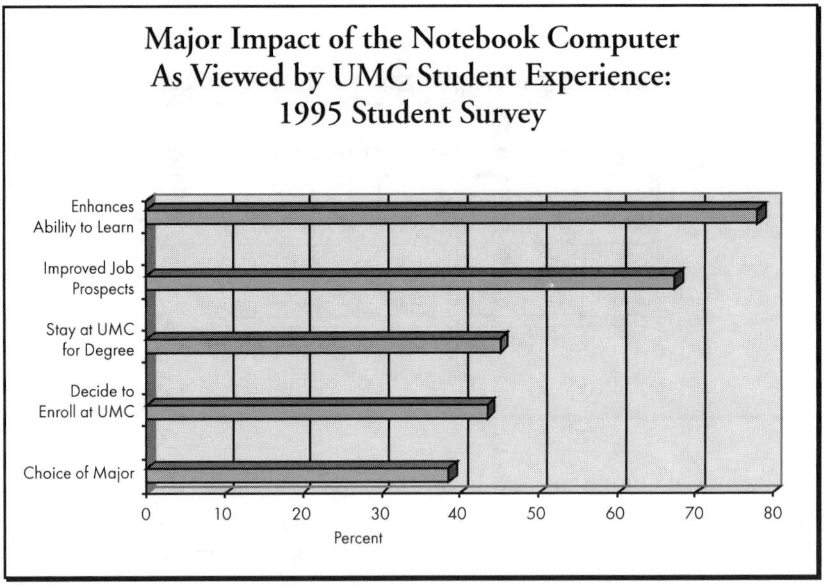

Major Impact of the Notebook Computer As Viewed by UMC Student Experience: 1995 Student Survey

Enhances Ability to Learn
Improved Job Prospects
Stay at UMC for Degree
Decide to Enroll at UMC
Choice of Major
0 10 20 30 40 50 60 70 80
Percent

Several of the students who were interviewed personally confirmed these survey results. For example, a UMC student from Winnipeg, Manitoba said: "The biggest impact is that we are looked upon as the pioneer, and it is a source of pride. It was a big factor in my choice to come to UMC." A non-traditional student noted: "If you have a strong understanding of technology, you have a great advantage in business." She indicated that UMC's technology commitment was a big factor in her decision to come back to school and in her decision to pursue a career in the information technology field. A freshman commented that: "A lot of students come to UMC because of the technology."

ASSESSING THE FACULTY EXPERIENCE

Widespread use of computing technology by the college's faculty became common during the 1980s, and by 1987 all full-time faculty members had desktop computers. During this time, faculty members were encouraged to incorporate computing technology into their teaching, research, and outreach. Their experiences helped to build support for a larger commitment to integrating technology into the educational process. In 1994, all faculty were provided with notebook computers. In December 1995, faculty were asked to assess their campus and their personal experience since the implementation of the notebook technology commitment.

Faculty Rating of the Benefits of Notebook Computer for Students

Ninety percent of faculty indicated that expanded learning opportunities and increased communications between faculty and students were major benefits of providing notebook computers to students. Both the faculty and the students indicated that the notebook computers provided increased flexibility, allowing students to do more course work outside of class and increasing student employment opportunities.

FIGURE 5.4

Faculty Rating of Major Benefits of Notebook Computers to UMC Students: 1995 Faculty Survey

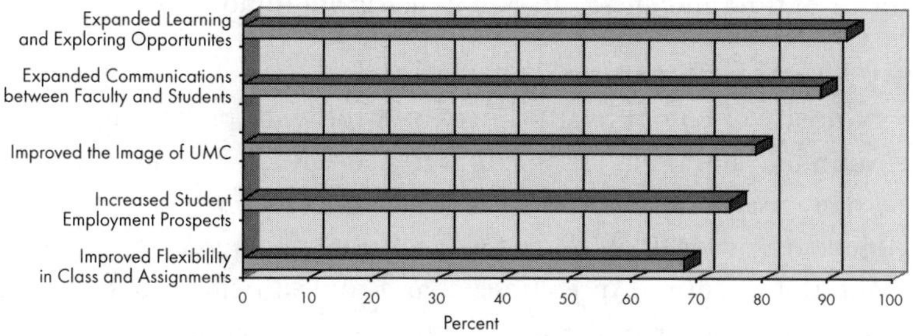

Expanded Learning and Exploring Opportunites
Expanded Communications between Faculty and Students
Improved the Image of UMC
Increased Student Employment Prospects
Improved Flexibililty in Class and Assignments
0 10 20 30 40 50 60 70 80 90 100
Percent

Faculty Perception of Changes Linked to the Notebook Technology Strategy

The most pervasive changes on the campus reported by faculty are directly linked to the use of technology. Technology skills and computer literacy have expanded across the campus. Faculty members feel pushed to keep ahead of the skills and expectations of students. The majority of faculty reported increased communications with students and other faculty, as well as linkages with other colleagues.

FIGURE 5.5

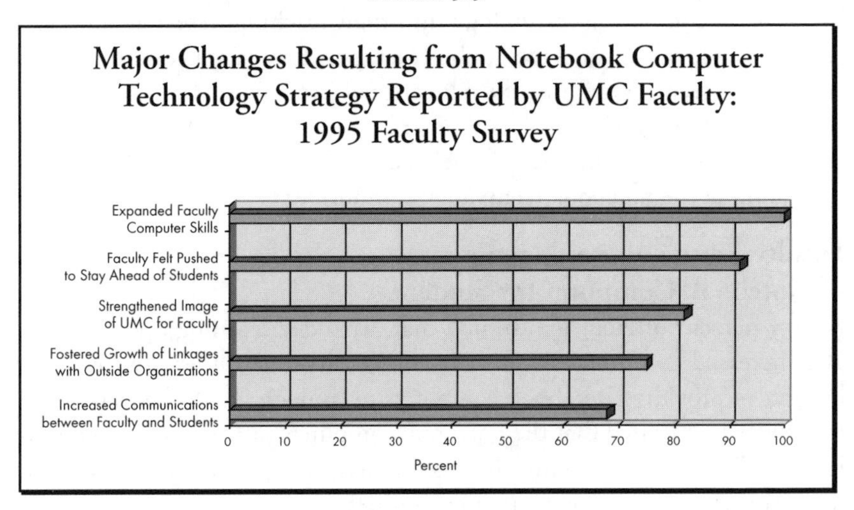

There is considerable evidence to suggest that the most significant short term impact is in the reallocation of time to learn and use different notebook computer applications. At this stage the majority of the faculty do not perceive an increase in productivity resulting from the technology. That is not surprising given the fact that faculty have made a considerable personal investment of time and energy in skill building and innovation.

Faculty Use of Computing Applications

The routine use of computers and networks for word processing and electronic communications has become universal at UMC, with nearly everyone making daily use of these tools. This could be said about many campuses today. However, at UMC, 90% of the faculty are now reporting regular use of presentation software, spreadsheets, and topical field related software. Nearly all faculty also report using the resources of the Internet and electronic libraries, technologies that were not readily available three years ago.

Although there is widespread use of the general tools, usage among faculty falls off for more specialized tools as the graph above shows. However, there is anecdotal evidence that there is an accelerating rate in the use of these tools.

FIGURE 5.6

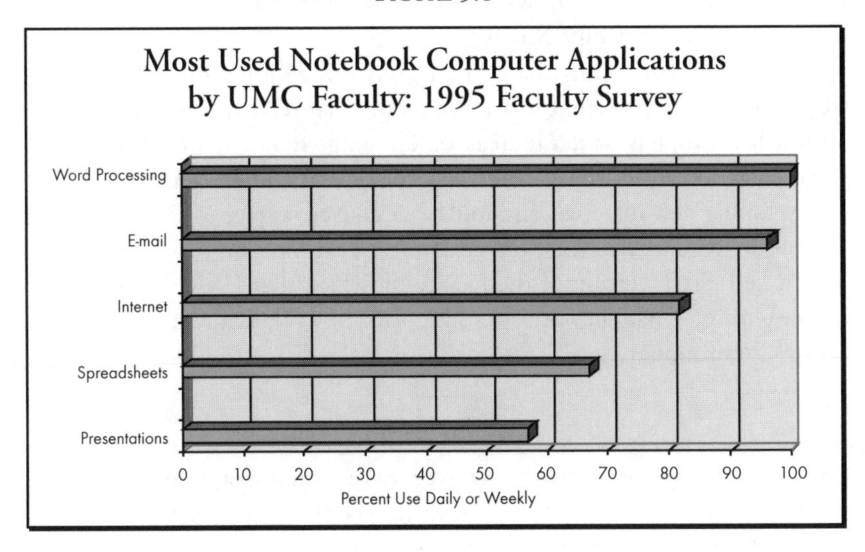

FIGURE 5.7

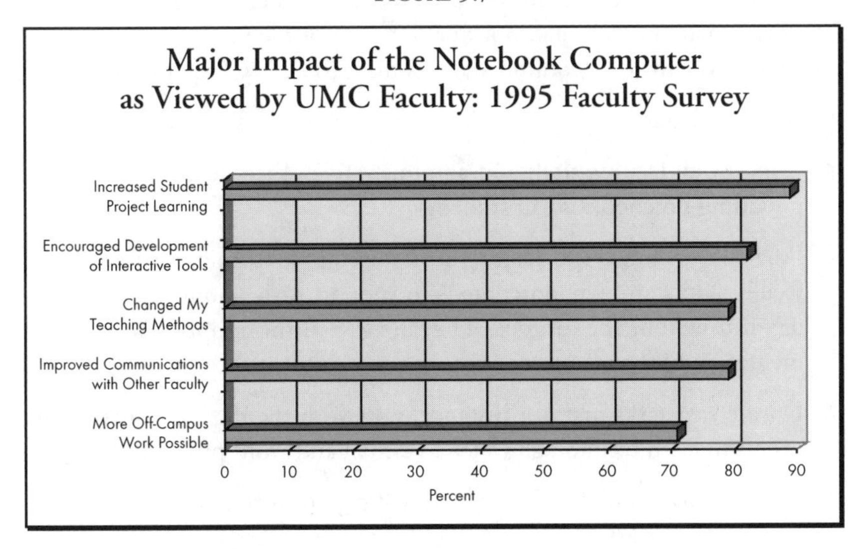

Faculty View of the Impact of the Notebook Computer Technology Strategy

There is agreement among the UMC faculty on the impact of the notebook technology. Ninety percent of faculty report that student opportunities for project learning have been increased. The large majority of UMC faculty perceive significant changes in the way they teach and are actively involved in developing new materials and tools that take advantage of the technology.

Improvements in intra-faculty communications and off campus work were noted. Sixty percent of the faculty indicated that UMC has become a more exciting, dynamic, and rewarding place to work as a result of the technology commitment.

SUMMARY

The 1993 commitment that the University of Minnesota, Crookston made to provide all students and faculty with notebook computers had an immediate and dramatic impact on the teaching and learning environment. Students have renewed self-confidence as they approach their careers, prepared with up-to-date technology skills and an approach for lifelong learning. Faculty made the time investment required to expand their own skills and evaluate their teaching, and they continue this commitment.

Among the major recommendations from the UMC experience are

- Begin with a plan.
- Connect all faculty, staff, and administrative offices to the LAN before providing notebooks to all students.
- Provide new sources of instructional development funds available to all faculty and staff. The outcome is to support early adopters of technology throughout the campus. They are key in the adoption and implementation of the technology strategy.
- Do the easy tasks first; for instance, start with the most productive and easiest to learn technologies such as e-mail and word processing.
- Students place a high value on and will pay for technology if it is incorporated into nearly every course and service on campus.
- Provide just-in-time training for faculty and staff in bite size pieces. This is a continual process.
- Establish work teams to gather input and respond quickly to the needs identified in the new notebook computer environment.

- Provide technology support services of a help desk and an Instructional Technology Center to increase use and user friendliness. Remember, students are paying more and expect more.
- Technology initiatives require continual attention. The technology strategy is only as good as the weakest link. Expect a crisis every week. Faculty, staff, and students learn quickly that problems may occur, but focusing on possible solutions is the order of the day.
- Adopting a successful technology strategy requires not only a commitment to reallocation of funds within each unit budget to implement the notebook network technology strategy, but also an ongoing commitment to keep technology current and to continue building technology capacity, along with critical training and support.
- Students are the most under-utilized resource in teaching and learning and in adjusting to change. In most cases, they have time, will take risks, are creative, and want to be more involved.
- Students gain valuable self-directed learning skills as a result of having 24-hour access, easy to use systems, and encouragement to work together with other students.
- Putting notebook computers in the hands of students and faculty is a broadly effective educational strategy.

The moral of the UMC story is that students are using technology to learn more as they prepare for their careers in the Information Age society. Faculty and staff are working smarter and becoming more effective by using new ways. Notebook computers were the focal point for responding to change. It just may be the catalyst needed by higher education institutions to retain their role in the Information Age.

6

Project Vision: Toward More Active and Collaborative Learning

Robert E. Dunham

Technological and social change will transform twenty-first century institutions from transmitters of knowledge—which characterizes education in highly stable societies—to creators of new paradigms—which is the norm in a rapidly changing society. Education today must, like any enterprise, be a bold or dangerous undertaking, preparing people for a changing world rather than one of permanence. The enterprising college or university must understand that its mission is not so much to teach as it is to create a culture—driven by technology—in which students, faculty, and staff are continuously learning.
Robert C. Heterick, Jr.

Introduction

In the spirit of transformation, The Commonwealth Educational System of The Pennsylvania State University has embarked on a bold venture called Project Vision with the hope of moving from a predominantly teaching environment to an environment where the emphasis is on students and faculty learning together.

Several factors cause us to move in this direction:

1. Students are beginning to demand a more active role in learning; schooling has become too bureaucratic as well as time and place bound. The

elementary school provides a very good beginning for students to become active learners. The teacher often moves around the room working with small groups of students rather than standing in front of the room lecturing to the group. As students progress through secondary school and into college, the teacher becomes more of a dispenser of information, students become more passive, and courses are packaged in restrictive time slots.

2. Older, nontraditional students often find it difficult to schedule courses at traditional times and places. Because these students often combine school and work or family responsibilities, the times that faculty prefer to teach are not always the times that students are available to take courses. If distances are involved, the "talking head" is no better today than in the early 1960s when television courses were in vogue.
3. A reexamination of the best use of faculty time is needed as costs of higher education continue to increase. With digital technology, we should reexamine whether it is the best use of faculty time to deliver the same lectures semester after semester. Or, at some smaller campuses it may not be cost effective to offer courses for a few students. A different mode of learning could help alleviate these concerns.
4. While the driving force for change should be the improvement of learning, the technology available today enables many of these changes.

Commonwealth Educational System

The Commonwealth Educational System (CES) of Penn State includes seventeen undergraduate campuses that offer the first two years of most of the university's undergraduate majors and some upper division baccalaureate programs. These campuses also offer associate degree programs and a wide array of certificate programs and courses as part of outreach efforts to the local communities. Penn State is one university, geographically distributed. It has one president, one board of trustees, and one university faculty senate. Students may flow from campus to campus in order to complete their academic programs. The faculty are dedicated to undergraduate education; they devote significant personal attention to students and classes are small.

Goals of Project Vision

The goal of the CES, beginning with Project Vision, is to reach out to more of the state's population with high quality learning opportunities at a cost most people can afford. Beyond this, CES hopes to become a model for transforming education in the twenty-first century, not only for multi-campus public university systems, but also for voluntary consortia of private colleges and for associations linking higher education institutions with elementary and secondary schools, social service agencies, hospitals, various units of local and state government, and international organizations.

The goals of Project Vision are to foster anytime, anywhere asynchronous learning, encourage active and collaborative learning, and support the faculty in the use of technology for learning. Project Vision is learner-centered, not instructor-centered. It uses faculty members as designers of learning environments and advisors to the learners. It is free from time constraints; students learn at times convenient to them. It is facilitated by virtual learning experiences. It fosters collaboration at each campus and among campuses.

Description of the Project

Project Vision was initiated in the Fall of 1995 at three of the CES campuses: Berks Campus in Reading, Pennsylvania; Delaware County Campus in Lima, Pennsylvania; and the Mont Alto Campus, in Mont Alto, Pennsylvania. These campuses were chosen because of the interest and background of the faculty, the support from the campus administration, and the technical support committed to the project.

At each campus twenty new first-year students and four faculty were chosen to participate in Project Vision. Each student enrolled in two Project Vision courses for the first and second semesters. In addition, each student took several traditional courses. Each faculty member and each student was provided with an IBM ThinkPad computer, equipped with appropriate software.

Selection of Students

A deliberate attempt was made to recruit and select a diverse group of students. Some were academically talented; others were academically respectable, but not gifted. Some of the students selected were users of computers; others had never used one. There was also diversity in gender and race.

A flyer was developed and sent to prospective students. Some of the students had applied for admission to one of the three campuses offering Project Vision; others had been offered admission, but had not yet accepted. An application was sent to all prospective students requesting completion and the submission of letters of recommendation. The Project Vision faculty at each campus reviewed all applicants and made the final selection. Applicants were asked to respond to two questions: "Why are you applying to Project

Vision?" and "What has been your most valuable learning experience to date?" Predicted grade point average, major, and ethnicity were used in order to select a representative cross-section of students.

Selection of Faculty

The faculty selection was a bit more complicated and difficult. Many faculty requested consideration for the project, but in the final analysis many were not accepted because of campus and course concerns, rather than individual qualifications. Having three campuses with a complement of interested faculty in three specific course areas was necessary in order to complete the selection. Because some campuses had faculty in two areas but not the third, selected faculty were recruited because of the courses they taught and their campus location. Interest in the project was deemed more important than experience using the technologies. Once the three faculty were selected at each of the three locations, all faculty agreed to be involved in the freshman seminar. Later, in the process of developing courses, it was decided that the librarians at each of the campuses should be included because the freshman seminar course had a heavy emphasis on information seeking and analysis. In the end, four faculty at each of the three locations were selected.

Courses

Since courses chosen for Project Vision were to be learner-centered, considerable time was devoted to the development of course materials and the design of the learning experience. Six faculty were released full-time from January until August to develop the courses. Three faculty were released for June and July, and the other three faculty joined them during the first semester. Library Studies 197-A and Health Education 48 were offered in the first semester and American Studies 100 and Science, Technology, and Society 200 were offered in the second semester. Three faculty, one at each of the participating campuses, were responsible for each course. All faculty participated in the Library Studies course.

Without released time for the faculty it would not have been possible to initiate this project. In the future, however, it may not be necessary to release faculty as much as we did for this initial effort.

Library Studies 197A: Learning strategies for the information age. Sometimes known as the freshman seminar course, this course is unlike the other courses in that it uses a more traditional mode of scheduled meetings for the first two-thirds of the course. This is necessary in order for the students to become comfortable with the technology and to wean students from the traditional classroom environment.

The goal of this course is to introduce students to learning strategies that are essential for success in the Information Age. Students, working individually and in groups, will be able to identify, procure, evaluate, and present information from a variety of sources and in a variety of formats. Some of the specific goals are to:

1. Use computer software for accessing information including Internet World Wide Web browsers such as Netscape, FTP, Archie, Gopher, and Veronica Telnet to on-line library catalogs.
2. Search the Penn State Library Information Access System (LIAS) to locate books, videos, and other information through The Cat (the on-line library catalog), and to locate citations to periodicals, newspapers, and other information sources.
3. Evaluate information for authority, relevancy, currency, and accuracy.
4. Discuss the impact of information technologies on individual and group learning, including the advantages and disadvantages of these technologies to the individual and society.

Health Education 48. This course explores values as they relate to ethical decision-making and health behavior. Its major objectives are to present and discuss ethical issues in reproductive health, to increase the students' awareness of the complexities of these issues, and to encourage an examination of value standards as they relate to certain ethical topics. This course was taught in conjunction with Library Studies 197-A and became the content area for using some of the skills learned in that course.

American Studies 100. This course provides a general introduction to major issues, ideas, and movements in American culture and has many opportunities for both independent and collaborative learning. One of the key goals of the course is to introduce students to conflicting interpretations of history and culture with an emphasis on critical thinking. The course was conducted primarily on-line and featured frequent on-line discussions of course topics during the first nine weeks, an individual family history paper, several group reports, and a major collaborative project, the *Multimedia Web Magazine.*

Science, Technology, and Society (STS) 200. There are two general objectives of Science, Technology, and Society courses. The first is to promote critical awareness through the interdisciplinary approach, and the second is to provide knowledge which includes interconnections, linkages, etc., for integrating education. These two objectives enable the student to weave an integrative web of understanding by examining the dynamics of science, technology, and society. Within our colleges and public schools, Science, Technology, and Society is becoming the new general education. Science, Technology, and Society is gaining recognition worldwide as a way to enable citizens to participate responsibly in modern democracies.

There are four themes in this course:

1. The whole is greater than the sum of its parts
2. Costs or harms using the concept of trade-offs and the heuristic that there is no free lunch
3. The concept of synthesis and the heuristic that there is neither value-free knowledge, nor knowledge-free value
4. Citizenship

Technology Support

The technological support for such an undertaking cannot be overemphasized. In addition to the computers given to the students and faculty, it was necessary to provide staff support. Each campus needed a local person who was technologically proficient and who also understood instructional development. Special equipment was given to each of the three campuses so that the project could be implemented.

A centralized staff was needed to train the campus staff and oversee the project and those that followed. A Center for Learning and Academic Technologies (C-LAT) was created centrally to support both the instructional development needs and the technological needs of those involved. C-LAT trained the campus staff, worked with the faculty, and prepared the computers used by the students and faculty. In addition, C-LAT now oversees the operation of Project Vision.

External Partners

Without the financial assistance, the collaboration, and support and encouragement of external partners, this project could not have been initiated. IBM and Bell Atlantic have been partners in Project Vision from the beginning. IBM has assisted in providing computers to faculty and students, and has been very helpful in reviewing the planning of the project. In addition, the Institute for Academic Technology in North Carolina (supported by IBM) was very helpful in training faculty and offering advice. Bell Atlantic, through a financial contribution, made it possible to provide released time and other support to faculty. Representatives from both IBM and Bell Atlantic have visited the project and offered advice and encouragement.

Evaluation and Outcomes

In order to test the goals for the project and to learn even more about this new learning approach, it was agreed from the outset to collect as much data as reasonable. Most of this was to be done internally. It was also felt that in order to get a more objective look at the project and the outcomes it was necessary and desirable to engage an outside consultant. Dr. Christopher Knapper, Director, Instructional Development Centre, Queen's University, Kingston, Ontario, Canada is conducting the external review. He visited with each student and faculty member during the first semester and will return again during the year to complete his interviews. He will also review the data collected and will draw some conclusions about the first year and make recommendations for improving the project.

From some of his preliminary findings and from other anecdotal information, we have already learned some things about the program. Generally, students spend more time on their learning pursuits in the Project Vision courses than in the more traditional courses. They seem to earn better grades than the original prediction formulae would indicate (Vision students earned first semester grade point averages above their predicted averages). Vision students report using their Vision learning skills and technologies in other classes. Despite the fact that they spend much of their time in asynchronous activity, they have developed a strong social bond with other Project Vision students and faculty. Their friendship with other Project Vision students has carried over into extracurricular activities.

They are learning to work in teams. As one of the Project Vision faculty concluded, "It is difficult to say who gained more from Project Vision this first year, the students or the faculty. In any event, the real winner is the learning process, which is the important result because everyone gains from that. Not all change results in progress, but progress only comes about through change, so projects like Project Vision are important to provide the assurance that the use of the new technologies can represent progress in education. I think we accomplished that."

Value to Students

After the first brief period of anxiety, students were quite positive about their experiences. Here is a sampling of student comments following the end of the first year.

> I felt that Project Vision was a truly rewarding experience. I feel that one of the reasons that it was so successful was that the students and the professors all seemed to be working together to achieve a common

> goal, that, of course, being a successful year and successful experiment. All of my classmates seemed to be quite enthusiastic about learning, this due in part to the computers that we were allowed to use, but also due to the relaxing atmosphere in which our classes were conducted.
>
> Many strong friendships were formed and the class as a whole performed well together. As for my personal experience, I am so grateful for the opportunity that I had to participate in Project Vision. It has opened so many doors for me that it is unbelievable. Not only have I gained extensive computer experience (that will undoubtedly be useful in the future), but I have also gotten a great sense of satisfaction from being a part of this newer style of learning, and from being successful in it!
>
> One great thing about Project Vision is that it defies the normal student-teacher relationship that one encounters in traditional classroom teaching. Through Project Vision, students learn from faculty, but faculty also learn from the students. Students are given a chance to share their knowledge with faculty, which is something I've found to be unique to Project Vision.
>
> In Project Vision students are challenged to find their own information rather than having it handed to them on a silver platter. The Project Vision students are forced to accept responsibilities that most students don't encounter till their junior and senior years.
>
> The students in Project Vision dealt with each other as colleagues and as friends. The Vision students here are a tight knit group of friends who not only work together, but play together as well.
>
> Project Vision is the single most exciting and interesting learning experience I've been a part of! It's really incredible knowing that you're working on the cutting edge of technology and learning.

Students are generally pleased and feel they have learned more than expected, have developed collaborative learning skills, are better prepared to enter the job market, have developed critical analysis skills when discovering and sorting information sources, and have carried their active learning over into their traditional courses.

Faculty Collaboration

One of the pleasantly surprising things to emerge from this project is the amount of collaboration among the faculty. Faculty who were very independent and accustomed to teaching autonomously have worked in teams to collaboratively develop the course materials and course design for the project. Some of the collaboration was done synchronously although much was done asynchronously. At first in a computer listserve, and later using a groupware product called FirstClass, the faculty expressed their concerns, fears, hopes, excitement, and questions, rave notices, etc., with each other. A review of those computer conversations serves as a reminder of the ups-and-downs that the faculty experienced during the evolution of Project Vision.

Much of the work done by Project Vision faculty has carried over into other courses they teach, and their advice has been actively sought by other faculty. There appears to be much more openness in what individual faculty are doing in courses as well as more interest and concern with helping students learn. As one of the Project Vision faculty stated, "By far the most outstanding advantage of my involvement with Project Vision has been the opportunity to collaborate with my faculty colleagues. Project Vision required us to collaborate in our disciplinary team—in my case the Health Education team, and interdisciplinarily with members of the Science, Technology, and Society; American Studies; and Library Studies faculty both on my campus and at other campus sites. This collaboration not only made the project courses better, but it also expanded my repertoire of teaching skills. These new skills have transferred into the other courses that I teach so Project Vision has had a broader impact than I expected."

Future Plans

Even before the final formal evaluations are completed, planning for the continuation of the move toward an active and collaborative learning environment continues. Project Vision I has admitted a new class of sixty first-year students at the same three campuses. The same courses with appropriate revisions will again be offered. In addition, at the Berks campus Music 7 will be offered, at York campus Political Science 1 will be offered, and at Mont Alto campus Psychology 2 will be offered. The Delaware Campus is proposing to make the Project Vision a full-year experience by adding Integrative Arts 1, English 15, Psychology 2, Earth and Mineral Sciences 150, and Library Studies 100 to the existing Project Vision courses.

Project Vision II has been developed to expand the first-year experience to three additional campuses in Altoona, Pennsylvania; McKeesport, Pennsylvania; and York, Pennsylvania. Project Vision II also provides two new courses for the second year at the three Project Vision I campuses. These courses are Speech Communication 100 in the Fall Semester and English 202 for the Spring Semester.

In order to speed up the process of getting faculty equipped to deal with asynchronous learning experiences, we have initiated Project Empower and also have focused on the development of core materials which might be available for a variety of courses. Project Empower was begun in the Spring of 1996 with approximately one hundred faculty (including some at every CES location). Each faculty was given a laptop computer (either IBM or Apple) and some released time to develop one or more courses. They were trained by C-LAT, and an instructional development staff person was provided at the home campus. This has created a great deal of excitement, and we are anticipating bringing another one hundred faculty into the program next year. By providing faculty time to develop materials, we are building a content base so that students will find it advantageous to acquire their own computers in the very near future.

Faculty Incentives

In understanding what motivates CES instructors, it is important to start with the understanding of why people choose to teach in the CES. The CES provides both affiliation with a respected university and a place for instructors who typically devote more time to the art and craft of instruction than to conducting research. Being part of Penn State, they can collaborate with and be stimulated by colleagues at University Park and other locations who take the lead in major research projects. At the same time, living and working on a small campus with 30-40 students per class, instructors find that teaching is a meaningful and rewarding experience, and teaching expertise is highly valued. Many of the incentives listed below function as incentives only because the faculty place teaching at the center of their careers.

The incentives to participate are numerous, and, judging from the tidal wave of faculty proposals coming in for the first Empowerment cycle, they are powerful motivators. The incentives include

- Use of a laptop computer
- The software required for an instructional innovation they want to try
- Training in the use of communications and instructional technologies
- Training and participation in dialog concerning active and collaborative instructional methodologies
- Ability to document instructional innovation as part of a promotion/tenure package

- Peer recognition
- Opportunity to collaborate with other faculty
- Some released time to concentrate on the design of interactive learning
- The chance to reach students across the state with courses that might be hard to fill at one small, local campus, bringing variety and increased job security

Future opportunities to expand Vision include K–12 institutions and international universities. We hope to collaborate with some of the school districts in Pennsylvania that are close to our campuses. Several institutions in other countries have expressed the desire to work collaboratively with our Project Vision faculty and to have students participate in the American Studies course from a distance.

Issues of Systemwide Vision Implementation and Experience

We think we are unique in tackling issues of scale in higher education. Issues such as copyright, faculty compensation for course development, enrollment credit, and distributed infrastructure that have hindered progress elsewhere are things our faculty and administrators are willing to work out as we go along.

The following activities are underway to remove potential obstacles:

- The university's legal expert on intellectual property is researching what we'll need to do to ensure everyone is treated fairly if and when we publish for-sale courses or modules.
- The Ben Franklin Technology Center, our small business incubator, is working on ways to set up a company that would market Penn State course packages. This could help our innovative process become at least partially self-supporting and continuous.
- CES campuses are developing programs that respond to their local markets, rather than remaining simply lower division feeders to the University Park campus. Thus, each campus can develop specialties which it can then offer remotely to students attending other CES campuses, where enrollment patterns may not justify housing the program.

Benefits and efficiencies we expect from these efforts include the ability to

- Offer courses on a systemwide electronic basis that help our campuses serve students better.

- Retain faculty who teach typically low local-enrollment courses by providing them electronic access to remote CES students. There should be less need to relocate faculty, or to deprive one campus of an instructor's services to benefit another.
- Increase enrollment without building more classrooms or parking lots. This will be accomplished by providing instruction electronically to worksites and homes in each campus' service area.
- Have a marketable competitive edge over competing institutions by having campuses that are recognized as being a distinctly more learner-responsive environment, including more thematic integration of courses with each other and with real world projects; more interpersonal growth for students working in teams, and more faculty interaction beyond the lecture mode.

Local market variations, along with declining resources for hiring more faculty and constructing more buildings, have generated tremendous faculty and administrative support for experimenting with new instructional strategies and for using distance technologies. CES faculty have expressed comfort with collaborating to create courses that then belong to the entire system, rather than to an individual instructor or campus. We are in a situation in which a campus may have too few students wanting a certain course, but wants to keep those students attending their campus. If we can make that course available to them via various technologies, taught by an instructor who resides at another campus and who is able to fill his or her class by including remote students, everyone benefits.

Strategic Activities

As we move into the future, strategic activities at three levels of program reengineering will make Penn State University's Commonwealth Educational System a national leader in high quality "anytime, anywhere" undergraduate education.

Empowerment. Faculty new to instructional innovation will be equipped with laptop computers and software, trained in learner-centered pedagogy and basic technology use, and assisted in completing a first small-scale project. The project must use appropriate technology to support more active learning. Empower-level activities are designed to create a large number of "power users" of pedagogical innovations, and to identify faculty interested in more extensive involvement in curriculum development.

VisionWorks. Faculty conversant with instructional technologies and interested in using them to develop more interactive, learner-responsive instruction will submit proposals requesting support for more extensive course development work. Approved projects will release faculty from some of their teaching responsibilities and provide technical, multimedia production, and instructional design assistance. Course segments developed to this extent generate courses that are ready for the curricular core.

The Curricular Core. Here, whole courses and/or major course segments are developed by teams of faculty and C-LAT staff. The Penn State CES Curricular Core may be adopted by faculty at the various campuses, used in an independent learning mode by off-campus students, or adapted by faculty who wish to use these resources in conjunction with other learning activities they have created.

The core resources are to be made available under a variety of delivery modes throughout the entire CES system. The more complete the core becomes, the more the CES will be able to respond to nontraditional learners, and to provide instructors' expertise wherever it is needed. Gradually, the CES will become more able to offer any course anytime a student wants it, and anywhere the student happens to be—at a remote campus, on the job, or at home.

This three-tiered approach should

- Increase faculty's ability to make the paradigm shift and make effective use of instructional and communications technologies
- Quickly and geometrically increase the number of faculty and students using these technologies—especially communications technologies—for teaching and learning
- Quickly and cost-effectively increase the number and quality of undergraduate courses that use technology to support active and collaborative learning
- Serve as a national model for large-scale educational reform

Critical Elements of Project Vision

The pedagogical emphasis in Vision is to assist faculty across disciplines in constructing curricula that engage students more fully in developing useful modes of inquiry, researching information, building strong communication skills, and becoming adept at collaborative problem solving.

Critical project elements include

- Identification, training, and specialist support of *development* faculty willing and able to develop curricula that effectively use these technologies to provide learner-centered, interactive instruction
- Identification and ongoing training and support of *power user* faculty who will pick up and use new curricular resources to fit their own teaching styles and students
- Support and training of on-site technical staff responsible for providing ongoing faculty and student user support
- Coordination with other PSU entities including the Center for Academic Computing, the Education Technology Services, the Schreyer Institute for Innovation in Learning, the Instructional Development Program, and Continuing and Distance Education

There were several critical elements that made this program possible and without which it probably could not have been successful. The released time for faculty is key. Most of the faculty expressed the opinion that they found this project different and very time consuming, and they could not have done it with other regular duties. After reviewing this more closely, it appears that the time for release could be shortened without adverse effect. This should be viewed as an investment rather than a cost. It has significant long-term benefits.

To depend on students' abilities to buy or lease a computer would have made this project very uneven. Providing every student with the same computer and software allowed them to concentrate on learning. It appears that sooner rather than later students will find it necessary and appropriate to buy or lease their own computer.

Surprisingly, most of the faculty were not experienced computer users. This meant that a great deal of time was spent learning the technology and getting used to a new tool. Technology training should take place before course development; otherwise course development time may be diminished.

Each campus designated a space for the learning studio. Often dubbed a clubhouse by the students, it provided a twenty-four-hour a day place for students to bring their computers and plug into the university backbone network and the Internet. It also had special equipment, including a scanner and laser printer; a Pictel unit and presentation hardware were also available nearby. This learning studio was the exclusive space for the students and faculty in Project Vision and proved to be invaluable. There was always a place to plug in—with people and technology.

Central support is vital in an organization like CES. Each campus cannot be expected to provide the special equipment and human resources necessary to guide and support a project. Faculty cannot be expected to create new learning paradigms without proper support. C-LAT devoted itself almost full-time during the first year to Project Vision. It now is able to turn its attention to Project Vision II, Project Empower, and other related projects.

Although some things did not work as well as anticipated, the overall format was successful. One faculty reported recently at a learning colloquy some of the lessons that faculty have learned:

1. Classroom technology is not the magic bullet needed to solve all of our problems with motivation.
2. It can serve to engage the student individually and in groups.
3. Using a computer based, asynchronous teaching model is quite different from the more traditional mode and requires significant time to develop.
4. It is still cutting edge, and everybody is learning, not just students.

Summary

One of our Vision faculty summed it up very well when he said, "I don't think I have ever seen a college-level class so excited about participating in a learning activity. They reveled in the experiment and really came together as a group. The Project Vision students felt that they were part of a group effort helping to take education into the twenty-first century. In fact, I was just as excited, and that is something for a veteran of twenty-eight years of college teaching."

We started Project Vision with a belief that dramatic, rapid change was necessary. Now, fully engaged, we find the process to be exciting, rewarding, and downright fun. We invite you to join us in the adventure of a lifetime.

(For information on Project Vision consult the website: http://www.clat.psu.edu/homes/projvis.htm)

References

Heterick, R. C., Jr. (1994, Spring). Technological change and higher education policy. *AGB Priorities,* 1.

7

REENGINEERING THE UNDERGRADUATE CURRICULUM

Jack M. Wilson

THE CHALLENGE OF CHANGE

It is impossible to pick up a newspaper without being bombarded by the news of the economic restructuring of industry worldwide. Many large industries, both in service and manufacturing, are radically restructuring themselves, often decreasing the numbers of employees. Many of these lost positions are coming from the ranks of middle management that tend to be populated by the graduates of higher education. At the same time there has been a surge of enthusiasm for new ventures that has pushed the stock market to new highs and propelled some high tech start-ups to values that represent unheard of multiples of either revenues or earnings. It is estimated that 60% of the venture capital going into these new businesses is targeted at software development. Yet, while all of this attention has been on the information sciences, American manufacturers have been able to restructure themselves to regain the global competitiveness that many had thought they lost in the '70s and '80s. In short: It is the best of times and it is the worst of times. Could it be any different in higher education?

Education itself is coming in for its share of criticism and pressure. Many point out that the cost of higher education is the only item that has outpaced the growth in health care costs over the last decade. Now that health care has changed substantially, all eyes are on education. At the Education Commission of the States meeting in 1995, Colorado's Governor Romer (a friend of higher education), called for the abolition or restructuring of tenure. There is legislation pending in 26 states to do just that.

Funding is very tight at the National Science Foundation (NSF), National Institutes of Health (NIH), and other agencies that provide support to higher education. Growth of research funding has not kept pace with the increases that we have come to expect since the end of World War II. The collision of a higher education system built on the expectation of growth with the reality of flattened funding and resources is causing a reassessment of many of our policies and practices. Several trends seem clear:

- A larger percentage of students are carrying on their studies while working.
- Corporations are assuming a larger role in the higher education of students. U.S. corporations spent an estimated 45.5 billion dollars on educational programs for their employees. German and Japanese companies invest 3–5% of their payroll in education and training while American businesses invest 1.5%.
- The pace of technological change is so great that many university graduates will need to be involved in continuous education.
- Resources are not available for universities to build new buildings and new campuses to accommodate the increasing demand for higher education.
- The communications infrastructure will be put to work to bring education to the home and workplace.
- Computing and networking technologies will change the way we learn as well as the way we work.
- New educational enterprises, both profit and nonprofit, will spring up to meet the demand for education.
- Cost will join quality as a measure of competitiveness in higher education.

What Will We Change To?

There are dissenters to these views. In *On Luddites and Liberty: Academic Freedom in the High Tech University* (1996), Virginia Fichera writes that computers are devices to replace (or enslave) people. Her conclusion that we should put people before progress follows inevitably from her premise. If that is the case, then we might ask ourselves whether the premise is indeed correct. I am reminded of a visit that I made to Tianjin, China several years ago. Tianjin was only then beginning the development that now makes it an industrial giant. As we waited out a twelve hour delay in our flight to Hong Kong, we watched the construction of a new runway. Hundreds of workers used shovels and wheelbarrows to excavate the area. I asked the government official with me why they didn't use a bulldozer to make quick work of the job. He looked at me in amazement, pointed at the workers, and asked, "Then what would they do?" A World Bank economist next to me just shook his head with a smile. It is a centuries old argument now being played out in the hall of academe. Changes in the tools empower people to be more efficient and to do new things.

In *Electronics and the Dim Future of the University*, Eli M. Noam paints a dismal picture of where technology is taking the university (Noam, 1995). He wonders: "Will it be more than a collection of remaining physical functions, such as the science lab and the football team?" His recipe for success calls on a rededication of the university to the role of the face-to-face learning community which focuses on the social development of its students during their education. There is no doubt that there will indeed be an important role for such traditional institutions, but one might expect that these would become an increasingly smaller percentage of the overall enterprise of higher education.

In a letter to the editor of the American Society of Electrical Engineers' (ASEE) *Prism* magazine, Steven Garret, Chair of United Technologies and an engineering professor at Penn State, complains that he would not want his child to ride in a car designed, fly in an airplane flown, or cross a bridge built by someone who was trained through computer simulation. He goes on to say, "There is always a point at which the reality is far richer and more complex than any simulation" (Schwartz, 1995). On the one hand, he is right. On the other, there is bad news for him. Simulation is rapidly displacing actual experience in a variety of settings. I was particularly amused since I had just returned from Boeing where I spent several days studying the extensive use of computing in the design, maintenance, and flight training for the Boeing 777. The design process has come so far that design moved from simulation to blueprints without the intervening prototyping of the past. Flight simulators have come so far that the first time a pilot flies a 777, the plane can be carrying passengers!

This issue of simulation versus hands-on experience is a red herring. The argument is not whether to include simulation as part of the training of an engineer; it is how much of the training can be done in simulation and how much requires real hands-on experience. The consensus of the community seems to be that much can be done in simulation, but that some hands-on is important. Our educational experiences might be informed by the way computing simulation is used in the workplace. No organization can afford to do every possible experiment to decide how to proceed on a technical issue. Today one begins by using or developing a model of the system at hand, exercising that model in simulation to understand how to do it better, and then doing an experiment to see if the model provides sensible results. You can't afford to work without computer simulation, and you can't afford to unquestioningly believe the results of computer simulations. Whether building new drugs, aircraft, cars, communities, or computer networks, the interplay of simulation and experiment provides the better, faster, cheaper way to do many things today. Education is not an exception.

A recent *Prism* article asks: "If a student can zoom the country's best professors into his or her living room, of what use are the rest of the country's professors?" (Schwartz, 1996). Perhaps the question to ask is what makes a great professor? Is it the ability to present material with wonderful slides and good jokes? Or, is it the ability to create an interactive learning environment that both enables and encourages students to work through (not just view) materials and discuss this material with others? If we think that the former (presentation) is the key to great teaching, then why hasn't TV education taken over higher education? Why hasn't "The Mechanical Universe," presented by Cal Tech's David Goodstein displaced all of the less talented introductory physics teachers? This is another of those tired old arguments that should have been laid to rest years ago. Teaching is not presenting.

The model of distance learning in which the best electrical engineering professor teaches all of the electrical engineering classes might be viewed in analogy to the mainframe model of computing. At one time the only model of computing was a powerful mainframe delivering information in response to inquiries from dumb terminals. The mainframe model of education is gone. Today's architecture is a network of diverse servers. Resources can be distributed across the network, and any particular node can act as a client or a server. All kinds of resources are found on all kinds of servers, and every client is responsible for providing a portion of the intelligence in the transaction. Modern educational architectures operate in much the same way. Every participant can be a resource as well as a client, and the clients must be actively involved in the process of learning. Just as mainframes have adapted to being servers on the Internet or intranet, outstanding teachers will adapt to being facilitators and resources on the educational net.

Will a CD-ROM replace your (fill-in-the-blank) professor? Surely any professor who can be replaced by a CD-ROM should be replaced by a CD-ROM as soon as possible. However, most faculty will not be threatened. Professors were not replaced by textbooks or by television. Professors will not be replaced by computers, CD-ROMs, the World Wide Web, or any other distance learning technology. Their lives and livelihood may change, their productivity might increase, but the need for the involvement of bright, knowledgeable, articulate, personable, and caring individuals in the learning process will not diminish.

Changes are indeed coming, and they will be profound. As Zemsky and Massy note, "Information technology will change teaching and learning profoundly, no matter what the response of traditional higher education institutions" (Massy & Zemsky, 1995). Education will change, technology will be accommodated, distance learning will occur. Those who choose to sit out the process will forfeit their opportunity to affect the process. History suggests that faculty will not be replaced by teaching machines. It also suggests that certain technologies are so powerful that they will change us in spite of ourselves.

Consider the automobile. The introduction of the automobile changed this country irreversibly within a few decades. It changed the way we work, changed the way we live, moved us from the cities to the suburbs, created the central industry of this century, changed the way we courted our spouses, created the shopping mall, and so on. Who was the great visionary who foresaw all of these changes? Who were the planners who guided us through the transition? The truth is it just happened. It overpowered us with the relentless force of a new paradigm. If we had planned even a little bit, we probably would not have chosen some of the outcomes.

Consider computing and communications technologies. Already they have changed the way we work and created the major industry of our times. For some, it has already changed the way they court and the way they work. There is preliminary evidence of changes in living patterns due to telecommuting. We can engage the process or we can just let it happen. In either case, happen it will.

RATIONALE FOR CHANGE

The introductory science courses at many of our large universities around the world can be an intimidating experience for the new student. It is not only the difficulty of the material, but also the experience of sitting in the large non-interactive lectures with an instructor who is mathematically unapproachable even when personally approachable. Sheila Tobias, in *They're Not Dumb, They're Different!*, provides one of the best chronicles of student reactions in the introductory course (Tobias, 1990). This format of large lecture, smaller recitation, and separate laboratory continues to be the dominant method of instruction at larger universities. The recitations are often taught by mixtures of teaching assistants and faculty with that mix varying widely from university to university. In spite of the uneven quality found in recitations, it is likely that most learning takes place in the recitation and problem sessions. The laboratories are a more dismal case. Taught by teaching assistants with minimal or almost no training, the laboratories are universally panned by the students. Because of this perception of low quality and the resources required to run laboratories, some universities have abandoned them altogether.

Recognizing the shortcomings of this system, faculty and staff at the major universities have devoted extraordinary attention to the improvement of it. Each meeting of societies like the Association of American Colleges and Universities (AAC&U), American Association for Higher Education (AAHE), American Association of Physics Teachers (AAPT), American Chemical Society (ACS), American Society for Engineering Education (ASEE), or Mathematical Association of America (MAA) is filled with ideas for how to improve the lecture. One recurring theme is the use of lecture demonstrations that range from the spectacular to the humorous. Faculty, students, and even the general public love and remember the best demonstrations and the best demonstrators. Over the years, we have turned to audio, video, and now computers to make the lectures more interesting and more instructive. Unfortunately, later interviews with the students often reveal that the memory of the demonstration is often not accompanied by an understanding of the concept behind that demonstration.

Many efforts to improve undergraduate courses work from an assumption that there are good lecturers and bad lecturers, and that students can learn more from the good ones. The strategy then is to improve the bad or replace with the good. Even many applications of technology are efforts to improve or replace the lecturer with electronic forms of lecture. Many institutions have used videotaped materials to replace the traditional pre-laboratory lecture with videotapes of good lecturers who can articulate in clear English the goals and procedures for the laboratories. Others have created computer based pre-laboratories (Wilson, 1980) toward the same ends. With the creation of the "Mechanical Universe," this approach of using technology to replace the lecturer may have reached its highest form. Each video opens with a scene of students filing into a large lecture hall and then listening attentively to the opening remarks of a truly outstanding lecturer.

Why is it when we hear educational institutions telling of their classroom of the future, it nearly always describes an instructor lecturing from a multimedia podium that resembles the bridge of the Starship Enterprise? Why don't they describe rooms in which it is the students who are working very hard and doing the interesting things, rather than watching teachers do them?

Clearly these are all worthy efforts toward noble goals, and many have undoubtedly benefited from these efforts, but perhaps it is time to do a more serious reexamination of our assumptions and approaches. Over the last few decades, evidence has been pouring in from those doing research in the cognitive sciences, but it seems to have had little effect on classes in most of our largest universities. There are, of course, some notable exceptions, and I hope to cite some examples.

The Rationale for the Status Quo

The first alleged rationale is, "Lectures can be an educationally effective method of teaching." Readers of any of the cognitive psychology or educational research journals know that the evidence is overwhelming against this contention (Halloun & Hestenes, 1985; Laws, 1991). That is not to say that a single lecture cannot be effective. When large groups are asked if they have ever heard a good lecture, (almost) all hands go up. When asked if they have ever heard 45 good lectures in one semester (a course), only about 1% say yes. There is rarely a hand when asked about 225 good lectures (a full semester program) or 1,800 (a four-year program). The problem is not the lecture itself; it is the scaleability of the format. Overreliance on the lecture, particularly the non-interactive lecture, is the problem.

Computing and communications technologies now give us ways of involving more and more students in their own education. Ron Thornton of Tufts (Thornton, 1990) compares more interactive methods using microcomputer based laboratories to traditional lecture approaches and shows that the interactive methods can reduce student error rates spectacularly. At Harvard, Eric Mazur felt that his students were really learning in his lectures, but conceptual testing of his students led him to his development of innovative interactive techniques for use with large enrollment courses. He provides an honest personal anecdote illustrating the statistical evidence amassed by Halloun (1985), Laws (1991), Sokoloff (1996), and Thornton (1990).

Providing good lectures is obviously superior to providing poor lectures, but there is little evidence that this leads directly to increased learning. A standard counterargument is that, "Lectures must work because students have been learning that way for centuries." The problem with this approach is that it fails to take into account the many other ways that students have been learning for centuries, such as reading, problem solving, discussion with other students, discussion in the recitations, performing laboratories, and so on. Frequently this counterargument is also based upon a generalization from the speakers' own experiences, which may be atypical. Do we ask what happened to those other students and why they were not successful?

Another rationale, often resorted to as the last bastion of defense against change in higher education, is: "The traditional course is the most cost effective way to educate hundreds or thousands of students per semester." We found, to our surprise, that this was not necessarily the case. Our introductory courses in physics, calculus, computer science, chemistry, and engineering analysis each educates 600–1,000 students per semester. Biology, at about 300, is a bit smaller. Until recently, the traditional approach was to divide the courses into two lecture sections with 300–500 students each and then subdivide further into about 25–30 recitation sections of fewer than thirty students and 30–40 labs of fewer than 25 each. The lectures are team taught by two or more faculty, the labs are taught by teaching assistants, and the recitations use a mix of faculty and teaching assistants. The mix varies from discipline to discipline with physics about evenly divided between faculty and TA's. In addition, these courses were supported by laboratory and lecture demonstration support staff. There were 57–72 events to be staffed each week in these courses.

This model is very typical of that found at most large Carnegie Research I Universities. After compiling the actual cost for this lecture-laboratory-recitation model in 1993, we were surprised to see just how expensive this course was. We were able to identify several alternatives that were economically competitive and promised far better educational effectiveness.

Designing an Educationally and Cost Effective Alternative

From 1988 to 1993, Rensselaer introduced a variety of courses, systematically incorporating the use of technology in a cooperative learning environment. In 1993 we convened a panel of nationally prominent educators, architects, and representatives of industry to review the status of our programs and to plan for future programs. Among these were Priscilla Laws, the primary architect for Workshop Physics, Bill Graves, the Director of the Institute for Academic Technology, and Joe Lagowski, the editor of the *Journal of*

Chemical Education. We invited six architects (including the architect for Bill Gates' new house in Seattle) who had gained national attention for their innovative designs for educational facilities. To complete the mix we added about six industry representatives from Perkin Elmer, AT&T, General Electric, IBM, United Technologies, and Boeing. With such a diverse group we thought that we might be able to gain a variety of perspectives on the issues but suspected we would not reach any kind of a consensus. We were wrong.

Although there were a variety of perspectives introduced by the participants, there were also strong areas of consensus. Among these was the need to reduce the emphasis on the lecture, to improve the relationship between the course and the laboratory, to increase the amount of doing and scale back the watching, to continue and expand the team and cooperative learning experiences, to integrate rather than overlay technology into all of the courses, and above all to do so while reducing costs!

A Brief History of the Studio Course Format

Course Structure

The experts' meeting led us to a design for the studio courses that incorporated a much more integrated use of computing with cooperative group learning techniques (Treisman, 1990). The physics course was a natural combination and extension of the Comprehensive Unified Physics Learning Environment (CUPLE) system (Wilson, Redish, & McDaniel, 1992), the M.U.P.P.E.T. materials (MacDonald, Redish, & Wilson, 1988), the Workshop Physics program (Laws, 1991), and cooperative learning techniques. The approximately 700 students enrolled in the large courses would be divided into 12–15 sections of 48-64 persons. Where there had been 57–72 events to be staffed, there were now 12–15. The courses were reduced from six contact hours (two lecture, two recitation, and two lab) to four contact hours and taught either in two periods each two hours in length or in two 1.5 hour and one 1 hour period. Each course is led by a team of one faculty member, one graduate student, and one or two undergraduates. The mentoring of graduate students and undergraduate students is an important side effect of the redesigned course structure.

The reduction from six to four contact hours is an important aspect of stewardship of both student and faculty time and resources. In spite of the one-third reduction in contact hours, the evaluations are demonstrating that students learn the material better and faster (Wilson, 1994). We also demonstrated that this approach could save $10,000–$250,000 every time these courses were taught.

Creating the Studio Classroom Software Environment

In the physics course, the workstations run the CUPLE software system, have full access to networked multimedia, and include a microcomputer-based laboratory system for data acquisition, analysis, and visualization. The calculus course makes heavy use of the Maple symbolic mathematics program. Biology uses the Bioquest materials from the Annenberg/CPB Project, while chemistry does microcomputer based data acquisition and analysis.

Creating the Studio Classroom Facility

The reengineering of the course led directly to a redesign of the facilities (see Figure 7.1). During 1993–95, we completely renovated seven classrooms for the studio courses. The classrooms accommodate 48 to 64 students in comfortable workshop facilities. There are 2 meter long work tables, each designed for two students, with open workspace and a computer workstation. Often the tables also contain the equipment for the day's hands-on laboratory. The tables form three concentric partial ovals with an opening at the front of the room for the teacher's worktable and for projection. The workstations are arranged so that when students are working together on an assigned problem, they turn away from the center of the room and focus their attention on their own small-group workspace. The instructor is able to see all workstation screens from the center of the oval, and thereby receives direct feedback on student progress.

FIGURE 7.1

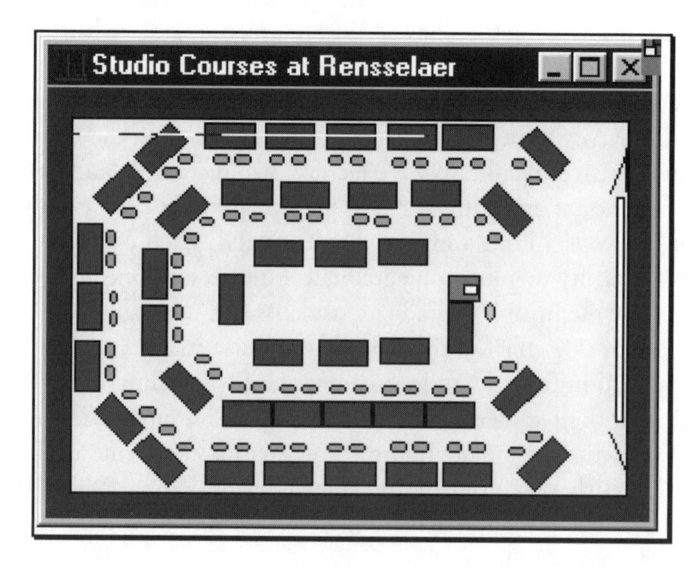

In any course, when the teacher wants to conduct a discussion or give a mini-lecture, he or she is able to ask the students to turn back toward the center of the room. This removes the distraction of having a functioning workstation directly in front of the student during the discussion or lecture period, yielding a classroom in which multiple foci are possible. Students can work together as teams of two, or two teams may work together to form a small group of four. Discussion as a whole is facilitated by the semicircular arrangement of student chairs. Most students can see one another with a minimum of swiveling of chairs. This is particularly important since only about 20–40% of the classroom time is actually spent on the computers; the remainder is devoted to group activities, hands-on laboratories, and discussion.

This type of classroom is friendly even to those instructors who tend toward the traditional style of classroom in which most of the activities are teacher-centered rather than student-centered. Projection is easy, and all students have a clear view of both the instructor and any projected materials. The classroom is unequaled as a facility in which the instructor acts more as a mentor, guide, and advisor. Rather than separating the functions of lecture, recitation, and laboratory, the instructor can move freely from lecture mode into discussion, can assign a computer activity, ask the students to discuss their results with their neighbors, and then ask them to describe the result to the class. Laboratory simply becomes one of the integrated classroom activities. This course uses the latest in computing tools and incorporates use of cooperative learning approaches. We have created a powerful link between the lecture materials and the problem solving as well as hands-on laboratories. This is a link that is tenuous, at best, in the traditional course.

Putting it all Together

A recent statement in *The Chronicle of Higher Education* claimed that it is harder to move a graveyard than to change the curriculum. The changes at Rensselaer are evidence that this need not always be the case.

The CUPLE physics studio is a natural outgrowth of the work of the CUPLE collaboration that was formed in 1989 (with support from IBM, the Annenberg/CPB project, and the National Science Foundation) to develop tools and approaches for innovative undergraduate physics courses and the program at Rensselaer to reengineer the undergraduate science curriculum for all students (Wilson, Redish, & McDaniel, 1992). The CUPLE software is now published by the American Institute of Physics as the Physics Academic Software Program and is in use at many other universities.

The theater-in-the-round classroom encourages extensive interaction among students and between students, faculty, graduate student assistants, and undergraduate student assistants. Cooperative learning techniques are designed into the structure and content. Many of the activities were introduced into the traditional classes in 1990–93. In 1993, the first full studio was deployed. During the Fall 1994 semester, the CUPLE physics studio was expanded to full deployment in all Physics I sections, Physics III sections, plus a pilot deployment in Physics II. In 1995 the physics department voted unanimously to end the traditional course in favor of the full deployment of the studio.

The studio calculus program grew out of the Maple calculus course which was first introduced in 1989 under the leadership of Professor William Boyce. Professor Joseph Ecker led the reengineering program which combined the studio model with the heavy use of symbolic mathematics introduced by the Maple calculus program. Harry Roy, Professor of Biology, introduced the studio approach to biology in his undergraduate genetics course. Alan Cutler and Tom Apple created studio chemistry. John Brunski and Robert Spilker in biomedical engineering led the development of the freshman Introduction to Engineering Analysis course. Frank DiCesare created an introductory engineering laboratory course, Laboratory Introduction to Embedded Control (LITEC), which requires students to synthesize their skills in the design of an electromechanical system (for example: an automatically navigating model car or a precision controlled temperature water faucet system) that is controlled by a simple microprocessor. All of these programs are team-oriented.

To some extent the studio format is designed to transfer some responsibility from the faculty to the student. The focus is on student problem solving and projects rather than on presentation of materials. The emphasis is on learning rather than teaching.

A Typical Course Day

Consider the students' experience in the typical Rensselaer studio class. Usually students come to class with a homework assignment of three to six problems to turn in. They almost always have questions about the assignment, and, since it is collected and graded, most have actually attempted the problems. The first portion of the class is most like a recitation. The problems are quite similar to those used in the traditional class except that there are more problems that might use the symbolic mathematics software (Maple, Matlab, or Mathematica), a spreadsheet, or even an object-oriented modeling tool. As we go over questions that they have about the problems, we often call on the students to present the solutions. Other students then comment on the problem. This usually consumes about 20 minutes.

Next we present a topic with a five-minute discussion followed by a laboratory on that topic. For example, we set up a video camera and have a student throw a ball. The video may be directly digitized into the computer and made available over the network to each work area. Students then analyze the motion using the CUPLE digital video tool and create a spreadsheet containing the position versus time data. The analysis proceeds in the usual fashion resulting in graphs of position versus time, velocity versus time, and acceleration versus time for each component. The final laboratory report remains in electronic format, although we often have the students record observations on a written worksheet.

Other laboratories are performed entirely at each work area. When we introduced Newton's Second Law, we had the students calibrate a force probe and then hang a spring and mass from the probe with an ultrasonic range finder under the mass to measure the position. Figure 7.2 shows the actual data presentation with a graph of distance versus time, force versus time, and force versus distance. From this, the students can calculate the acceleration versus time and compare it to the force divided by the mass.

FIGURE 7.2

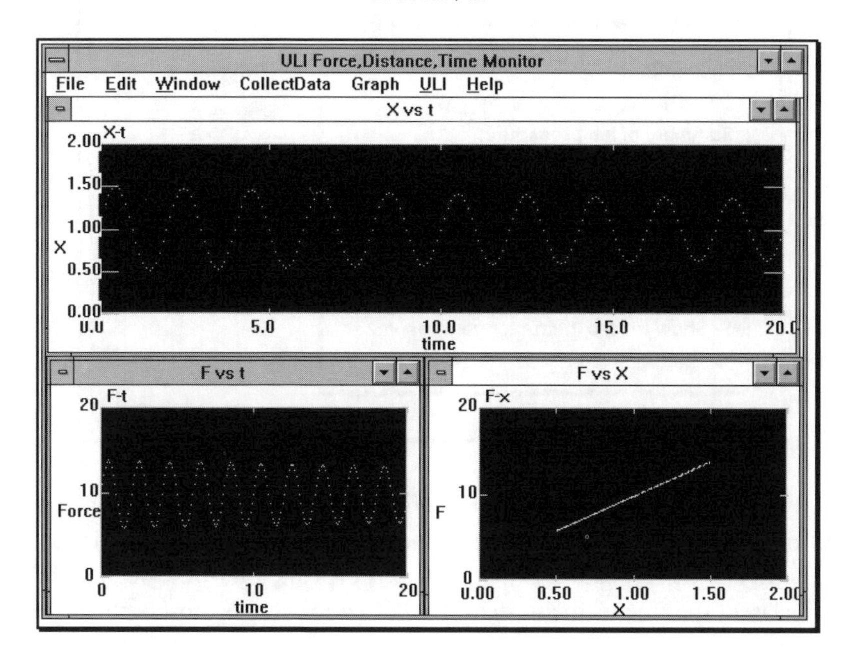

You may notice that this experiment foreshadows the introduction of Hookes' Law and the topic of oscillations, both of which come later in the course. There are questions on the worksheet that ask the students to observe and comment upon each of these phenomena, but we do not attempt to name them or introduce theory at this time. We try to introduce the concept and work with it before naming it.

In both examples given above, the computer based laboratory data acquisition and analysis tools are embedded into a hypermedia text that introduces the topics, links the students to related materials, and poses questions for the students to answer with the tools. These hypermedia activities were created by a consortium of schools led by Rensselaer and the University of Maryland. Funding has come from the Annenberg/Corporation for Public Broadcasting, the IBM Corporation, and the National Science Foundation. Most of these materials were created by teams of faculty and students working together. The student involvement has added a fresh approach to many of the materials—an attribute appreciated by students taking the course.

FIGURE 7.3

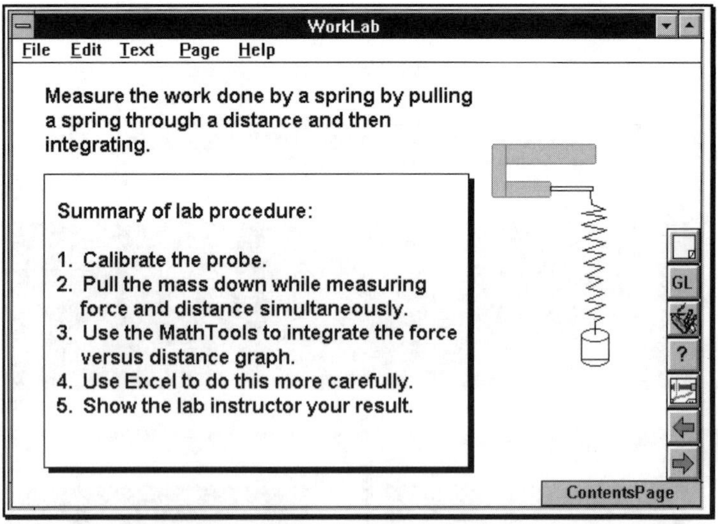

WorkLab
File Edit Text Page Help
Measure the work done by a spring by pulling a spring through a distance and then integrating.
Summary of lab procedure:
1. Calibrate the probe.
2. Pull the mass down while measuring force and distance simultaneously.
3. Use the MathTools to integrate the force versus distance graph.
4. Use Excel to do this more carefully.
5. Show the lab instructor your result.
GL
?
ContentsPage

Figure 7.3 shows a page from the first laboratory on work. This is the summary page for the experiment that is covered in more detail in later pages. In the earliest experiments, the lab is explained in some detail, while in the later experiments the student is expected to provide most of the experimental design.

Notice that the student has access to the full range of CUPLE facilities during the session. She may annotate the book with marginalia by pressing the yellow post-it note button. This allows her to insert typed yellow post-it notes or freehand scrawls across the pages. The glossary button (GL) brings up a large glossary of physics terms. The Swiss army knife launches the CUPLE toolbox that allows the student to use MAPLE, Excel, the CUPLE mathematical function tools, or any of a variety of references. References include an electronic periodic table, the String and Sticky Tape low cost experiments, the Lecture Demonstration Handbook, and even access to all of the materials in the Physics InfoMall (see Fuller & Zollman), assuming you have purchased the InfoMall separately.

The Window on Physics (WinPhys) object-oriented modeling system provides both a collection of models and materials for constructing your own models and simulations. The object-oriented nature of the WinPhys system provides for all functions to inherit certain behaviors, among them the ability to differentiate or integrate themselves.

FIGURE 7.4

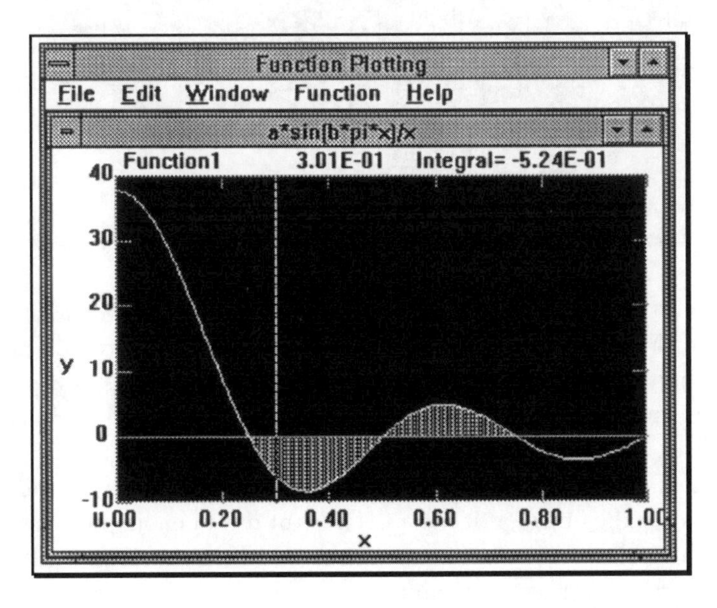

Figure 7.4 shows the graph of the sin(x)/x with the integral displayed both graphically and numerically. The ability to read out, differentiate, integrate, and take the Fourier transform is of great use to the student in both laboratory and problem solving. Of course, the early laboratories have the students calculate this explicitly just to ensure that they understand the process.

Hands-on activities are an integral part of the CUPLE physics studio. In fact, there are more than twice as many hands-on laboratories than in the traditional course. Each activity is shorter than the traditional laboratory but is tightly integrated with both the homework and class discussion. The laboratory portion of the class ranges from 20–40 minutes and is often combined with a computational activity.

FIGURE 7.5

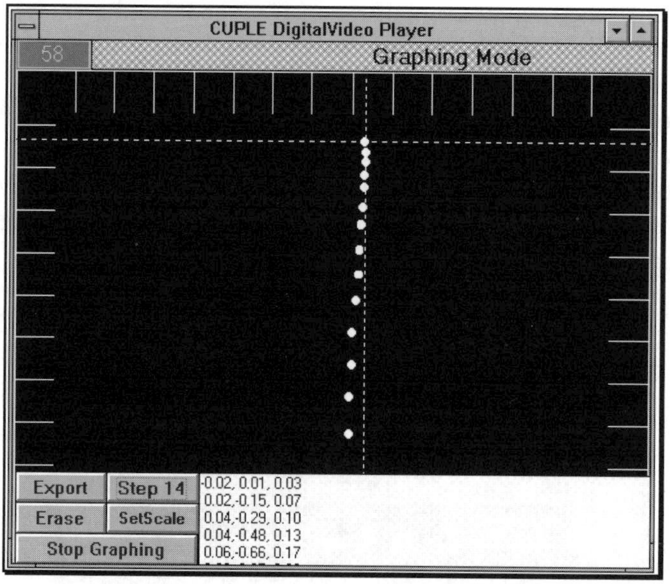

Lab activities fall into three major categories: microcomputer based laboratories (MBL) as described above, video laboratories, and model simulation projects. The video laboratories allow the students to take live video of an event (from a handi-cam) directly into their computer and then play that event back as video on each student's computer screen (Figure 7.5). They bring up a graphical overlay on the screen and place points on the graph directly over the object as it moves. Those of us old enough to have done this with spark marks on waxed tape or with a Polaroid camera will recognize that this is conceptually quite similar and leads to the same kinds of data analysis that we performed. On the other hand, the relationship between the marks and the moving object is far more obvious to the student than it was in the earlier cases. Since we use similar equipment each week, set up for this lab is limited to bringing in the handi-cam and plugging it into the network. This is also far less cumbersome and less expensive than the specialized equipment that we previously used to do the spark tapes or strobed Polaroid pictures.

The class ends with a discussion of the material assigned for the next class. At this time we often call attention to the foreshadowing that has occurred in the problem solving and laboratories and pull this together to introduce the next topic.

As noted earlier, the studio course has been recognized as a significant breakthrough in providing high quality cost effective courses in articles in *Newsweek* (April 29, 1996), *The New York Times* (January 8, 1995), *The Wall Street Journal* (November 13,1995), and the ASEE *Prism*. The Rensselaer Satellite Video Program (RSVP) distance learning program won the 1993 US Distance Learning Association Award for best University Distance Learning Program and the 1996 US Distance Learning Association award for its cooperative engineering and management distance learning program with General Motors. The studio course model won the 1995 Theodore Hesburgh Award from TIAA/CREF and the American Council on Education, the 1995 Boeing Outstanding Engineering Educator Award, and the 1996 Pew Award for the Renewal of Undergraduate Education. At this time, we are one of the three finalists for the Pew Foundation Award.

The Studio at a Distance: Distributed Studio Courses

We also see the boundaries blurring between on-site and distance learning. Rensselaer Polytechnic Institute presently educates about 800 students per semester in interactive distance learning formats, and we are among the leaders in research on this format. We want the distance learning student to have the same learner-centered studio experience as the on-campus students. Toward that end we worked in collaboration with AT&T and Bell Laboratories in the creation of the first prototypes of the Interactive Multimedia Distance Learning Environment. In that 1994 program, we offered interactive multimedia distance learning courses in linked sites at Dallas; Chicago; Cincinnati; Holmdel, NJ; and Troy, NY. We then worked in collaboration with IBM and Interactive Learning International (ILINC) to deploy a much improved version of the system at Kent State University to teach English, nursing, and graduate business to the branch campuses and corporate sites. For the last two years we have run faculty workshops as part of the National Science Foundation Chautauqua program. This program links sites at the University of Pittsburgh, Rensselaer, and Cal Poly-San Luis Obispo.

A distributed studio classroom (StudioLinc@Distance) is a studio classroom in which students work together in groups at multimedia, networked workstations (Wilson & Mosher, 1994). The workstations have access to the multimedia and other computing resources for the course and also provide multipoint video, audio, and collaborative software. Students have a live video window on their screen in which they can see the teacher or other students in any of the linked classrooms on the network. A studio classroom is one in which the emphasis is on the student's activity rather than on the teacher's (Wilson, 1994). Studio classes incorporate extensive use of integrated hands-on activities with mini-lectures, and small group problem solving and discussion sessions. StudioLinc@Distance studio classes combine the best features of the synchronous (live or real time) use of interactive compressed video and the asynchronous (flexible time) components of the Web or other multimedia based environments.

Rensselaer has been a pioneer in the development and deployment of full curriculum multimedia courses that have gone into commercial distribution. Of particular note in that regard are the CUPLE Physics Course (Wilson, Redish, & McDaniel, 1992; Wilson & Redish, 1992), published by the American Institute of Physics, and the Studio Calculus course, published by HarperCollins College Publishing. Now these multimedia courses can be delivered over the network combining interactive multimedia materials in an asynchronous environment with live interactive network video conferencing to introduce a synchronous component.

Figure 7.6 illustrates how the teacher's screen might look at some point in a StudioLinc@Distance studio course. The student, Nicole, who appears on the teacher's screen at the moment, has the floor. Perhaps she has requested attention by raising her hand electronically to signal the teacher. The teacher sees a list of all those who have raised their hand and selects Nicole as the next to speak. To the right of Nicole's live video is multimedia educational material. Nicole can lead us through that material while annotating it on everyone's screen. Notice that the teacher has a window (lower left) that shows a complete list of all students registered in the class. Those students with their (electronic) hands raised are marked with the hand icon. The teacher can pass the floor to anyone or take it back and lead the students through the material. Whatever the teacher opens on the teacher's screen is also opened on the students' screens. This is not merely a bitmap that is sent (as in white-boards or screen sharing): This is the fully functional application. This means that the student can go ahead or go back and review, but the teacher can always bring everyone together onto the same page.

FIGURE 7.6

Our work has shown that the asynchronous techniques can be made to work much better if a small portion of the course is done synchronously. This tradeoff of synchronous versus asynchronous time is not yet well understood. The experience with fully asynchronous courses is often that the percentage of students who complete the course satisfactorily is not high enough to be acceptable. On the other hand, it would be desirable to have as much of the course done asynchronously as possible to give the students the any time flexibility and to allow economies of scale. We intend to study this aspect of the course to determine the optimal ratio of synchronous to asynchronous activity in particular situations.

In 1995 the new software was put into use for the first time in an NSF Chautauqua program that linked Rensselaer Polytechnic Institute and the School of Engineering at the University of Pittsburgh into linked virtual classrooms. Faculty from around the nation (and three from Hong Kong) came to the three day workshop on multimedia in science, mathematics, and engineering education. Using the CUPLE Physics multimedia course, I taught from Pitt on the first two days. The following day I taught from Rensselaer. Students felt that the other instructors and I were in the room with them no matter where our actual location. Observers noted that the students at Pitt would often communicate to one another while making eye contact through the system rather than trying to do so across the room!

Since then, HarperCollins College Publishing has published a calculus text that will include a multimedia version created in the LearnLinc environment. Ernst and Young, AT&T, IBM, GTE, and other companies have licensed the software to create virtual classrooms for corporate education and training. With the assistance of IBM, Kent State University has deployed LearnLinc to teach classes in English, nursing, and business across its extensive branch campus system. Skidmore College, Cal Poly, Curtin University of Technology (Australia), and Hong Kong City University are in the early stages of deployment and testing.

Conclusion

Our experiences thus far with the studio courses have been very encouraging. Student response is particularly satisfying. They have been quite enthusiastic about the course as measured by responses on the end of semester surveys. Nearly twice as many students agree that they enjoyed the studio course as compared to the traditional lecture/recitation/lab format. The studio mathematics course was the first of the freshman courses to be conducted and has been through several complete cycles of evaluation. The physics course is only one semester behind.

One question on an external survey conducted by the dean of the undergraduate school last semester stirred quite a bit of interest in the administration and faculty. When students were asked whether they would cite a particular course as "a positive reason to attend Rensselaer," over 90% of the students taking studio math agreed! This compares to 63% who agreed with this proposition in the other mathematics courses that had been downsized but did not abandon the traditional lecture approach. When student responses were controlled for popularity of the teacher and course, there were significant (actually spectacular) gains in students' satisfaction.

Our initial experiences indicate that faculty are rated far higher in the teaching evaluations in the studio courses. Faculty ratings are a significant issue at institutions like Rensselaer where student evaluations and research results play equally major roles in salary, promotion, and tenure decisions. More and more research universities are revamping these criteria to re-emphasize the teaching aspects of the professor's role and this trend is expected to continue—even accelerate—in the next few years.

Students in these courses are performing as well as or better than students in the traditional courses in spite of the 33.3% reduction in class contact time. This was demonstrated by student performance on tests matched in difficulty, length, and content to tests from previous years and those given this year in the traditional course. In both mathematics and physics, more topics were covered in the studio courses than in the lecture courses.

With the support of an anonymous donor, we have now launched a longitudinal study of student performance and attitude that will follow the students through their undergraduate career and two years into work or further study. We recognize just how difficult it will be to measure and document these changes and also how difficult it will be to convince the university community to consider restructuring its courses. However, the preliminary results are so encouraging that we are optimistic.

References

Fichera, V. (1996, January). On Luddites and liberty: Academic freedom in the high tech university. *AAUP New York ACADEME, 23* (1), 9.

Fuller, R., & Zollman, D. *Physics InfoMall.* Information is available from R. Fuller, Department of Physics, University of Nebraska.

Halloun, I.A., & Hestenes, D. (1985). The initial knowledge state of physics students. *American Journal of Physics, 53,* 1043-1055.

Laws, P. (1991, July/August). Workshop physics: Learning introductory physics by doing it. *Change,* 20-22.

MacDonald, W.M., Redish, E.F., & Wilson, J.M. (1988, July/August). The M.U.P.P.E.T. manifesto. *Computers in Physics 1,* (1), 23.

Massy, W.F., & Zemsky, R. (1995). Using information technology to enhance academic productivity. *An EDUCOM National Learning Infrastructure White Paper.* Washington, DC: EDUCOM.

Mazur, E. (1996). Understanding or memorization: Are we teaching the right thing? *Conference on the Introductory Physics Course.* New York, NY: Wiley.

Noam, E. M. (1995, October 13). Electronics and the dim future of the university. *Science, 270,* 247-249.

Schwartz, R. (1995, December). The virtual university. *ASEE Prism,* 22-26.

Sokoloff, D., & Thornton, R. (1996). Learning physics concepts in the introductory course: Microcomputer-based labs and interactive lecture demonstrations. In *Conference on the Introductory Physics Course.* New York, NY: Wiley.

Thornton, R. (1990). Learning physical concepts with real-time laboratory measurement tools. *American Journal of Physics, 58* (9), 858.

Tobias, S. (1990). *They're not dumb, they're different!* Tucson, AZ: Research Corporation.

Treisman, P. U. (1990). *Teaching mathematics to a changing population.* Report of the Professional Development Program at the University of California, Berkeley, and Mathematics Achievement Among African American Undergraduates at the University of California, Berkeley: An Evaluation of the Mathematics Workshop Program. *Journal of Negro Education, 59* (3), 1990.

Wilson, J. (1994, December). The CUPLE physics studio. *The Physics Teacher, (32)* 9, 518-523.

Wilson, J.M. (1980). Experimental simulation in the modern physics laboratory. *American Journal of Physics, 48,* 701.

Wilson, J.M., & Mosher, D.N. (1994). Interactive multimedia distance learning: The prototype of the virtual classroom. *Educational Multimedia and Hypermedia, 94,* 563.

Wilson, J.M., & Redish, E.F. (1992). The CUPLE project: A hyper- and multi-media approach to restructuring physics education. In E. Barrett. (Ed.). *Sociomedia: Multimedia, hypermedia, and the social construction of knowledge.* Boston, MA: MIT Press.

Wilson, J.M., Redish, E.F., & McDaniel, C.K. (1992, March/April). The comprehensive unified physics learning environment. Part I: Background and system operation. *Computers in Physics, 6* (2), and Part II: Materials. (1992, May/June). *Computers in Physics, 6* (3).

Young, J. (1996, January). The studio classroom. *ASEE Prism, 15.*

8

Collaborative Legal Education

Steve H. Nickles and Craig Runde

Introduction

Legal education values active student participation in the learning process. Recent technological advances coupled with expanded student access to computers have provided the opportunity to experiment with formats to stimulate student involvement and bridge the gap between theoretical knowledge and the practical elements of law practice.

This chapter describes one such experiment involving the creation of collaborative environments and virtual classrooms to supplement in-class discussion. It describes various communications and publications applications used in the virtual classroom and analyzes faculty and student reactions to the concept.

The Nature of Legal Instruction

Law school instruction has long incorporated techniques meant to encourage active student participation. The best known of these is the Socratic Method, a form of dialog, "a conversation between teacher and student–in question and answer form–where the teacher asks the questions, and, in so doing, provides some direction. By selecting the questions, she produces discourse at varying levels of generality with varying degrees of focus. By adjusting the generality and focus of questions she adjusts the conversation to the learning goal of the moment, allowing her to move from one goal to another or back and forth between goals during a single class hour" (Marshall, 1994). As Professor Don Marshall from the University of Minnesota Law School puts it, "[The] ultimate purpose of the dialog [is] to maximize learning by encouraging participation in the process of discovery."

While dialog has been the prime technique for teaching students to "think like lawyers," it has been supplemented in recent years by simulation, skills training, and clinical programs. Development of these courses and techniques have provided a more hands-on approach to learning important lawyering skills in the areas of problem solving, legal analysis and reasoning, legal research, factual investigation, communication, counseling, negotiation, litigation, and alternative dispute resolution procedures, organization, and management of legal work as well as recognizing and resolving ethical dilemmas (MacCrate, 1992). Although they differ in approach, each of these techniques actively engages students in the learning process.

Simulation courses use a "learning by doing" method pioneered by the National Institute of Trial Advocacy. While initially developed for litigation training, the technique's popularity is spreading to other upper class courses such as legal research and writing. Skills training involving courses has become increasingly important as law firms' expectations of young graduates have increased. The skills courses require students to actually use the tools of the lawyer's trade to solve sample legal problems. Clinical courses enable students to work with real clients while under the supervision of clinical faculty.

While these newer teaching methods have become very popular with students, they pose problems for schools because they require smaller student/teacher ratios and more overall resources than traditional classes.

Technology in Legal Education

While law schools have often adopted conservative approaches to curriculum development, they have been surprisingly willing to use new technologies. Apart from standard office applications, the first major technological innovations in schools appeared in the 1970s with the advent of computer-assisted legal research services and computer-assisted legal instruction programs.

The WESTLAW and LEXIS services revolutionized legal research in law practice and in law schools and have become widely relied upon by both faculty and students (Mersky, 1980). All faculty and students are able to obtain individual passwords to access these databases from both school and home. The databases contain most of the statutory and case law needed by legal researchers together with a wide variety of non-legal information sources.

Pioneering professors began developing computer-assisted legal instructional programs in the 1970s as well (Burris, 1980). Law schools themselves have created a membership organization called the Center for Computer Assisted Legal Instruction, which has fostered the development of over 100 lessons for use by students (Teich, 1991).

The next wave of technological innovation in law schools arrived in the early 1990s, largely as a result of more widespread access to equipment. In the 1980s student access to technology was often limited to school computer labs. This has changed markedly in the 1990s as more students have bought their own computers. Some schools have even begun to require students to own computers. This wider access has, in turn, led to a desire to do more with computers and a growing interest in e-mail, electronic textbooks, and other educational tools.

An Experiment in Collaborative Learning

It was against this pedagogical and technological background that faculty members at the University of Minnesota Law School, who were interested in exploring new uses of technology in the curriculum, began meeting with representatives of West Publishing in the fall of 1993. West, one of the world's leading legal publishers, is headquartered in Minnesota and made a natural potential partner. They had long been involved with law school publishing and had developed a number of technology-based products including their WESTLAW on-line research service. West proved receptive, and a collaborative project was begun in the spring semester of 1994.

While a number of different models were pursued, perhaps the most interesting experiment involved the creation of virtual classrooms. The first implementation of the concept occurred in the fall semester of 1994. Approximately 165 students in several first year classes were chosen to participate.

In the past, professors had used Internet, e-mail, and listservs to facilitate communication outside of class but had experienced a number of practical problems using these tools. The law school and West used several approaches to improve the quality of the virtual classroom experiment over earlier efforts. First, students and faculty were provided with Lotus Notes client software which provided a richer, easier-to-use interface for communications. A number of lab computers were also made available for students who did not own computers. Finally, West staff provided training for students and faculty involved in the experiment.

Virtual Classroom Databases

Several separate databases were developed for each class participating in the virtual classroom project. Some typical databases included a discussion forum, course materials, and professors' problems. (See Figure 8.1.)

Figure 8.1

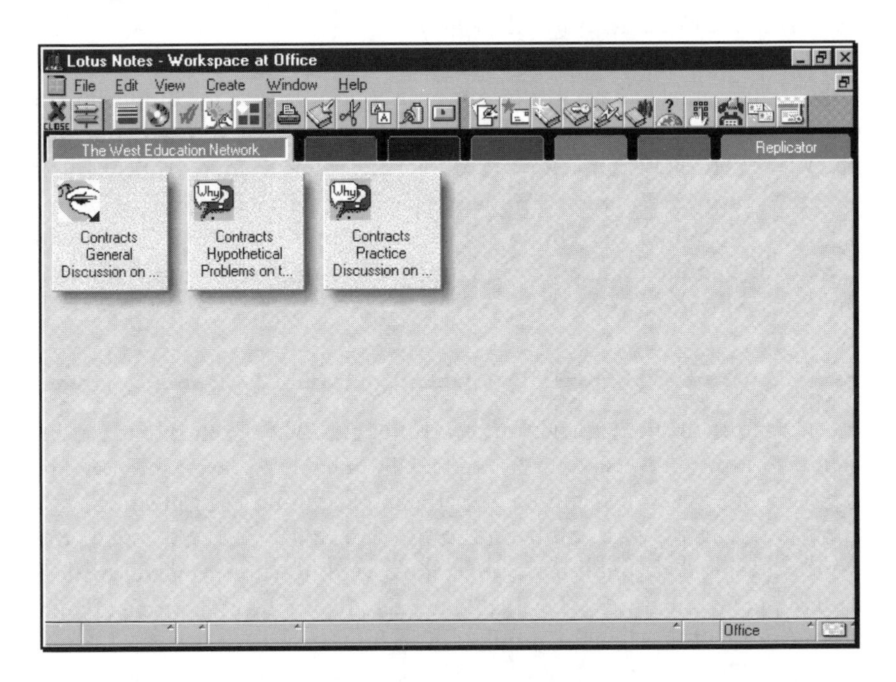

Each professor was able to structure each of the databases according to his or her own preferences. For example, a discussion forum could be made anonymous or not according to the professor's desire. Likewise, a professor could determine whether students or only faculty members could post to a particular database.

The discussion forum database was used most frequently by students to raise questions and discuss issues that arose in class. A typical student entry would ask a question about a particular point raised in class that day. Other students and the professor would have the ability to read and respond to the student's question or raise new points on their own. The threaded nature of the discussion enabled students to easily see when a particular message was in response to a preceding one. Unread messages were highlighted to facilitate browsing through new postings.

The course materials database provided professors with an easy method for distributing supplemental materials that otherwise would have been photocopied and distributed in class. It was particularly easy to locate new materials for the course on WESTLAW and then download those materials into the course materials database.

The professors' problem database gave faculty a convenient method for distributing problem sets to students. It also served as a unique feedback mechanism for students' answers. The students' answers could be posted directly within the professor's problem database for the entire class to see. It gave students an opportunity to practice answering questions similar to those which would be found on an exam. It also enabled other students in the class to discuss and debate sample answers.

Guest Participants

One of the most interesting aspects of the virtual classroom was the ability of the professor to incorporate guest participants in class discussions. This becomes important in bridging the gap between the theoretical knowledge learned in school and the practical elements of law practice.

One experiment with a first-year contracts class showed the power of this capability. Students had been using the discussion forum in their virtual classroom to discuss particular elements of contract interpretation. On one particular point the class was divided in its interpretation. After considerable discussion the professor issued a sample ruling, similar to that of a trial court. He then assigned students to prepare legal briefs on each side of the issue and post them to the forum. A third group of students was assigned to act as an intermediate court of appeals and pass judgment on the two student briefs. The professor then contacted several state supreme court justices who agreed to serve as a final court of appeal and issue written judgments on the students' work.

Throughout the process, the level of student interest grew. They became particularly attentive when the actual judges began to issue their opinions. The students were excited that during their first class in law school their work was being judged by state supreme court justices. This motivation gave considerable momentum to the rest of class exercises.

The use of guest participants in the virtual classroom was not limited to judges. Lawyers, business people, other law professors, faculty from other departments within the university or from other schools could also be brought in as guest participants. This capability is not limited to the United States, and a number of professors have shown interest in bringing in guest participants from other countries.

New Publishing Medium

The virtual classroom also provided a new medium for professors to publish. This electronic publishing made it easy to supplement traditional printed course materials. One simple method was distributing course materials electronically. Beyond that, the professor also had the capacity to use the databases to publish her own notes or outline of the course. If new cases or other materials came to her attention, the notes could be easily updated by editing the earlier postings.

Lotus Notes made it easy to build hypertext links between materials in the databases so professors were able to link their own content to discussion threads created by students. West also created a template that enabled professors to build links from references in their notes to primary legal materials on WESTLAW. These capabilities greatly enriched the professors' own online publishing.

Dynamics of the Virtual Classroom

The asynchronous quality of the virtual classroom enabled professors, students, and guests to participate when and where they found it convenient. Beyond this fundamental characteristic, the virtual classroom experiment also discovered several other unique dynamics.

First, the virtual classroom was professor driven. At this point student usage was influenced by the degree to which professors promoted use of the forums. This was often done by professors making references to the databases in class or discussing questions which were posted on them.

Professors could control the degree of their own participation. This was important to a number of faculty who were concerned that the virtual classrooms not take too much extra time. Most professors found that it was well within their capacity to control their level of participation. Even those who preferred not to spend much time with the electronic conferences found them to be helpful as an alternative to traditional office hours toward exam time.

Although the virtual classrooms were professor driven, student participation increased during the semester. As students became more comfortable with using the software, they began to participate in greater numbers.

Unlike the questions asked of professors in the hallway after class, the postings in the discussion forum were available to everyone. The questions and responses also seemed to have a greater reflective quality. Although most of the postings were short, they did suggest that students put thought into them before posting to the forum.

Most of the discussion forums were made anonymous so that students could feel comfortable in posting questions and comments. This anonymity lead to a greater percentage of participation in the virtual classroom than in the regular classroom. Students are often reticent to volunteer comments in the regular class for fear of appearing inadequate. This greater student participation provided professors with better insight into student comprehension of materials taught in class.

Some professors were concerned that the virtual classrooms would take away from student participation in class. The actual experience, however, was that students were more responsive than usual.

Faculty/Student Perspectives on Collaborative Learning

Professors consistently felt that the virtual classroom provided them with a better grasp of how students were understanding the materials presented in class. This diagnostic quality enabled faculty to use precious class time to focus on those concepts that were most difficult for students. They could cover basic and often routine matters in the virtual classroom, leaving more regular class time to deal with difficult subjects.

Professors also found they could encourage more student participation through the use of the virtual classroom conferences. This increased participation, in part promoted by anonymity, also made its way into the traditional classroom.

Some professors were uncomfortable at first with the technology, but since it is similar to e-mail, they quickly were able to master it. There was also concern about the virtual classroom taking more professor time. Designed so faculty had control over the amount of time they wanted to use, with the virtual classroom they could also control when they chose to participate. The flexibility of the asynchronous communications of the virtual classroom tended to offset the concern about additional time.

From a student perspective, the major benefit of the virtual class experience was additional access to the professor. Not only could they ask questions of the professor in an anonymous fashion, but they could also look for professor participation in the discussion forum as an additional method for determining what the professor felt was important.

The students also benefited from the asynchronous quality of the virtual class. They could ask questions whenever they arose, even if it was late at night or when they were working from home. They also had the opportunity to practice answering questions. This is particularly helpful in the law school setting where the only feedback is often an actual exam.

Students had some of the same technological concerns about using the virtual classroom as the professors. Students who did not own their own personal computer also were concerned about having access. The use of the student labs and provision of training for students helped to overcome these issues.

Students were concerned about the time associated with the virtual classroom. In this experiment the virtual classroom was seen as additional work not compensated by either additional credits or a reduction of some other work required for the course. Although students recognized that the additional work resulted in better comprehension of the course materials, they were still concerned about the overall time commitment.

The Future of Collaborative Learning

Based on the results of the experiment at the University of Minnesota Law School, use of virtual classroom technology was expanded to 20 schools in the 1995–96 school year. The concept, now called the West Education Network, was used by more than 100 professors and 5,000 students. While they experienced many of the dynamics of the original experiments, they also explored new ways of using virtual classroom technology. A number of new approaches to using the technology for simulation, skills, and clinical courses are beginning to be tried.

Collaborative learning will become an increasingly important element of legal education. Technological barriers are falling as student computer use and school technology infrastructures improve. Students, faculty, and publishers are all showing increasing interest in the collaborative learning model.

The practice of law fundamentally involves the creation and communication of ideas. Collaborative learning techniques, such as the virtual classrooms in law schools, provide excellent training for the future law practice experience. Virtual classroom technology will facilitate both communication and the creation of work product. Increasingly professors will use conferencing to publish electronic course materials, link those materials to on-line primary source materials and distribute the materials to their students and others. They also will be able to use virtual classrooms to incorporate feedback and participation by judges, lawyers, and other professionals to help bridge the gap between academe and the world of law practice. Collaborative learning has a bright future in legal education.

REFERENCES

Areeda, P. (1996). The Socratic method. *Harvard Law Review, 109*, 911.

Burris, R. (1980). *Computer network experiments in teaching law.* Princeton, NJ: EDUCOM.

MacCrate R. (1992). *Legal education and professional development—An educational continuum.* Chicago, IL: American Bar Association.

Marshall, D. (1994). *Socratic method and the irreducible core of legal education.* Law Alumni Distinguished Teacher, University of Minnesota Law School.

Mersky, R., & Christensen, J. (1980). Computer-assisted legal research instruction in Texas law schools. *Law Library Journal, 73*, 79.

Teich, P. (1991). How effective is computer-assisted instruction? An evaluation for legal educators. *Journal of Legal Education, 41*, 489.

9

Transforming the Community College From a Teaching to a Learning Institution

Terry O'Banion

More than any other institution of higher education, the community college has appropriated the moniker "the teaching college" as most descriptive of its innate character and culture. *Building Communities* (AACJC, 1988), the report of the Commission on the Future of Community Colleges, is a tribute to the community college's commitment to teaching. One of the most significant documents ever written on the community college, *Building Communities* has been widely distributed by the American Association of Community Colleges and has had great impact on hundreds of community colleges across the country. The report references the value of teaching again and again. "Building communities through dedicated teaching is the vision and the inspiration of this report" (p. 8). "Quality instruction should be the hallmark of the movement" (p. 25). "The community college should be the nation's premier teaching institution" (p. 25). These sentiments regarding the value of teaching in the community college are echoed throughout the national literature on the community college.

It is not surprising, therefore, that the campus literature also reflects this emphasis on teaching. Accreditation reports, grant applications, and annual reports on the state of the institution all reflect this emphasis. College mission statements which reveal the core values of an institution also reflect this emphasis on teaching. Barr (1995) studied the mission statements of California's 107 community colleges and noted that teaching was always listed as a key purpose and mission of the institution. In contrast, he discovered that "community colleges never used the word 'learning' in a statement of purpose except when it was bundled in the phrase 'teaching and learning' as if to say that, while learning may indeed have something to do with community colleges, it is only present as an aspect of teaching" (p. 2).

More and more community colleges are adding the word *learning* when they use the word *teaching*, but careful reading reveals the emphasis is still on teaching over learning. Lauridsen (1994) conducted a survey of a random sample of 100 community colleges to determine the purposes and activities of their teaching and learning centers. Lauridsen noted that the words used to describe centers, in addition to *teaching* and *learning*, most frequently included *development* preceded by *faculty*, *staff*, and *professional*. Another rather common title was faculty *resource center*. Interestingly, the most frequently mentioned purpose for teaching and learning centers in their mission statements is to improve teaching, followed by to encourage faculty development, and last to improve learning. So while community colleges tend to link teaching and learning in the titles of centers that help faculty with their work, the focus is primarily on teaching with learning last.

Community colleges often take great pride in comparing their commitment to teaching in contrast to the university's commitment to research. To drive the point home, community college advocates often note the university's propensity to use graduate students to staff large lecture sessions while they, more committed to quality teaching they say, make teaching the priority of professional staff. In the early 1990s community colleges began to establish endowed teaching chairs, their version of the university's endowed research chairs. Endowed teaching chairs have now been established in dozens of community colleges across the country as one of the most visible expressions of the community college's commitment to teaching. Valencia Community College in Florida is an excellent example, having established 24 endowed chairs through 1995. "The purpose of Valencia's endowed chair program is threefold: to recognize and promote teaching excellence at the college; to spotlight outstanding members of Valencia's teaching faculty; and to provide the college with financial resources to support teaching excellence" (Gianini, 1995). All of the language reflects the emphasis on teaching rather than on learning.

There is nothing inherently wrong with placing great value on teaching except that it has led to placing more value on teaching than on learning, on teachers than on learners. As a result, educational institutions tend to accommodate the needs, interests, and values of their employees more often than the needs, interests, and values of their customers. The value placed on teaching by community colleges will be a challenge for those institutions that plan to realign their missions, programs, and practices to reflect the learning revolution emerging across the entire higher education landscape.

THE TRANSFORMATION BEGINS

A Nation at Risk (1983) left most higher education institutions untouched by significant reform, but it set the stage. The nation's community colleges were ripe for a revolution in the 1990s. A second wave of educational criticism emerged in the early 1990s, cresting in *An American Imperative* (Wingspread, 1993). This, and many other reports in the early 1990s, found many community colleges ready to address major new changes, such as placing primary emphasis on learning and learners as the key focus for the educational enterprise. *An American Imperative* called for "a seamless system that can produce and support a nation of learners, providing access to educational services for learners as they need them, when they need them, and wherever they need them" (p. 19). The report went on to say "putting learning at the heart of the academic enterprise will mean overhauling the conceptual, procedural, curricular, and other architecture of postsecondary education on most campuses" (p. 14).

Community colleges have been preparing for just such a revolution for over a decade. They have been national leaders in modeling the concept of the learning community, a curricular intervention designed to increase opportunities for student-to-student collaboration and student-to-teacher collaboration.

Community colleges have led in applying concepts of total quality management and continuous quality improvement, preparing their institutions through new processes and definition of values to focus on learning as their primary goal. Community colleges have also been leading national experiments in applying technology to improve teaching and learning on their campuses. For example, community colleges have been experimenting with distance learning models, taking their educational programs off-campus to be delivered on-site at the plants and factories of local business and industry.

In other words, community colleges have been actively involved in creating innovative programs that reflect the new emphasis on learning even though they may not have coalesced these individual efforts around a comprehensive institution-wide initiative focused on the learning revolution. A number of community college leaders, however, are beginning to focus on learning as the heart of the educational enterprise, and it is only a matter of time before many community colleges begin to explore the implication of this increasing emphasis on learning and learners.

Since 1990, there has been a groundswell of interest in the learner from community college presidents, trustees, faculty, researchers, and state policy makers. This new focus on learning is captured best perhaps in a statement from Myran, Zeiss, and Howdyshell (1995):

> There is something magical about the year 2000. We hear, as you do, the siren call of new beginnings and new possibilities. We feel we are entering a period of profound and fundamental change for community colleges, the most sweeping period since the 1960s. Then, we transformed campus-based colleges into community-based colleges; today we are becoming learner-based colleges. As we enter the new century, we will combine the forces of learner-based and community-based education to shape a powerful and new definition of the community college. (*Preface*)

George Boggs and Robert Barr of Palomar College in California have been among the earliest advocates to urge community colleges to move toward a new paradigm of learning in contrast to the old paradigm of teaching. Boggs (1993) notes "The new paradigm says that community colleges are learning, not teaching, institutions. The mission is student learning. The most important people in the institution are the learners. Everyone else is there to facilitate and support student learning" (p. 2). Barr and Tagg (1995) make the same point: "In the instruction paradigm the mission of the college is to provide instruction, to teach.... In the learning paradigm the mission of the college is to produce learning" (p. 15).

The Maricopa Community Colleges in Phoenix, Arizona, is one of the leading institutions in the country exploring how to apply the new learning paradigm. Paul Elsner (1993), Chancellor of the Maricopa Community Colleges, has raised a number of key questions:

> How can the faculty facilitate the actual rhythms of learning, verification, expansion, and conceptualization? Is this an elusive process even when we witness it in our own labs and classrooms? Will technology drive a formidable learning paradigm that will eclipse all traditional learning? Will students discover their own navigational route to such learning processes and live outside and on the edges of our traditional colleges? (p. 26)

A number of California community colleges are beginning to focus on implementing the philosophy of placing learning first. The theme has captured the interest of Fred Colby (1995) a trustee in the San Diego Community College District who declared "To meet the challenge, we must develop new instructional methodologies which focus on learning, not teaching, and make use of new technologies at every level of education" (p. 4). This theme is reflected most clearly in a new document developed by the California Board of Governors, *The New Basic Agenda: Policy Directions for Student Success* (1995). This key document says unequivocally "Student learning is essential to the social and economic development of multicultural California" (p. 2).

This sampling of perspectives from community college leaders, all recorded in the last five years, is confirmation that the learner and learning have emerged more clearly than ever as the key priorities of community colleges. The priority has always been assumed, but now it is articulated as the most visible cornerstone of reform efforts in policy, programs, and practices.

Emerging Models of the Learning College

Community colleges have begun to rally around an emerging concept, "the learning college," as a framework for the reform efforts to place learning first. "The Learning College places learning first and provides educational experiences for learners anyway, anywhere, anytime" (O'Banion, 1995–96, p. 22). The learning college is based on a series of principles that place learning as the central focus of the entire educational enterprise. The following four principles are examples of this focus on learning:

- Learners must be engaged as full partners in the learning process, assuming primary responsibility for their own choices.
- The learning college must create and offer as many options for learning as possible.
- The roles of learning facilitators are defined by the needs of learners.
- Learning facilitators succeed when improved and expanded learning can be documented for learners.

The concepts and principles of the learning college are elaborated upon in detail in a new book, *A Learning College for the 21st Century* (O'Banion, 1997).

A number of community colleges are already beginning to explore these concepts and to initiate emerging models of the learning college. None of the leaders in these colleges claim they have designed the definitive model of a learning college. They are just beginning their journeys, reworking the present to create the future. The brief descriptions of their early efforts outlined in the following sections do not do justice to the extensive changes occurring in these colleges. The descriptions here represent a point in time; they are continually evolving their definition of the learning college. The colleges are different in the way they approach their tasks and design their structures and measure their outcomes, but there is a common bond, a common commitment to placing learning first, as a central value and guiding light for everything they do.

Community College of Denver

Perhaps longer than any other community college in the country, in fact for over a decade, the Community College of Denver has been creating a learning college. In 1986, under the leadership of President Byron McClenney, faculty members were asked at a fall convocation to participate in setting goals for the future of the institution. To no one's surprise, the goals reflected an emphasis on placing students first and on collaboration as a way faculty and staff would achieve their goals. A self-study process for the reaffirmation of accreditation and a new state law requiring accountability reports from all public institutions of higher education provided platforms for the college to focus its efforts on comprehensive institutional change.

From these early efforts emerged an annual planning activity in which strategies for the coming year were agreed upon by college constituents. These strategies are reviewed annually against the strategies of the year before as a way of refining new goals and directions. In addition, the annual accountability reports were woven into the annual planning cycle; thus the college had built in an inescapable opportunity to review its progress and plan for future progress on an annual basis.

Soon a Statement of Values for Teaching Excellence was created, reflecting the institution's strong commitment to placing learning at the center of all of its activities. The statement of values includes the following elements:

- Enables students to become independent learners
- Demonstrates a commitment to student outcomes (job readiness, skill levels, mastery of subject matter)
- Provides an opportunity for critical thinking and problem solving
- Provides linkages between instruction and real world applications
- Demonstrates an excitement about teaching and learning
- Maintains high but realistic expectations

- Demonstrates appreciation of a diverse student population
- Encourages growth in students' self-esteem

Using this statement of values as a guide, the faculty at the Community College of Denver created exit competencies and a way to assess the competencies for all certificate and degree programs. The college also issued guarantees of job competencies for employers and guarantees for the transferability of its Associate of Arts and Associate of Science courses. In addition, the majority of courses and programs are offered in an open-entry/open-exit and self-paced mode. Most laboratories are open and in many cases provide computer-assisted learning options. The case management process in which faculty members and students work as teams to ensure learning is operational throughout the institution.

These changes toward an improved learning climate have had considerable impact on student learning and retention as documented in the annual accountability report to the state. For example, between 1987 and 1995 the total number of graduates from the Community College of Denver increased by 98%. In that same time period, people of color (as a percent of total graduates and transfers) increased from 13% to 43%. Of vocational graduates who completed their educational goals, 98% either continued their education or were employed within one year.

The institutional climate has developed to the point that faculty and staff now look forward to the annual feedback regarding their progress. In addition to the accountability report to the state, the college has instituted evaluations from students on an annual basis which are printed in the semester schedule of classes. Institutional data about student progress and high ratings by students are validated by external evaluations that also confirm that the college is on the right track. The Community College of Denver was one of the public institutions in the state to be recognized by the Colorado Commission on Higher Education for an exemplary annual accountability report. The North Central Association Evaluation in 1993 found "exemplary planning and accountability activities" that are "a part of the college fabric."

In 1996 the college initiated perhaps its toughest challenge on the journey to become a learning college. The college is designing a pay-for-performance program for faculty salaries, and a 25-member task force has developed a statement of philosophy and an evaluation plan to be instituted in the near future. This development is rare in community colleges and is further evidence of the strong climate of trust and collaboration that has become embedded in the culture of the Community College of Denver. The

Community College of Denver is well on its way to becoming a learning college for the 21st century.

Lane Community College

Since 1993, Lane Community College (Oregon) has been involved in an institution-wide restructuring process designed to make sure the college changes in response to changing times. In a memo to all college employees, President Jerry Moskus noted there had been major changes in the environment, technology, politics, leadership, and growth in the past five years, and urged, "To continue to be a strong, effective community college, Lane must rethink nearly everything it does." To begin that task, all faculty and staff members at Lane were invited to participate in special sessions to create a new organizational structure based on a new vision of the future.

That new vision has been developed, accepted by faculty and staff, and approved by the board of trustees, and is captured in a brief statement: "Lane Community College provides quality learning experiences in a caring environment." Throughout the document on restructuring, the language of learning reflects the values and focus of the emerging vision:

- Above all, Lane must put the learner first by shifting more and more to a learner-focused organization. This means that our structure should help customers and clients accomplish their goals as easily as possible. In some cases, it means organizing around whole processes; in others, this means that our structure must be transparent to those who use our services and must not cause obstacles.
- Change must be built into our organization; we must become a learning organization. Bureaucracies are not amenable to change. Organizations that move routine decision-making and problem solving to work teams are better able to adapt to continual change. We must break down the walls between departments by designing our processes and services around work teams that cut across artificial organizational lines.
- Our ideas of management and supervision must change. As employee groups are empowered to problem solve and make decisions in their work areas, managers must learn to be coaches, advisors, and consultants rather than bosses and day-to-day decision-makers.
- We must put more emphasis on training and socialization of Lane employees. The new Lane described here will require intensive training for many, if not all, current employees.

- Finally, it is clear that we must rely more and more on technology to help us do our jobs. In order to do that, our organization must facilitate cooperation and collaboration among the various units that provide and support the use of technology.

Lane has made measurable progress in restructuring the college to carry out this new vision. The college has been organized into four groups: executive services, college operations, student services, and instructional services. Each of the four main groups is made up of subgroups of two or more departments with common elements. The groups and subgroups are displayed in a circle on the organizational chart to indicate that Lane is no longer a hierarchical, bureaucratic organization. All four of the main groups contribute members to strategic teams, defined as "cross-functional, vertically-integrated assemblages to pursue ongoing institutional objectives." Project teams are vertically-integrated groups that address short term, limited objectives. Strategic teams address topics such as marketing and diversity, whereas project teams are formed to address, for example, a specific construction project. In making these organizational changes, college leaders have been very sensitive to past organizational structures and have been careful to explain the reason and need for change.

Aware that symbolic actions or ceremonies are a useful way of marking new beginnings, college leaders held a restructuring ceremony to explain and celebrate the new directions. One of the activities considered for the restructuring ceremony was the symbolic burning of the college's large procedures manual. As an indication of the sensitivity of leaders to past allegiances, this act was rejected because it was felt that many who had developed or used this manual would have seen it as an attack on their departments.

With a new vision statement and a restructured organization in hand, college leaders began to make changes in programs, processes, and practices. A project team addressed the problems of high faculty turnover expected from retirement and made recommendations regarding faculty hiring, orientation, and staff development. The team recommended a revised faculty hiring process and developed an annual hiring calendar. They envisioned a future faculty that would form a learning community, play a more active role in college governance, better reflect the diversity of society, and be substantially full-time. An Organization Development Action Team has been created with representatives from faculty, classified staff, and administrators to develop and manage a series of training programs designed to improve communication skills, team effectiveness, meeting effectiveness, conflict resolution, and customer service.

The new focus on learning at Lane is creating a demand on campus for more and better information, and technology is helping to meet the need. A college-wide network now links most staff with each other via e-mail and with the Internet. Many staff have taken the e-mail and Internet classes taught by college instructors as part of the staff development program.

New uses of technology are also serving students. A touch-telephone registration system—already the service rated highest by students—has been enhanced to give student callers their grades, thereby saving mailing costs. When registration is in progress, the college broadcasts the class schedule live on cable television so that students can monitor open and closed classes as they register by telephone. The use of a bar code system in the book store is beginning to eliminate long lines. Kiosks provide students with personalized information such as their schedules, grades, transcripts, and with general information such as campus maps. Counselors and advisors are developing a system to aid them in serving students, and the library has been computer-automated. "Smart cards" are currently being field tested as future passports to the learning college, a means by which students gain access to what the college offers, while at the same time creating a permanent record of where they have been.

Lane is making considerable progress toward becoming a learning college. That transition was given a real boost when voters approved a $42.8 million bond measure which will enable the college to make current facilities more learner friendly and to build and equip small learning centers at ten of the high schools in the college's 5,000 square-mile district.

Palomar College

Changing the language it uses to reflect and encourage new values and behavior, Palomar College (California) has also been a leader in moving toward "the learning college." In 1989, Palomar created a Vision Task Force whose work lead to the notion of shifting its mission, indeed, its driving paradigm, from instruction to learning. President George Boggs has said "The new paradigm says that community colleges are learning, not teaching, institutions. The mission is student learning. The most important people in the institution are the learners. Everyone else is there to facilitate and support student learning."

The Vision Task Force included 16 members representing all segments of the college and a representative from the community. The Vision Task Force studied national and state documents about the state of education; reviewed vision statements from businesses and other colleges; interviewed faculty, staff, students, and selected community members; surveyed business owners regarding their needs in terms of a workforce; and completed an environmental scan on social and economic changes in the community and in the state of California. The new vision statement and a revised college mission statement required 18 months of study and development by the members of the Vision Task Force.

The foreword to the vision statement captures the essence of the vision:

> Readers of these statements will note that they reflect a subtle but nonetheless profound shift in how we think of the college and what we do. We have shifted from an identification with process to an identification with results. We are no longer content with merely providing quality instruction. We will judge ourselves henceforth on the quality of student learning we produce. And further, we will judge ourselves by our ability to produce even greater and more sophisticated student learning and meaningful educational success with each passing year, each exiting student, and each graduating class. To do this, we must ourselves continually experiment, discover, grow, and learn. Consequently, we see ourselves as a learning institution in both our object and our method.

With a new vision statement approved by all college constituencies including the board of trustees, things began to change at Palomar. Recruitment brochures were revised to attract a faculty and staff committed to promoting and supporting student learning. Employment procedures were revised to help select faculty and staff who shared the college's values and beliefs. Orientation for new full-time and part-time faculty and new members of the governing board now emphasize the principles of the learning paradigm.

Student learning forums have been designed to bring together faculty, staff, and students to listen to student suggestions about improving their opportunities for success. Learning communities that have been developed in the state of Washington have also been implemented widely to provide a multidisciplinary approach to learning and to encourage collaboration between and among students and faculty. The board of trustees now sets the district's annual goals in the context of the Palomar College vision statement. The vision statement and the new learning paradigm are the theme of the annual faculty convocation in which innovative faculty and staff members who contribute to the paradigm shift are recognized. Palomar's annual planning process is now also guided by the vision statement. For the first time, the 1995 goals of the Palomar College Faculty Senate included a stated commitment to enhance student learning. At all levels and in many ways, Palomar College personnel are moving forward in creating a learning institution.

Maricopa Community Colleges

In 1993, Maricopa (Arizona) was invited to participate as one of 30 institutions of higher education in the Pew Higher Education Round Tables. The purpose of the Pew Round Tables is to assist colleges and universities in a restructuring process intended to address rapid change. In the earliest discussions at Maricopa, participants agreed that profound, systemic change was needed which focused on: 1) the need for a new learning paradigm that is learning-centered and student-centered, and 2) the need for more collaboration and integration within the Maricopa District.

Round table members began discussions by contrasting characteristics of the traditional learning paradigm and the desired learning paradigm. These discussions confirmed the need for a new vocabulary and resulted in agreement on key concepts of the desired learning paradigm:

- Learning is a process that is lifelong for everyone and should be measured in a consistent, ongoing manner focused on improvement.
- Everyone is an active learner and teacher through collaboration, shared responsibility, and mutual respect.
- The learning process includes the larger community through the development of alliances, relationships, and opportunities for mutual benefit.
- Learning occurs in a flexible and appropriate environment.

Throughout 1994, the results of the round table discussions were shared with all faculty and staff in the Maricopa District, and several projects were initiated to move the district toward "a learning college." An example of the scope of these efforts, Project Apollo is a $6 million plus partnership with Oracle Corporation designed to develop and implement learner-centered financial records, human resources, and electronic mail systems. This is a major undertaking that will capitalize on the sophisticated technology base already established at Maricopa to make it more learner-centered. Chancellor Paul Elsner has said, "The learner-centered system will result in greater opportunities for students who will be empowered to serve as navigators of their own learning paths."

In addition to Project Apollo, in January 1994 Maricopa launched "Strategic Conversations" with its governing board members as well as internal and external communities. The Strategic Conversations represent a significant shift in the way Maricopa's governing board conducts its business. These conversations, up to two hours long, are now open to active participation from members of internal and external communities and have been used to develop and revise new statements of vision, mission, goals, and values. Each strategic conversation is a structured process in which a cross-functional team prepares a brief background paper, conducts interactive exercises, and facilitates the participation of everyone present. The purpose of the conversations is to promote learning and a greater understanding of the issues challenging Maricopa and its communities. The focus of each conversation differs. Some conversations have been on creating definitions of learning organizations, reviewing examples of established programs at Maricopa that already reflect the learning organization, changing roles for staff, and assessing individuals and the Maricopa organization as a reflection of the learning college. This new process encourages individual and organizational learning. People are recognized as the primary source of new solutions and creative ways of doing things.

As Maricopa has undertaken a massive effort to move to a learner-centered organization, collaboration has emerged as a key value in overcoming the compartmentalization of old structures. Two significant enterprises have emerged as the primary mechanisms to ensure that the college becomes a learning organization or a system of learning colleges. The two enterprises are the Learner-Centered System Steering (LCS) Team and the Organizational Analysis Team (OAS). These two teams have different paths, different goals, and different processes, but they constantly interact and change their goals and processes based on their interaction with one another. The LCS Team coordinates a fairly massive reengineering effort by identifying, analyzing, and recommending changes in the process cycles that support students from registration through graduation or completion. Twenty-eight representatives from 22 departments form the design team which is chaired by a student. Reviewing the past activities of the college and conducting a series of student focus groups, the team identified 17 cycles related to learning support systems for students and grouped these into four key categories: the learning plan, financial aid and support, scheduling, and curriculum approval and articulation. While these cycles reflect somewhat traditional approaches to providing student support, they are being viewed from a new perspective that places learning first. The intention is to reengineer all strategies supporting these four cycles and automate as completely as possible the services provided for students.

The Organizational Analysis Team consists of many college leaders, policy analysts, president, consultants, faculty, deans, and staff at all levels of the organization. Its purpose is to analyze the impact of change on Maricopa and to suggest processes and programs that will lead to an appropriate adaptation to that change. The team acts as a cushion and interpreter of change which makes it easier for the stakeholders to understand the transformation. The Organizational Analysis Team will play a key role in helping individuals and groups with the complex challenges involved in adjusting to new changes.

Maricopa recognizes that technology will play a major role in assisting students to navigate more of their learning options and support faculty in their efforts to provide a more meaningful and challenging learning environment. Maricopa has tracked the introduction and development of new applications of technology throughout its history as a way of visibly communicating the impact of this force. Maricopa is well along the path of a major journey toward using technology to become a learning-centered institution.

Sinclair Community College

As early as 1985, staff members of Sinclair Community College (Ohio) began discussing how they could develop learning outcomes for each of the college's programs. The discussion was fueled by President David Ponitz who suggested that the college should offer a guarantee for Sinclair graduates. The idea was that each graduate's level of performance in the workplace as well as the transferability of courses would be guaranteed. To put such a guaranteed program in place, the college needed to develop learning outcomes and methods for assessing learning. An Assessment Steering Committee adopted 12 principles of assessment, and the first principle illustrates that Sinclair was well on the road to becoming a learning college: "The primary reason for assessment is to improve student learning and development." Through its work on assessment and guaranteed programs, Sinclair has developed one of the most substantive programs in the nation.

In 1991, the college took a second major step toward becoming a learning college by initiating a Quality Initiative. Using processes of total quality management, and with the assistance of an external consultant, the college created and adopted the following vision statement.

Sinclair Community College Vision

Before us lie uncharted worlds of opportunity. Sinclair will be the bridge into that future, giving open access to opportunity, intellectual challenge, and self-discovery for students with diverse needs:

- With Sinclair, people will pursue their quests for lifelong learning through affordable, high quality education.

- At Sinclair, people will benefit from a caring approach to teaching and learning that provides personal attention and encourages individual growth.
- Through Sinclair, people will be empowered with knowledge and skills for their journeys into tomorrow.

Our success shall hinge on turning these values into action:

- Dedication to quality and excellence
- Reliance on anticipation, imagination, and innovation
- Commitment to responsible citizenship within our community
- Adherence to the Sinclair credo—"Find the need and endeavor to meet it"
- Confidence in the courage, determination, and diversity of our students, employees, and supporters
- Belief in unlimited human potential

Following the completion of the vision statement, core indicators of institutional effectiveness were developed in six areas: access to success, lifelong learning, student development, community focus, quality workplace, and stewardship. Critical success factors, which are actions or outcomes, have also been defined for each of the core indicators and provide a way to measure and document performance and achievement toward a learning college. Each of the college divisions has also refined its mission in light of the overall values statement, the core indicators, and the critical success factors. The college now has in place a framework for measuring the extent to which it will achieve its goals of becoming a learning college.

From these initial activities has emerged a statement on Vision for Learning Excellence for Sinclair. This statement places in perspective the future that Sinclair will face and notes the strategies and processes that Sinclair will use to continue its journey to become a learning college.

Conclusion

The concept of the learning college is an attractive idea in an embryonic stage that, if nurtured properly, can address many of the current problems facing higher education. It even has the potential of changing the entire architecture of higher education. As has been illustrated in these brief summaries of practice in five of the leading community colleges in the country, the community college may be the ideal crucible in which the concept of the learning college can take form. After 100 years of experimentation, the community college has emerged as an institution with a strong penchant for innovation and for risk taking. The community college is not afraid to reach out and explore new ideas and new concepts as these colleges illustrate. Building on their strong commitment to teaching, community colleges in the future will be transformed into learning colleges as a more visible expression of their basic commitment to placing learning first.

This chapter is adapted from *A Learning College for the 21st Century* by Terry O'Banion (ACE/American Association of Community Colleges, 1997).

References

American Association of Community and Junior Colleges. (1988). *Building communities: A vision for a new century.* Washington, DC: AACC.

Barr, R. (1994, February). A new paradigm for community colleges. *News: The RP Group.* The Research and Planning Group for the California Community Colleges.

Barr, R. (1995, March). From teaching to learning: A new reality for community colleges. *Leadership Abstracts, 8,* 3. Mission Viejo, CA: The League for Innovation in the Community College

Barr, R., & Tagg, J. (1995, December). From teaching to learning—A new paradigm for undergraduate education. *Change,* 12-25.

Boggs, G.R. (1993, September). Community colleges and the new paradigm. *Celebrations,* An occasional publication of the National Institute for Staff and Organizational Development (NISOD), Austin, TX.

California Board of Governors. (1995). *The new basic agenda: Policy perspectives for student success.*

Colby, F. (1995, August 28). Breaking down the walls in education. *Community College Week.*

Elsner, P. (1993). *Encyclical III: Effective teaching and learning and the quality transformation.* Phoenix, AZ: Maricopa Community Colleges.

Gianini, P. C., Jr. (1995, December). Endowed chairs for instructional leadership. *Leadership Abstracts, 8,*12. Mission Viejo, CA: The League for Innovation in the Community College.

Lauridsen, K. (1994). A contemporary view of teaching and learning centers for faculty. In T. O'Banion & Associates, *Teaching and learning in the community college.* Washington, DC: American Association of Community Colleges.

Myran, G., et al. (1995). *Community college leadership in the new century: Learning to improve learning.* Washington, DC: American Association of Community Colleges.

The National Commission on Excellence in Education. (1983, April). *A nation at risk: The imperative for educational reform.* Washington, DC: U.S. Government Printing Office.

O'Banion, T. (1995-96, December/January). A learning college for the 21st century. *Community College Journal.*

O'Banion, T. (1997). *A learning college for the 21st century.* Washington, DC: American Council on Education and American Association of Community Colleges.

Wingspread Group on Higher Education. (1993). *An American imperative: Higher expectations for higher education.* Racine, WI: The Johnson Foundation, Inc.

10

Tradition and Change in Quest of Excellence

Thomas K. Hearn, Jr.

From its founding more than a quarter century before the War Between the States, Wake Forest College grew from the Baptist beliefs in freedom of conscience and the tensions between faith and reason. Young men and later women came from the fields and small towns of eastern North Carolina, usually the first in their families to attend college. They were tended by teachers of moral and intellectual substance who embraced the Socratic principle that education was the conversion of the soul to wisdom. The people and the setting created an environment of sustained personal relationships. There was little campus housing, and many students boarded with faculty families. There was no town-and-gown problem; the town *was* the gown. Implicit in the school's motto of *Pro Humanitate* was the conviction that the purpose of education is to prepare one for a life of service. And its bedrock values of honesty, integrity, and faith nourished a close and caring community.

For more than a century Wake Forest preserved this character and pursued a defined mission. Then, after the Second World War, it was uprooted from the small town with which its name was shared in the rolling farmland of "down-east" North Carolina and was transplanted a hundred miles to the west at the threshold of the Blue Ridge in the industrial city of Winston-Salem.

Suddenly, this country school had moved to town and confronted an institutional identity crisis. Was this the old school in a new place? Or was it a new school with the old name? That question lives at Wake Forest to this day. The removal also exhausted the institution, its resources, and its people. The outcome of this exhaustion was a cautiousness, a tentative approach to change. With the benefit of hindsight, this caution served Wake Forest well. The school had no energy or capacity to pursue the trends of the sixties and seventies which threatened and, in some instances, seriously compromised American higher education. Wake Forest retained its core curriculum, its commitment to undergraduate teaching, and its core values from the old campus.

Challenges

Even the most focused of institutions cannot remain completely unaffected by its greater social and scholastic environment. The ascension of the research university in America in this past half century has engendered a system in which senior faculty members mentor a handful of graduate students and engage in their own highly specialized areas of research while doing little or no undergraduate teaching. Many undergraduate courses, especially crucial introductory courses, are taught by teaching assistants. The shared values and context of the liberal arts has given way to more specialized, career-oriented majors. There is frequently little connection between what takes place inside the classroom and the co-curricular lives of students. And as scholastic standards on the elementary and secondary levels have declined, greater numbers of students are coming to college unequipped with adequate writing and critical thinking skills.

These and other problems are causing a new and vigorous public scrutiny of higher education, public and private. Colleges and universities have historically been largely exempt from external accountability. That has changed. No longer do Americans perceive their colleges as pet institutions whose primary purposes are football, fraternities, and fun. The public is demanding outcomes from colleges—in the quality of teaching and the results of teaching in demonstrable student outcomes.

Especially for private schools with high tuition, a consumer culture now requires that we provide superior academic outcomes which justify the extra cost. The efficient and effective use of scarce resources—what we do with what we are given—and the ability to provide distinctive educational advantages are the most urgent challenges confronting private institutions today.

THE PLAN

Wake Forest follows a regular academic planning cycle. The issue for this iteration was the enhancement of an already outstanding undergraduate program. This effort began in early 1993 with formation of a sixteen-member task force of faculty, students, and administrators which was chaired by the provost. They were charged with charting the university's academic course into the new century. The task force gathered information and opinions from a consulting panel of administrators and students and through 200 faculty questionnaires, an all-day faculty retreat, 82 hearings, numerous open forums, visits to other universities, and special sessions with a host of key university bodies and constituents. It also sought campus reaction to a preliminary white paper and an interim report issued in January 1994.

Harking back to the origins of the Wake Forest culture, enhancement of the personal relationships between teachers and students emerged as the single most important priority for the enhancement of our undergraduate program. College is about student learning, and students learn most when motivated by dedicated professors in an environment calculated to promote intellectual and personal development. The special challenge for a college or university is to create an environment with the people, policies, and traditions that motivate learning and growth.

Based on this principle, Wake Forest formulated The Plan for the Class of 2000, a blueprint to provide more personal opportunities for faculty and students to collaborate in learning. Wake Forest recommitted itself to its liberal arts program, the development of stronger writing and critical thinking skills, the appreciation of global perspectives, computer competency, and small class sizes across the curriculum.

To enhance personalized learning, the plan called for forty new faculty positions, a 15% increase in the undergraduate faculty, underscoring our commitment to dedicate more resources to students in smaller classes. We will retain the size of the undergraduate student body at its present level. The plan introduced a rigorous, mandatory seminar for first-year students, assuring each of an in-depth intellectual encounter in a class no larger than 15 students. We will add more than a hundred class sections. We increased funds for the library and scientific instrumentation.

An annual symposium theme of substantial intellectual or creative value was established to provide common learning opportunities for the entire community. To take advantage of opportunities to promote learning and communication with technology, we will provide a notebook computer to every incoming student.

Approval

Approval of the plan was a complex process. Because significant changes and costs were involved, the faculty and the Board of Trustees had extensive information sessions and discussions.

For the faculty, there were at least two points of controversy: whether computing technology should be mandatory at a traditional liberal arts institution, and whether our investment in technology was the best use of academic resources.

For the Board of Trustees, a major concern was the effect of a $3,000 tuition increase required to finance all of the plan's provisions. Wake Forest has traditionally had a lower tuition than its peer institutions, and there was concern about sacrificing a portion of our price advantage. The trustees required that Wake Forest's need-blind admissions policy be maintained. That policy has served to maintain economic diversity in the student body and has been an important competitive advantage.

All of these concerns were worthy—indeed, essential—points for debate, and there were disagreements at every level of the institution. For example, a small group of students held a protest regarding the computer component. Mostly seniors, they objected to the tuition increase for their successors and feared that the technology provision would compromise our tradition of intensive faculty-student interaction. Even so, the plan was approved or endorsed in a series of five votes over an eight-week period in the spring of 1995 by the college faculty, the student legislature, and the Board of Trustees.

The plan's ultimate approval by the faculty resulted from a core of leaders who championed the advantages of mobile computing for their students and their colleagues.

Final approval by the Board of Trustees came in April 1995, after detailed information and carefully constructed financial plans were examined at two meetings. During the 1995–96 academic year, the plan was tested and refined in a pilot program.

The Freshman Experience

Central to the plan is the restructuring of the freshman experience. The first year of college is crucial to socialization and formation of intellectual habits. Most academic and social problems at Wake Forest occur in the first year. Away from home for the first time, many first-year students must cope with personal adjustments, new social pressures, and the use of unsupervised and unstructured time.

The first-year seminars, which enroll no more than 15 students each, are drawn from various departments and subjects. But all of them share the common goal of enhancing skills in writing, critical thinking, and oral presentation. The expectation is that the seminars establish faculty-student and student-student relationships around a common learning experience. The seminars also provide a forum for technology training and enhancement.

Some of the seminars are conducted in residence halls where first-year students share living quarters with seminar colleagues. Coffee hours and other co-curricular programs are also part of dormitory life. The aim is to promote peer learning through formal and informal interaction among students, to achieve educationally purposeful connections between what goes on in the classroom and what goes on in the residence halls, and to assist students in forming friendships and exploring positive social experiences early in their college careers.

The addition of 40 faculty positions swims against contemporary currents in higher education. We are lowering the faculty-student ratio which many institutions are working to raise. New faculty and more classes will enable almost all students to graduate in four years. Above all, more faculty will enable Wake Forest to enhance, through smaller class size, the quality of its student-teacher relationships.

TECHNOLOGY

The technology component generated the liveliest debate on campus, and has attracted wide interest. In planning for technology, the advice of Pope's couplet is wise: "Be not the first by whom the new is tried / Nor yet the last to lay the old aside." Pioneers pay a high price in technological innovation. Wait too long, and you may be laid aside.

Wake Forest concluded that it was timely, even necessary, to make computers uniform and universal. We had been making the infrastructure investments over the last dozen years. Information technologies are not about the future; they are defining the present. Vast academic resources are available on-line, and these resources are growing exponentially. Computing competency has become an essential placement skill for college graduates today, whatever the profession or vocation.

We are enrolling a generation of students who expect to use this technology. As part of a five-year longitudinal study on the impact of computers on the culture of the university, Wake Forest's Department of Communication surveyed in August 1995 the hundred first-year students who used

ThinkPads as part of the pilot program conducted in the 1995–96 academic year. Although the survey was conducted before they actually experienced using their computers as part of their courses, the results were revealing. Among the findings: 80% indicated they welcomed increasing use of computer technology; 83% said they believe the technology should make learning easier; 65% felt that the computers were not being introduced into the classroom too early; only 19% feared that the computers would make the teaching process too impersonal; and only 30% felt that the computer would be an added burden.

During the planning we considered whether owning a computer ought to be optional, and whether flexibility in platform and hardware ought to be available. Our answer to both matters was negative. If ownership were made optional—that is, not made available to each student—the inequality we now have between the computer have's and have-not's would remain. Moreover, without universal adoption and standardization, this technology could not be assumed as a basis for the teaching program. Nor could we afford the cost of supporting various hardware and software options.

After negotiation with several vendors, we entered into a long-term agreement with IBM. Beginning in the fall of 1996, every first-year student at Wake Forest received an IBM 365XD, a powerful notebook computer which can travel with them from residence halls—all of which have direct network access—to classrooms, laboratories, the library, and out into the field. The computer includes 16 mb RAM, an 810 mb hard drive, a 100 mHz Pentium processor, Ethernet/fax/modem connections, 4X CD-ROM, and an external floppy drive.

Software includes Windows 95, Microsoft Office Suite (Word, Excel, Power Point), Lotus Notes, and Netscape. All computers have a custom-designed Notes-based course and project filing system. Technically, the computers are leased to our students when they enter as freshmen. At the start of their junior year, the students get a new machine to replace that one. When they graduate, they take the newer machine with them.

The technology is no better than the support provided. Faculty members receive a computer with the standard load upon completion of training. Twenty academic computer specialists were hired and assigned by departments to assist students and faculty in their disciplines. Student computer technicians who receive scholarship aid will work in each residence hall, and a corps of student technology support personnel will assist the faculty in the use of the computer for teaching. (The latter arrangement will, of course, itself foster the kind of faculty-student collaboration that undergirds this entire initiative.) A help desk is open, and there are on-line and phone help lines and training.

The computers will become an integral part of each student's academic experience. After the university completes networking the campus this summer, students can plug into the network in virtually every building to communicate with each other, their teachers, and information sources worldwide. Every residence hall has direct connections—two in shared rooms—to the network. Network connections also will be available for instructional purposes in more than half the classrooms.

Special laboratories have been equipped in the departments of music, English, physics, chemistry, romance languages, the Calloway School of Business and Accountancy, and elsewhere. Wherever they are, students, faculty, and staff have remote access to the network. Whether on a vacation or a trip, our students will be able to access the files being used in courses and submit work. By the time a Wake Forest student graduates, he or she will be competent in those technologies which are shaping every profession and vocation as well as public life.

The provost and the dean of the college, together with an elected faculty committee on technology, developed a 25-point strategy to assist faculty training in the uses of instructional technology. Funds are available for training and course development.

Many courses will emphasize electronic access to library materials and distant experts as well as in-classroom collaboration. Some courses will be paperless. The potential applications of computers in the curriculum are practically limitless. ThinkPads will come with Lotus Notes, a powerful groupware which provides ready database and information retrieval and links students with each other and with off-campus experts in interactive forums.

An art instructor can construct a customized textbook of images on a server which students can access from anywhere at any time. A physics class can use a program that performs the time-consuming mathematical calculations, freeing more time for theoretical instruction. An English professor can provide an on-line newsgroup, assign a different student to post a summary of a chapter or a poem before each class session. Other students can post responses and other commentary, engendering lively on-line discussions that invariably will carry over into the classroom.

Benefits

As with any complex effort, this plan carries risk. Wake Foresters have been willing to take these risks because of the major benefits we believe it carries:

- Wake Forest's academic advantage rests with providing education that is both personal and individual. Prior to the computer, this kind of academic experience required that vast quantities of faculty and student time be spent on seeking information. Now, faculty time can be more directed to the analysis and discussion of information, a higher order intellectual activity.
- The computer has become a basic tool of scholarship in every discipline. The ability of professors and students to delve more deeply and to analyze larger and more complex data sets means that most research now requires these technologies. Our capacity to attract the best and brightest faculty over the next decade depends on our capacity to provide for them the tools their professions will require.
- Students are intellectual nomads, spending parts of each year in a residence hall, in their homes, traveling abroad, visiting friends. Wherever they are, they now have access to the instruments of scholarship. The instruments they learn to use are theirs upon graduation.

We were concerned about maintaining an environment in which some students could afford computers while others could not. Computer laboratories could not remedy this inequity. We must offer the best education with the best tools to all our students.

Conclusion

Our conviction is that information technology does not replace the traditional classroom transaction, but enriches it. A community depends upon communication. This technology has the potential to relieve faculty of the traditional need for skill development, review, and rote learning. Technology is thus designed to preserve and promote Wake Forest's time-honored adherence to the principle that the personal engagement of students by professors yields the promise of wisdom.

[I would like to express my thanks to David Fyten, University Editor, for his help in preparing this chapter.]

PART 3

LOOKING TO THE FUTURE

11

The Library of the Future

Suzanne E. Thorin and Virginia D. Sorkin

Traditional Libraries

Libraries are indispensable adjuncts to education, a base for generating innovative thinking, a stimulus to culture, and an aid to individual self-development. They are collections of history, culture, and insight, offering access to information and knowledge representing diverse sources and viewpoints. Libraries acquire, organize, preserve, and make available materials in all media. Today, most library materials are stored in site-specific facilities and are available to those who can come to the facility.

Reviewing the 20th century, one can see the importance of the growth of the public library in our cities that occurred through the support of Andrew Carnegie's philanthropy. Similarly, the number of universities, and thus the availability of higher education for the average person, grew in part because of the Morrill Act of 1862. Justin Morrill, U.S. Senator from Vermont, sponsored legislation that created a system of land grant universities: The heart of these universities is the university library. During this same period an explosion of journal publications occurred, reflecting and facilitating the creation of academic specialties.

United States institutions of higher education are rich in resources, such as research libraries. Today, the academic research library works hand-in-hand with faculty and students to supplement course materials and to provide the necessary foundation materials for new investigations and basic research.

Does the evolving digital library supplement or replace this well-established set of relationships? This chapter argues that the evolution of digital libraries will not supplant but rather extend the reach of libraries.

Paralleling the expansion of the boundaries of the research library is the role of the university librarian. The role of librarian as knowledge navigator, a term coined by the Librarian of Congress, James H. Billington, is already expanding to include the on-line resources of institutions worldwide. Librarianship in the new digital age requires computer literacy as well as a knowledge of subject matter and the profession of librarianship.

LIBRARIES AND EDUCATION

Libraries' Traditional Roles in Education

Libraries serve three critical roles in education. The first role is the practical one of sharing expensive physical resources such as books, motion pictures, and CD-ROMs through both interlibrary loan and digitization. The second role is that of cultural guardian as collector, organizer, and preserver of the artifacts and ideas of culture. The role of community or interdisciplinary center, where people and ideas from all disciplines are brought together, is the third (Marchionini & Maurer, 1995).

Libraries' Economic Imperative to Adapt to Digital Resources

The role of the library in education continues to evolve. While libraries have always adapted to social and technological evolution, libraries today are actively embracing and hastening the shift to the digital world. The reasons for this are both economic and practical.

While the number of publications is increasing, from 1981 to 1991, the typical research library lost an average of 27% of its buying power in real dollars. The cost of some serials during this time, particularly those in the sciences, increased more than 20% per year. According to Brian Hawkins (1994), "If one assumes that information is doubling every four years, then by the year 2001, the combined impact of inflation and the growth of information would result in our libraries only being able to purchase 2% of the total information acquired only two decades before."

The demand by scholars, students, and lifelong learners for current information—on-demand—pressures libraries. The growth of knowledge creates additional pressure. It is not only the growth of knowledge that presses libraries to adopt the digital world. It is also the practical problem of how to avoid the loss of our civilization's accumulated knowledge base. There are slow fires burning within the walls of libraries as the acid within the paper destroys some books containing the intellectual history of our civilization (Hawkins, 1994). Preservation of the artifact is an expensive ideal, but preservation of the content is a practical necessity. Digital preservation is one pragmatic and potentially cost effective solution.

Visions of Digital Libraries

There are many definitions of a digital library. Terms such as *electronic library* and *virtual library* are often used synonymously with the term *digital library*. Common elements in the definition of a digital library, as identified by the Association of Research Libraries, include the following:

- The digital library is not a single entity.
- The digital library requires networking technology to connect many entities.
- All linkages are transparent to end users.
- Universal access to digital content and information is a goal.
- Digital library collections are not limited to document surrogates but can include digital artifacts not extant in traditional formats (ARL Fact Sheet, Boston Conference, May 1995).

The federal government views digital libraries as a way to provide its citizens with access to information (IITF Report, 1994). This is also the traditional role assigned to public and depository libraries in the United States. The Depository Library Program (DPL), administered by the U.S. Government Printing Office, is a national resource network designed to ensure free public access to all government-produced and government-published information. Depository libraries are located in each state and congressional district to assure wide distribution of government information. This commitment to public access of government information can be traced back to 1857, when Congress resolved that printed documents could be made available to the public through official sources. Having access to government information digitally will enable a larger number of citizens to have a part in informed governance and to enrich their lives.

A taxonomy of physical library elements as applied to a digital library is supplied by Nurnberg et al. (1995). The taxonomy consists of data, metadata, and processes. The authors' conclusion is that physical libraries provide a starting point for defining digital libraries. There are, however, digital library elements with no physical library analog. These include

- New digital data types (e.g., hypernovels, scientific visualizations)
- New metadata (e.g., dynamically generated indexes, personalized structures)
- New processes (e.g., retrieval by agents, personalized presentations, knowledge navigator support for novice users)

The library of the future will no longer be just a physical place where information is kept. It will also be a logical entity made up of many physical entities that provide content, expert support, and a passageway through which students, faculty, and lifelong learners access the information resources of the world.

Problems to Surmount

Some major problems with which the digital world must contend are the creation of substantive content, the costs of conversion, the resolution of intellectual property rights, as well as the fear publishers have of competition by digital libraries and the loss of revenues due to the ease of copying of digitally published materials.

Content

There are two major sources of data for digital libraries: content acquired in digital format and content converted from existing holdings.

The first type is controlled by publishers. Today, more than 99% of all printed works exist in digital form at some point during their life cycle from creation to publication. Of the 856,000 items the U.S. Copyright Office received for registration and offered for addition to the Library of Congress' collections in 1995, however, only 11,000 were received in machine-readable format (i.e., CD-ROM, diskette). Not only do publishers fear releasing digital items that support their revenue streams to the federal government, but less than 10% of print items created digitally are in non-proprietary formats.

While traditional-format publishers are beginning to venture into electronic publishing, new authors and publishers spawned by the Internet are adapting with ease to electronic publishing as they bypass editors and publishers. The academic presses are also moving toward adopting this new and potentially cheaper mode of publishing.

Commercial publishers are testing the Internet as a delivery mechanism, but cautiously. Since anyone with access to the Internet can become both author and publisher by putting up an original article, musical composition, or image, the status quo of the traditional publishing cycle is threatened. Proofreading, editing, and typesetting are not necessary to create and make available a simple World Wide Web (WWW) page. Similarly, the rules of fair use that have been vital for U.S. libraries in supporting research and creativity are still being debated for materials published electronically.

Digitization of existing content is vital to create a content core for the new digital institution. This effort is under way not only by the Library of Congress' American Memory project but by projects around the world. For example, the Library of Congress offers Lincoln's draft of the Gettysburg Address and the rough draft of the Declaration of Independence in Thomas Jefferson's own hand. The Royal Danish Library is preparing to digitize the original manuscripts of Hans Christian Andersen.

Cost

A major consideration of the digital library is the cost conversion effort to create a core of digital content. On the average, it costs six dollars to digitize one page of a book. This does not include the cost to create the necessary description for indexing and retrieval, or the cost of handling an item during the conversion process. And this six dollar cost does not apply to the digitization of sound recordings or motion pictures, major creative outputs of our culture during the 20th century.

Intellectual Property Rights

Copyright issues in the electronic environment are identified but not resolved. Publishers are unsure how to protect their authors, their users, and themselves in this new medium. Issues of access rights, fee collection mechanisms, fair use, security, and authentication are only a few of the questions to resolve before commercial entities might consider adopting the network for publishing.

Competition

Traditionally, libraries represent the interest of end-users, whether the academic community of students and faculty, the employees of an organization, or the general public. Commercial publishers represent the interests of their shareholders as well as the needs of their customers, both authors and users of their publications (Kahin, 1994). If a library acts as broker between user and author, has the function of the digital library replaced the function of the publisher? The traditional relationship between publisher and libraries is changing. The new economic relationship has yet to be modeled to the satisfaction of all stakeholders.

THE LIBRARY OF CONGRESS AND THE DIGITAL WORLD TODAY

The Library of Congress (LC), the *de facto* U.S. national library, is experiencing massive changes in its organizational structure, in how it does business, and in the rapidly changing mode and type of information it disseminates because of the evolving digital world. It is facing the need to reorganize the processing of materials to prepare for the time when digital objects rival—in number and content—the traditional formats it now processes. In addition, the World Wide Web now delivers some materials electronically to those patrons who prefer to connect to the Library of Congress' systems electronically rather than come to Capitol Hill. For more than a decade, the Library of Congress has relied on its Library of Congress Information System, LOCIS, to search the automated card catalog. Today, the Library is actively using WWW forms-based searching predicated on the Z39.50 protocol for the books and serials catalogs.

In January 1995, at the request of the 104th Congress, the Library of Congress implemented a new on-line legislative system named THOMAS after Thomas Jefferson, the so-called father of the Library of Congress. Prior to THOMAS, the *Congressional Record,* containing all of the discussion and record of the legislative process, was most easily available through printed form delivered every morning following a congressional session to its subscribers. Today, this on-line index of legislative activity is updated daily and is available for anyone in the world to search freely. This presents a major change in the quality and timeliness of legislative information available to U.S. citizenry. Currently anyone with electronic access can search the 103rd or 104th editions on-line and have associated materials, such as the full text of legislation under consideration, displayed by the system immediately.

The U.S. Copyright Office at the Library of Congress receives over 600,000 registrations each year. To process this flow of materials the Copyright Office is actively working with the Advanced Research Projects Agency (ARPA) and the Corporation for National Research Initiatives (CNRI) to support and guide the development of a Copyright Office Registration, Recordation, and Deposit System (CORDS). CORDS will enable the processing of electronic copyright registration, deposit, and recordation of materials transmitted in digital form over communications networks. The project will also evaluate how the process of electronically assisted copyright works, including the establishment of policies and procedures to create secure digital repositories for copyrighted materials. On February 27, 1996, the project officially received its first electronic registration and submission.

American Memory

The Library of Congress' major obligation for nearly 200 years has been to preserve the history of the nation—items that document and celebrate the creativity, ingenuity, and vibrancy that is America. By combining the richness of the Library of Congress historical collections with the power of the new interactive electronic systems, American Memory is making core Americana materials accessible in schools, libraries, and homes across the country. LC's goal is to digitize millions of original items by the year 2000.

The Library has already become one of the largest providers of serious content on the Internet, recording more than a million electronic transactions every working day. The demand keeps growing. With the click of a mouse, students, teachers, and lifelong learners already have access to elements of our history:

- Mathew Brady's Civil War photographs
- The notebooks of Walt Whitman
- Some of the earliest American documentary films (San Francisco before and after the earthquake and fire of 1906 and of President McKinley at the Pan-American Exposition of 1901)
- One-of-a-kind sound recordings of American leaders during World War I and the presidential election of 1920
- Rare African-American pamphlets from Reconstruction to World War I
- Broadsides from the Continental Congress and Constitutional Convention, ca. 1774-1790, and much more

The Twentieth-Century Evolution to Digital Research Libraries

Michael Gorman recently noted in the book *Future Libraries: Dreams, Madness and Reality* (Crawford & Gorman, 1995) that "there seems never to have been a time in which libraries were not under one gun or another." Today, the fear is that networking will make museums of libraries. Whether this is a real fear or not, both the technology and the inevitability of change are real, and plans must be made for what lies ahead. Today's transition is greater than any other faced by libraries in this century, and it is most uncomfortable for many. Libraries' services have become more complex due to the extent of information being offered on-line at the same time that budgets continue to shrink or, at best, stay level.

The Library of Congress' public clients once were categorized as three groups of users: 1) people who were above high school age and who could come to Washington (after using local and regional resources), 2) catalogers in libraries across the country who depended on LC's bibliographic data, and 3) public library borrowers who never knew or cared that LC supplied the Dewey numbers with which they found their books. The research university's clients have traditionally been the faculty and students in their institutions.

Today, libraries must serve a much broader clientele. Accurate bibliographic data are only the beginning of what clients want. They expect full text and photographs—even sound and moving images. If a library does not own these materials, clients want access to them electronically or through interlibrary loan—immediately.

Within the university community, not only can students now access information in their dormitories and all over the campus, but some universities and library schools (e.g., the University of Michigan) are consciously expanding their clientele to include the residents of their state and beyond. In fact, each Web site is often a window on resources of multiple institutions.

The lines of responsibility in education no longer form a neat organization chart of grade schools, junior and senior high schools, colleges, and graduate schools served by teachers, librarians, and professors dedicated to a particular group. With access to electronic information, public and research libraries as well as library schools are now active participants at all levels of learning. And all levels of learning are expanding—from youth to elder hostel.

Yet the prospect of financial support for these new endeavors in our libraries is bleak. The hard truth is that libraries are cost centers, not profit centers. Libraries are taking various approaches to being seen as offering, at best, intangible benefits, and, at worst, no return on investment. At one extreme, Columbia University closed its library school, in part, as a result of low contributions from its alumni when compared with the graduates of its law and medical schools. Others are trying to increase income. For example, the San Francisco Public Library is recouping some costs by charging fees for selected services. The George Washington University Libraries run a successful fee-for-service operation available to anyone inside or outside the university with the wherewithal to pay. To increase capital for innovation, the Library of Congress is building its digital program through public-private partnerships and making all electronic content freely available.

The study *University Libraries and Scholarly Communication*, sponsored by the Mellon Foundation (Cummings et al., 1992), makes it clear that academic research libraries are not receiving the funding they need to support their clients. The first finding in the report is that "libraries have not taken a larger percentage of the university budget; their percentage has shrunk." Ann Okerson, associate university librarian at Yale University, states that "contrary to the conventional wisdom, library budgets have tended to increase less rapidly than other university expenditures. The library's percentage of total expenditures has tended to decline" (Cummings et al., 1992). Other findings reflect the reality of daily life: Because of the continuing inflation in the cost of serials and the fact that book and serial budgets have not grown, fewer materials have been purchased at a time when domestic and international publishing produced greater and greater numbers of new titles each year. While budgets have diminished and prices have skyrocketed, the Mellon study finds that the scholarly community has continued to tie scholarly publishing to academic prestige and reward. This practice has contributed to the so-called information explosion.

To summarize the issue: Academic library budgets have not been able to purchase as many of the proliferating journals as necessary because of the rising cost of the journals and the libraries' own shrinking budgets. At the same time, the prevailing reward system for scholars continues to focus on publication being a "defining criterion for rank and status." Although problems are still with us, there are signs of change.

First, technology has made rapid strides. An example is Elsevier Science's announcement that the journal *New Astronomy* would go on-line. "In a video simulation accompanying one paper on binary pulsars," says Elsevier editor Michiel Kolman, "You will see how two stars rotate around each other: they evolve. One star sucks up matter from the other, explodes in a supernova explosion, and so on. It is a very beautiful way to illustrate a theoretical model" (*Science*, 1996). This description captures the imagination. What a wonderful way for students to learn and for scholars to share their research.

Second, because of these technological advances, the old model of publication is changing. The number of serials on the Web (which itself did not exist in 1992) is proliferating. Gary Taubes, who wrote the article in *Science*, notes that at the end of 1995, over a hundred peer-reviewed science, technical, and medical journals were available on the Internet. Some exist only in electronic form, others are electronic with a paper edition for archival purposes, still others are electronic versions of paper journals, some of which do not yet offer the full text found in the paper version. And, Taubes states, "By the end of 1996, the number of electronic peer-reviewed journals may increase by another order of magnitude."

Yet librarians are still responsible for what some have called the "library as place." They continue to buy and catalog books and serials, and to invest deeply in the special collections: rare books, manuscripts, music, sound recordings, prints, photographs, motion pictures, and maps. Scholars in the arts and humanities read those books and serials, and they use—and will continue to use for the foreseeable future—primary source materials in their investigations. The idea that a digital image can substitute fully for the original document is no more acceptable to scholars than is using a microfilm copy instead of the original.

Moreover, scholars respect being able to work in a library and to explore ideas they find there. William G. Bowen, former president of Princeton, captures this idea movingly in his foreword to the Mellon Foundation Study on university libraries and scholarly communication:

> Why do great libraries have such a hold on so many of us? In part, I think, because of their ambience, the sense they give of the power of ideas and the luxury of being stimulated and encouraged to think for one's self. Libraries are humbling places, because they remind us of the vast store of knowledge which we can approach but never really control. They are humanizing places, because we are brought into contact with so many lives lived in the past as well as in the present. They are symbols of the continuity of learning. They stand for such basic principles as freedom of expression, the need to recognize and respect a diversity of view, and the obligation finally to come to one's own conclusions—and then to be held accountable for what one has written.
>
> No one believes that new technologies will, should, need to, or can supplant the pleasure of holding a book and turning its pages. Still, full advantage of the power of high-speed processing and communication must be taken advantage of without losing sight of the larger purposes of the enterprise. It is true that the library is under significant pressure not only to change but also to accelerate its rate of change. It is no less true that the processes of change must respect all the functions and attributes of the library if it is [to] remain a vital center of learning in the broadest sense.

If, as Northrop Frye stated, our only crystal ball is a rear view mirror, those words must be taken seriously and used to chart the future.

There are no easy solutions to the situation libraries and librarians face today—a situation with broadening responsibilities constrained by ever more limited resources. This potentially grim situation is also one full of opportunity and exploration: The most exciting and challenging time for libraries, surprisingly enough, has come at the end of this century just as it did at the end of the nineteenth century. Change in how library work is to be conceptualized and accomplished must occur both at the individual and at the collective levels.

The key principles and assumptions encouraging change that Jim Neal and Pat Steele cite in their article "Empowerment, Organization and Structure: The Experience of the University Libraries" (*Journal of Library Administration*, 1993) give guidance. Their recommendations indicate that librarians are most comfortable with structure, predictability, hierarchy, and their own definition of space and responsibilities. Many of the profession's accomplishments have come about because of attention to details and accuracy.

Librarians are now being asked to make radical changes in the way they work. They are being asked to

- Eliminate hierarchy
- Work in teams
- Consider and meet clients' needs
- Learn to communicate with information technologists
- Implement business practices such as long-range and yearly planning and be accountable for implementing those plans
- Change long instilled work practices and organizational structures
- Keep their eyes on "the big picture"

If one believes in the centrality of the library to the learning process and to the support of scholarship, then, uncomfortable as change is, it is imperative that librarians and scholars work together to ensure that libraries endure and prosper.

THE TWENTY-FIRST CENTURY LIBRARY

It is clear that no one believes that the 21st century library will arrive one day over the Internet and that on the next day we will close the doors of all library buildings or redefine them as museums. The users, the sites, the functions, and the staff will all look very much as they do today with some differences beginning to be discernible.

Users

Research libraries' communities and boundaries will expand. Faculty and students will remain the most important group research libraries serve, but other audiences will also emerge to take advantage of these rich resources. The great research and national libraries of today will be the great collaborators of the 21st century, sharing resources to develop new collections only possible in the electronic world.

University and college libraries will reach out more to the communities in which they reside. The public library and the research library in college towns will be much more closely linked, sharing information with their users seamlessly. The depository library network will assure access to government information for all citizens without having to visit the library site. Users unwilling or unable to physically enter a library building will have access from home or some other convenient location. Both the mission and outreach of all libraries will broaden to audiences currently excluded.

Collections

None of the traditional formats will disappear, with the possible exception of the not very traditional CD-ROM, which may well be replaced. Books, serials, motion pictures, and recorded sound will continue to be published and stored on library shelves and archived for posterity.

The access capabilities of the library will begin to rival collections in importance, however, as more content becomes electronically available. Breadth and depth of electronic content in various areas, such as history, mathematics, and the sciences, will be common in the 21st century.

Site

Site specificity will slowly decline in importance. Lending libraries are unlikely to disappear soon, but it is not unrealistic to expect textbook publishers and the academic presses to adopt and adapt to electronic publishing quickly once the issues of copyright and royalty payment are resolved.

Functions

The functions of libraries will remain. They will continue to select, collect, describe, store, and manage information. Large areas will be electronic and may or may not be on-site but will be accessible. Navigation and assessment of electronic information will be the most important new function users will expect libraries to perform.

Staff

Librarians will retain their traditional function as organizers of knowledge, but the great reference librarians of today will be joined by computer experts with particular expertise in electronically accessible bodies of materials.

MIGRATION TO THE TWENTY-FIRST CENTURY

In building the digital research libraries of the 21st century, we should consider the following.

Reconfirm the Mission of Libraries

Assess how closely what is being done now supports the mission of the institution. Mission discussions bring out differences of opinion and can lead everyone to new clarity. After agreement is reached on the mission, identify priorities within the mission: Who are the people to be served, and what are the services to be provided? Budget allocation should match the priorities. No one has sufficient resources, but many are adding services while book and personnel budgets continue to fall.

A Library's First Duty is to Serve Its Clients

It is a myth that the electronic age will make libraries obsolete and that books are outdated. This is borne out by the difference between the expectations of humanities and social sciences scholars, artists and performers, and scholars and researchers in the sciences. Before a decision to move from a paper to an electronic resource is made, the researchers who will use the resource should be consulted.

Librarians must talk with students and professors regularly about how well libraries are serving them. Librarians must know the literature and trends in research, must reach out to the internal clients always and the external clients when possible, and must aim for 100% satisfaction.

Use Technology to Help Meet the Library's Mission

Reading library literature is important, but librarians need to read the popular literature on the emerging digital world too. Librarians need to read what scholars are saying about how they use and expect to use technology in the future and what information technologists suggest about future possibilities. All of this should be applied to the mission of the library. Librarians should use the technology first so that they know what is hype and what is real.

Examine Old Assumptions

Understand what "the other side" thinks and how they speak. Many technologists cannot understand the language of librarians, and some librarians have no interest in learning and speaking the language of technology. Librarians must be willing to clarify their business practices prior to automating them. Similarly, technologists must recognize that many librarians today are also capable technologists. The gap between information technologists and librarians has narrowed, but it must close completely, since the need to understand each other will only increase.

Librarianship has traditionally segmented certain specialties. Distinctions between reference work and cataloging are blurring today because of the increasing ability to search and retrieve full texts and other materials online. Emphasizing the similarities in library specialties will lead to cross-specialty learning, which in turn will help strengthen library services overall.

Break Old Patterns

Through digitization, different formats can be displayed together or in close sequence: maps, recorded sound, text, motion pictures, and photographs. Exercises such as visualizing how the layering and combining of information are changing research and learning and hence are changing librarianship must expand the profession's thinking.

There are so many possibilities for scholars to enrich and broaden their research through the access to and use of digital images. The ability to study a particular manuscript, then to call up the pertinent maps and photographs on the topic is a powerful one. For example, it is much easier today to understand how the Thirty Years War affected the musical careers of Heinrich Schuetz and his contemporaries. Thanks to digital libraries, it is possible to study German music history in context through the study of images of war scanned from paintings as one reads accounts of the war or compares scanned maps of the period. Music students have traditionally been concerned first (and sometimes only) with music. Such isolation, as rich as it is, can be broadened easily today through the availability and use of digitized documents.

It is time to mine parochial library resources to enrich the digital collections being created. It is critical that current information be linked to historical and cross-cultural resources to promote understanding.

Do Not Close the Buildings Yet!

The old model will not go away. People will continue to cherish the feel of a book in their hands, the ambience of doing research in a library, and the sense of community that using a library produces. Library buildings and collections are unlikely to disappear.

Enjoy

Last, and not least, librarians need to stop occasionally and look at the privilege of being a part of this landmark change in the way the world communicates. Some days the venerable glass truly is half empty. But, for the most part, days in libraries are full of empowerment—librarians can make sure that the coming changes are for the better. K. Wayne Smith, OCLC's chief executive officer, said it just right: "Whether your view of the Information Superhighway is optimistic, pessimistic, or simply mystic, I submit that libraries are already in the fast lane of that road to the future. It will indeed be a new era for academic libraries, but it will be an era that is built on thousands of years of library tradition, and on an enduring purpose."

References

Association of Research Libraries. (1995, May). *ARL Fact Sheet.* Presented at ARL Conference, Boston, MA.

Billington, J. H. (1994, Winter). The electronic library. Columbia University: The Freedom Forum Media Studies Center. *Media Studies Journal*, 109-112.

Buschmann, J. (1994, May). Librarians, self-censorship, and information technologies. *College & Research Libraries,* 221-228.

Crawford, W., & Gorman, M. (1995). *Future libraries: Dreams, madness & reality.* Chicago, IL: American Library Association.

Cummings, A. M., Witte, M. L., Bowen, W. G., Lazarus, L. O., & Ekman, R. (1992). *University libraries and scholarly communication.* Published by The Association of Research Libraries for The Andrew W. Mellon Foundation.

D'Elia, G. In collaboration with The University of Minnesota Center for Survey Research and The Gallup Organization. (1993). *The roles of the public library in society—The results of a national survey: Final report.* Prepared for the U.S. Department of Education, Office of Educational Research and Improvement, Library Programs.

Davis, E. (1992, February-March). Cyberlibraries. *Lingua Franca.*

Hawkins, B. L. (1994). Creating the library of the future: Incrementalism won't get us there! Co-published simultaneously in *The serials librarian.* The Haworth Press, Inc. *24*, 3/4, 17-47, and *New scholarship new serials: Proceedings of the North American Serials Interest Group, Inc.* G.

McMillan & M. L. Norstedt. (Eds.). New York, NY: The Haworth Press.

Information Infrastructure Task Force (IITF). (1993). *The national information infrastructure: Agenda for action.* Washington, DC: Department of Commerce.

Information Infrastructure Task Force (IITF). (1994). *Report of the information infrastructure task force committee on applications and technology.* Washington, DC: Department of Commerce.

Journal of Library Administration. (1993). Empowerment, organization, and structure: The experience of the Indiana University libraries, *19*, 3/4, 81-96.

Kahin, B. (1994, April). *Institutional and policy issues in the development of the digital library.* International Conference on Scholarship and Technology in the Humanities, Elvetham Hall, England.

Lynch, C. A. (1993, April 5). *The roles of libraries in access to networked information: Cautionary tales from the era of broadcasting.* A paper based on a presentation given at the Data Processing Conference in Champaign-Urbana.

Marchionini, G., & Maurer, H. (1995, April). The roles of digital libraries in teaching and learning. *Communications of the ACM*, 67-75.

Mitchell, M., & Saunders, L. M. (1991). The virtual library: An agenda for the 1990s. *Computers in Libraries, 11*(4), 8-11.

Neal, J., & Steele, P. (1993). Empowerment, organization, and structure: The experience of the university libraries. *Journal of Library Administration.*

Nurnberg, P. J., Furuta, R., Leggett, J. J., Marshall, C. C., & Shipman, III, F. M. (1995). *Digital libraries: Issues and architectures.* Center for the study of Digital Libraries, Texas A&M University, (http://www.tamu.edu).

Taubes, G. (1996, February). Electronic journals: The coming explosion. *Science.*

12

A Learning Enterprise for the CyberCentury: The Western Governors University©

Michael O. Leavitt

In the spring of 1897, word came to the pioneer town of Cedar City, Utah, that the legislature would establish a branch of the state university in the southern part of the state. After a lively competition by the towns in the area, Cedar City was awarded the school, on the condition it would deed over land and construct a building by the next fall. The citizens believed an existing structure could temporarily house the school until the permanent building was completed. Classes started in September, but in late December the State Attorney General denied the payment of teachers' salaries because the permanent building had not been constructed. He further declared that unless it was completed by the following fall, the school would go to a different community.

Here was a genuine crisis. Cedar City was a town of 1,500 people without even a bank. Teachers were paid with wheat and oats, or meat, eggs, and cheese. Undertaking such a challenge in the middle of the winter with no money and no materials was overwhelming. These people were largely uneducated themselves. They had come from the coal mines of Wales and the iron mines of England. But they were people of strong basic values who hungered for education and could foresee the importance it would have for their children. This school mattered to the community more than almost anything else. Against all odds, citizens united to construct the building. They made bricks in freezing weather. Families provided food, bedding, and warm clothing to the men who hauled timber down from the mountains.

Today in Cedar City stands an inspiring sculpture of Old Sorrel, the only horse powerful enough to break through the barriers, the deep snowdrifts that blocked the logging trails into the mountains. By the fall of 1898, the school was built that later became Southern Utah University. Those pioneers were prepared to enter the 20th century with a school that became the heart of their community. In the nearly 100 years since then, countless lives have been blessed from the university's establishment, my own included.

Today, a century later, the opportunity to create a new university for a new generation has arrived. This university, however, is quite different from the traditional university. It will not be made of bricks and mortar. It will not be bound by time or place. Classes will be delivered using advanced technology. It will be competency-based, with student success not measured by "seat time." Like a century ago, the task may seem overwhelming, with significant barriers to overcome. But if we maintain our hunger for education, its creation can be accomplished. We must show teamwork and leadership and demonstrate a pioneering spirit the way those settlers did 100 years ago. If we stay on course, we will enter a new century and a new millennium with a new learning system that will also benefit countless lives.

The western governors advocate a new enhancement to learning and formally announced their support for a Western Governors University (WGU) on June 24, 1996. Since then, a great deal of discussion has occurred, and many questions have arisen about what it is, about what it isn't, and about the background, vision, goals, and organization of this new learning enterprise.

How is the Digital Age Impacting Higher Education and Creating a Need for New Approaches?

For many centuries, control over formal education has been accomplished by two means. First, access was controlled because students, depending on the era, had to come to the temple, library, or university to obtain education. Second, individuals and institutions that teach were required to be credentialed or accredited in some fashion. Control of access and control of faculty/institutions was justified to ensure quality of instruction so that a degree or certification earned by a student would be marketable, something of value. This process has served admirably for many years and will continue in effect for many more. But today, as we enter the Digital Age, a new century, and a new millennium, we must expand our vision of the education enterprise and be willing to consider new methods to ensure the quality outcomes we desire.

In the years ahead, it will be impossible to control access to and delivery of educational services as completely as we have in the past. Students no longer need to travel to the university to obtain knowledge and information. It flows freely to wherever they are. And the sources of information and knowledge are becoming so numerous and ubiquitous that it will be impossible to credential or accredit all of them. A new model of higher education, which will complement and support the traditional model, is embodied in the Western Governors University. This development is important not just for the sake of higher education.

The world is rapidly changing due to the sweeping transformations of the Digital Age. Learning and knowledge are the foundation of the new information-oriented economy. Much of our country's and states' economic success or failure will be the direct result of how well we address the lifelong learning needs of the 21st century. The Western Governors University can play two important roles: First, it can increase access to lifelong learning and job training services for students of all ages, no matter where they are. Second, it can help open distribution channels to a burgeoning world-wide market for education services to both public and private educational institutions. We simply must align our public policies with what is occurring in the marketplace.

Eventually, the inexorable forces of advanced technology will drive many of the changes contemplated in the Western Governors University. But we can make the transition faster, and in a more organized fashion—and with less disruption to and more collaboration with traditional institutions—if all segments of society concerned with education cooperate in this development.

How Did This Project Get Started?

I had been encouraging distance learning in public and higher education in my own state of Utah for a number of years, as it had become clear that course development costs are extremely high, and that a great deal of duplication was occurring among institutions both within Utah and in other states. Then I had an interesting experience that led me to begin looking at this issue on a broader scale. I was visiting Northern Arizona University in Flagstaff in 1995 and met with NAU President Clara Lovett. She showed me the innovative and successful distance education initiatives underway in Arizona. I described our similar efforts in Utah. Then I suggested, perhaps naively at the time, that it might make sense to connect our two systems, so that Arizona students could take advantage of the courses and degrees Utah institutions are offering, and Utah citizens could likewise enjoy the array of offerings from Arizona. Dr. Lovett smiled and said that while she would love to connect our two systems, there were four reasons it couldn't occur. "And what are those reasons?" I asked. She was quick to reply: "Bureaucracy, tradition, regulation, and turf." I noticed that she did not list technology.

In the next few weeks I thought a great deal about President Lovett's list of barriers, and how they could be overcome. I thought about Old Sorrel breaking through the snowdrifts in the mountains above Cedar City so a new school could be built. When the Western Governors' Association convened in Park City, Utah, in June of 1995, I raised the issue of distance learning and a wide-ranging discussion ensued about this exciting new approach to education. I asked whether there was interest in collaborating and linking our systems together. Around the table, heads nodded and 11 or 12 hands went up. I suggested to my fellow governors that they, more than anyone else, were best positioned to break through the barriers that we would confront.

They agreed, and the Western Governors' Association staff was assigned to develop a preliminary plan for the enterprise. A design team that included higher education experts was impaneled, and work began. The governors met again six months later in December 1995, and spent a day and a half discussing the prospects and possibilities of the new institution. They approved the design team's preliminary work and unanimously agreed to go ahead. The design team then began work on specifics of organization and implementation. In June of 1996, the western governors met again in Omaha, Nebraska and unanimously approved the Implementation Plan. At the time of this writing, 13 governors have signed a memorandum of understanding committing them to fund the project and personally serve on the Steering Committee.

What Makes This Project Different From the Distance Education Initiatives Underway in Many Institutions?

It is much bigger both in size and in scope. We are attempting to coordinate efforts among numerous institutions in several states. In addition, we are introducing a new element not found in other initiatives. At the June, 1995, Western Governors' meeting, Gov. Roy Romer of Colorado suggested taking this project to a level far beyond simply teaching courses across state lines. He proposed that the new institution emphasize student competency and assessment of learning, moving away from the old measures of "seat time" and credit hours. Thus, our focus is on whether learning has occurred, not on who provided the learning, the credentials of the provider, or how long a student sat in class. This shift takes the Western Governors University into the realm of the revolutionary, into a challenging new paradigm for post-secondary education.

This shift is crucially important, and it takes into account the world-changing forces of the Information Age. In the Industrial Age, people had to go to campus to get information. In the Information Age, information and knowledge will flow wherever the people are. The monopoly, which existed for some 2,000 years, is broken. In the 21st century Digital Age, as learning becomes a lifelong pursuit, there will be so many different sources and opportunities to gain knowledge and learning that in some cases the seat-time, credit-hour measurement system will be obsolete. In an era when information and training services are delivered through so many different methods—interactive video, e-mail, satellite, the Internet's World Wide Web, CD-ROM, 500 television channels, and so forth—it will be impossible to ensure the quality of each individual, school, or business that delivers courses, or the courses themselves. Thus, the focus must be changed from who provided the course, and how many hours it was taught, to assessment of whether true learning occurred. Instead of trying to hold back the onslaught of education and training opportunities, we must develop sophisticated assessment methods to measure and certify learning and competency. This would allow us to recognize learning achieved through life experiences and on-the-job training. Should not an entrepreneur who has run a successful business for ten years have an opportunity to qualify for a business degree along with the 22-year-old who has sat in classes for four years? We should care whether competency has been gained, not how or from whom the competency was gained.

Do You Have a Practical Example Demonstrating the Need for This Shift?

During a visit to San Juan High School in the southern, rural part of Utah, I met a teacher whose experience demonstrates why we need to change our focus. The high school has large populations of Native American children, many of whom live in poverty. The school is making innovative use of advanced technology. A teacher there began working several years ago to deploy computers and networks at the school. He doesn't have a degree in computer science or engineering, but he took training seminars, studied a lot, and was basically self-taught. He was able to obtain grants to buy computers and network equipment, and he saved money by installing the networks himself. He then trained other teachers to use it. He and his students installed a local area network. They pulled the fiber optic cable through the school and installed the equipment. San Juan is in a remote area and getting repair service was a problem. So he trained and certified 12 of his students as factory-authorized repair personnel, using video courses from hardware and software companies. These 12 students passed the repair specialist's certification test. They left high school with exceptional skills and also provided their school with superior service. The teacher, with his specialized knowledge, began teaching computer classes for a local community college on an adjunct basis. He then decided to obtain a master's degree in computer science and applied to a major university in the state. They told him he had not taken the proper prerequisite computer courses to be accepted in the program. He described his experience and informal training. But rules were rules. Ironically, if he had received credit for the classes he taught others, he would have been qualified. But the traditional university system would not acknowledge those classes because he taught them, he didn't take them. This new institution will measure and assess knowledge and proficiencies and then recognize them no matter what their source. Students deserve to have their knowledge recognized. They will go elsewhere for recognition if higher education does not develop good assessment methods, then recognize learning and competency.

How is the Private Sector Involved in This Initiative?

In several ways. Telecommunications companies and vendors of educational services are involved in the creation of the Western Governors University, along with public colleges and universities. Private colleges and universities are invited to fully participate by offering courses through this institution and to serve as local centers for students. Private businesses that offer high-tech courses and job training services are also invited to participate. Some large corporations that engage in significant employee training have caught the vision of how this institution can be of great benefit to them and their employees. How this might work in a real-life situation is described by Ray Waddoups, an executive with Motorola and a member of the Regional Advisory Committee. Mr. Waddoups notes that Motorola is presently training more than 140,000 workers annually in the discipline of microelectronics/computer chip manufacturing. While the skills they are learning are highly useful and marketable in today's business environment, the workers are not receiving any formal certification or credit toward a degree or vocational credential. They are getting good training, but have nothing to show for it in the form of certification or credential. By working as a partner with this new institution, Motorola and other microelectronics companies like Micron and Intel can work with universities and other entities to develop courses for their employees, complete with assessment methodologies. The employees could then not only gain valuable skills through the courses, but also obtain a formal credential or certification and credit toward a degree if they wish to pursue one. Those who already have the required skills could demonstrate competency and obtain the credential or credit without having to take a course. Such an arrangement would be very attractive to Motorola and many other companies that provide job training, Waddoups said.

Do the Western Governors View Themselves as Higher Education Experts? Why are Governors Doing This?

No. Governors do not view themselves as higher education experts, but we do hold the keys to being able to break through the barriers of regulation, bureaucracy, tradition, and turf of which Dr. Lovett spoke. Our role is to serve as a catalyst, to bring the combined power of several state governments behind a new concept. It will take enormous political clout and some pretty good battles in the arena of public policy to break through the barriers. This could not be accomplished by one governor alone, but several governors joining forces can provide the leadership to get the job done. Also, change and reform don't come easily from within major institutions of society, especially one with as much tradition and convention as higher education. Pressure and impetus for change must often come from the outside. Governors are uniquely positioned to serve as catalysts for change.

Will the WGU Eventually Replace Traditional Higher Education Institutions?

No. This initiative is not meant to replace traditional institutions. It merely adds a new element. I fondly recall the autumn day not long ago when my wife and I dropped our oldest son off at his college dorm and helped him unpack, make his bed (probably the only time it was ever made) and stash his suitcases under the bedframe. I drove away with a lump in my throat, but excited for him, knowing the many growing experiences and challenges he would face. This is not about eliminating those campus experiences, those rites of passage. Sitting at home in front of a computer would not have met my son's needs at that time in his life. Teachers will not be replaced by technology nor will the traditional classroom be replaced. Many students will continue to enjoy the traditional four-year experience with sports, activities, and clubs. On the other hand, there are numerous nontraditional students and those who need retraining, many with jobs and families, whose needs are not met through the traditional campus experience.

What is the Value of the Traditional Institutions That Will be Participating?

A few in higher education view this project as a threat, but most see immense opportunities. A stated purpose of the Western Governors University is to open new, worldwide markets to public and private educational institutions. The corporate job-training market alone is valued at more than $200 billion annually. With technology changing so rapidly, the need for employee training and retraining grows commensurately. The worldwide market for educational and job training services is about to explode. We sometimes view distance education too narrowly, as merely a way to save money. We should expand our vision and look for opportunities to make money. But what institutions will provide this training? The reality is that traditional higher education institutions are presently not well-positioned to take advantage of these opportunities. A November 1995 study by the Social & Economic Sciences Research Center at Washington State University concluded that while "lifelong learning has become a reality for most Americans," most traditional colleges and universities "have shown little interest in meeting this demand."

The study also concluded that "teaching conducted only in the traditional campus classroom will not meet the public's demand for tailored educational services." The study says "colleges and universities must change how they do business to meet the demand for life-long learning." But to this point they have structured themselves to serve one main customer: the undergraduate student who seeks a first-time college education, usually full-time and on-campus, where courses are scheduled between 8 a.m. and 5 p.m. Monday through Friday. These constraints make it difficult to serve the burgeoning market for lifelong education and job training. "If colleges and universities do not recognize lifelong education as part of their mandate and assign it higher priority, the private sector will certainly fill the vacuum," the study says.

While it might be difficult for an individual institution to restructure and tap into these new opportunities, it will be easier if the institution works through the Western Governors University. Corporate education and individual lifelong learning needs will be coordinated through the Western Governors University, and education providers will have access to these emerging and existing markets. The institution can provide new distribution channels for learning services, courses, and educational products. In addition to opening a new world-wide market for the institutions involved, participating institutions will also be staying ahead, or at least keeping up, with these powerful new forces and trends in society. I believe that time will prove that those institutions which do not add this distance learning component in their offerings will be at a competitive disadvantage. Being involved with the Western Governors University will be a very efficient way of learning how to survive and thrive in this new world.

What is the Value to Students?

This institution will provide many new choices, a means to take numerous elements and opportunities and organize them into something greater than the sum of the parts. It will provide many students with a more convenient way of accessing educational opportunities. It will also enhance quality. Every student should have at least a portion of his or her education delivered through technology, because this is the way the world will work in the future. I participated in a three-way video conference on this subject with the Chancellor of the Open University in the United Kingdom and a Minister of Education in Mexico. I thought to myself, the day will come soon when Utah students will study international relations with students in Mexico and students in England at the same time. That's a powerful enhancement of basic quality. Another benefit will be cost. The average cost of an education at a state university today is over $9,000 per year. There is much concern that the cost of higher education may soon be beyond the grasp of many of our citizens. We believe that in time this institution will provide broad access to people who may not otherwise receive it.

How Important are Lifelong Learning, Job Training, and Retraining Needs?

A new workplace, with a new kind of worker, has appeared in the Information Age. Lifelong learners are the students of the 21st century. They are unique in comparison to their predecessors in several ways. First, the average

Information Age worker will retrain often. Three of four workers who lost their jobs in 1994 required additional skills to obtain new employment. An institution that requires a student to attend classes between 8 a.m. and 5 p.m. will have difficulty satisfying that need. Many of these workers have families and jobs; they need educational opportunities that cater to their schedules and are accessible at any time from any place. Second, the average worker will change jobs ten times in his or her lifetime. They will need training quickly to adapt to new employment. Finally, the worker in the Information Age needs technology skills that are constantly updated. High-tech skills swiftly become obsolete. Business demands that workers use technology to solve problems. Moreover, high-tech skills should logically be delivered via interaction with technology. Through the WGU, students will have access to lifelong learning opportunities to acquire the necessary skills for employment in the 21st century.

Is Anyone Involved in the Design and Implementation of This Institution Who has Higher Education Expertise?

Governors immediately went to the Western Interstate Commission on Higher Education, the National Center for Higher Education Management Systems, and to our land grant institutions and various university and college presidents. All of them have been involved in the development of the implementation plan. The professional expertise behind the planning and implementation of this institution is first-rate and highly accomplished.

What Will be the Nature of the Entity Itself?

It will be a non-profit, independent corporation, not operated by the Western Governors' Association. It will be established as its own entity with a board of trustees. The Implementation Plan lists criteria that will guide the institution. It will be

- Market-oriented, paying particular attention to developing education markets and needs
- Independent, not controlled by those who represent established institutions
- Client-centered, focusing of the needs of students and employers
- Degree-granting and accredited, empowered to grant degrees that are recognized by employers and academia

- Competency-based, certifying learning and competency, not seat-time
- Non-teaching, having no faculty of its own, drawing from other institutions and other sources
- High quality and cost-effective, enriching education with expanded opportunities, while holding costs in check
- Regional, sharing resources and taking advantage of economies of scale
- Quickly-initiated to meet current demand and continue the momentum

Will Western Governors University Actually Teach Classes?

No, all classes will be taught by institutions of higher education, public and private, in addition to nontraditional providers of education services.

Who Will Accredit the Institution and Ensure Quality?

Quality is the highest priority of this endeavor, and work is ongoing with accreditation agencies to develop a process of accreditation. We're pioneering, and the accreditation agencies we're finding are as anxious to determine how to do this as we are. They see this as the wave of the future and something they have to adapt to, so we're working together to assure quality and to develop the accreditation process.

Will the Western Governors University Compete for Funds with Other Public Institutions? Are You Going to be Diluting an Already Thin Resource?

We expect there will be very little direct appropriation going from state governments into this institution. Whatever public funds are invested will be more than offset by benefits to public institutions created by the opening of new, world-wide markets for educational services through the Western Governors University.

How Will it be Financed?

This institution is an entirely new concept and will require a unique economic equation and business plan. The capital and revenue sources could include investment capital, a base of appropriated funds, donated capital, for-profit vendor involvement, and fees and tuition. It seems very clear however, that it will primarily draw its operating revenues from fees and tuition that will mostly go back to the providing institutions with some small portion for the administration of the institution itself.

How Will the Institution be Organized?

The design team recommends that it have a small central office, with numerous local and regional centers that will provide services for students. The functions of the central office will include financial management, maintenance of academic records, quality control, arranging assessments, auditing the local and regional centers, overseeing student services, and establishing requirements for degrees and certificates. The local and regional centers will provide pre-admission services, interim and final assessments, counseling and advising, information services, help with local programming and needs assessment, and access to the technology-delivered courses.

An exciting element of this learning enterprise will be the World Wide Web site or virtual catalog that is being developed as the university's nerve center. The catalog or "WGU Advisor" as some call it, is being developed by IBM Corporation with guidance from the design team and Sally Johnstone of the Western Cooperative for Educational Telecommunications. While it will list courses offered through the Western Governors University and will provide students with a wide range of information, it is much more than a catalog. It will link learners and providers of advanced technology-based courses, programs, and learning modules. It will provide information on the assessment of specific competencies leading to certification in a variety of fields. It will also provide initial advisement services, such as assessment of learners' readiness for specific learning experiences. While flesh-and-blood student advisors and counselors will still be required, the catalog will make their jobs easier, helping them take a prospective student through the entire process, from class selection to financial aid to delivery methods, to assessment of competencies and the granting of certification or degrees. The catalog is fully interactive, allowing a student to customize an entire post-secondary program that best suits individual needs. The catalog will also be heavily used by educational service providers and by industry and business representatives to enroll their employees in job training programs. The catalog will exist on-line only; there will not be a printed version. It will be available 24 hours a day from any location with Internet access.

How Will Courses be Delivered? Is This Just Watching Television?

This is a very important point. This institution is not being designed simply on the basis of the technologies that exist today. We're designing this institution to take advantage of the technologies that we know will exist tomorrow. Delivery methods will include interactive two-way video, satellite, television, e-mail, CD-ROM, the Internet's World Wide Web, and traditional classrooms. In the future, as bandwidth increases, it's very clear that new and better technologies will broaden WGU's delivery options.

How Many Courses Will be There?

We don't know precisely, but hundreds of courses that meet the requirements have already been offered by various institutions. There will be hundreds, perhaps thousands, that will be listed in the virtual catalog.

Will the Western Governors University Offer Degrees?

Yes, the university will assemble courses that may be offered through a variety of different institutions into academically coherent groups that will constitute certifications and degrees. Students will also apply courses taken through the Western Governors University to programs and degrees offered at traditional institutions.

Will a Degree From the Western Governors University Have Real Value?

It will be a fully accredited degree. That's a standard that we want to maintain to ensure quality. Ultimately, it will not be accreditation agencies that will determine the success of this endeavor; it will be the marketplace. Is this institution good enough to attract students? And will industry and business recognize degrees and hire graduates? We firmly believe the answer to both questions will be affirmative.

What are the Largest Obstacles?

We don't know yet. This is pioneering; we don't know what's over the next hill. But clearly, our greatest obstacle will not be the technology. Our greatest obstacles will be the sociology and working through the "people" element—the regulation, bureaucracy, tradition, and turf. I had a conversation with a member of a faculty who said, "This virtual university idea scares the heck out of me." My response was, "I've got an easy solution—don't do it. If this is not something you find intriguing, you don't need to get involved. This is all voluntary. But if you're prepared to innovate, if you want to step forward and pioneer, if you want to be part of the next wave of educational innovation, venture forward with us." That is our message to those who are concerned and fearful. After all, this is not a replacement for the existing system, it's a new and very exciting element.

Do the Western Governors' Actions to Date Mean This Institution is Absolutely Going to Happen?

No, it means we're engaged in the next phase of analysis. To use a business venture analogy, we have spent some money doing research and development and concluded that this concept is worthy of our further investigation and investment. We now must raise some additional capital, and develop it further. If we aren't able to raise the capital, that would be a pretty good indication it might not fly. But I think there's a very strong feeling that we will raise the capital and that we will be able to turn the vision into reality.

Conclusion

It is heartening to see many individuals in higher education begin to understand what is represented by the Western Governors University. Consider these excerpts from comments published by Robert M. Threlkeld, dean of learning and technology at California State University, Fresno, on the Internet's Distance Education On-line Symposium:

> We can choose to ignore developments like the Western Governors University. It's not in California—*yet.* We can fight boundary-spanning satellite instruction, and try to establish signal-jamming Maginot Line policies which prevent other institutions from getting a foothold nearby—*for a while.* We can ignore the chorus of malcontents who trash higher education and who propose technological box-top solutions to complex problems—*a bit longer.* If we follow that strategy, public higher education will begin to be seen like a rock in a river. Events will flow around us, wearing us down in the process. Campuses will become smaller, poorer, and more marginal to the social mainstream.
>
> A more optimistic future is to embrace, not reject, the use of new technologies. Use technology to create new learning environments both on and off the campus, environments which let students

and faculty learn together. Free professors from being confined to the role of the "sage on the stage," the tedious requirement to be experts in a world of information that is growing too quickly to totally comprehend. Support faculty to work on the development of technology-based education programs which will increase learning effectiveness. Create structures so that professors have more time to interact with students. Build the educational enterprise around student outcomes and rigorously evaluate achievement.

Dean Threlkeld has nicely caught what I believe is the spirit of the Western Governors University. I heard an interesting comment about change made by Ray Noorda, a pioneering entrepreneur in our state and founder of Novell, the networking software company. He said this about change: "You can fight it and die; you can accept it and survive; or you can lead it and prosper." I believe we must lead change if we are to prosper in the Digital Age. Let us enter the new century with a new learning enterprise, much as those pioneers did 100 years ago in my home town of Cedar City. Let us be as courageous as they were in breaking through the barriers of regulation, bureaucracy, tradition, and turf. This can be the legacy of our generation. Others have stepped up in the past with big ideas to create great institutions for society. Now it is our turn.

References

College Board Report. (1991). *Education and the workforce.*

Dillman, D. A., Christenson, J. A., Salant, P., & Warner, P. D. (1995). *What the public wants from higher education: Workforce implications from a 1995 national survey.* Technical Report 95-52. Social and Economic Sciences Research Center, Washington State University.

Victor, K. (1994). *National Journal, 16* (1), 6-10.

[Several important documents regarding the structure and design of the Western Governors University are available on the World Wide Web at http://www.westgov.org/smart/vu/vu.html.]

13

Life on the Wired Campus: How Information Technology Will Shape Institutional Futures

William F. Massy

Colleges and universities pride themselves on their sense of sustaining mission and the stability of their modes of operation. Many within the academy see themselves as holdouts against such "business fads" as restructuring and reengineering—not to mention the substitution of capital for labor that has driven two centuries of business productivity improvement. What banks, retailers, manufacturers, hospitals, and governments have undertaken cannot be taken for granted within the academy. This aphorism, coined by Clark Kerr and the Carnegie Commission, brings home the depth of higher education's sense of constancy:

> Taking, as a starting point, 1530, when the Lutheran Church was founded, some 66 institutions that existed then still exist today in the Western World in recognizable form: the Catholic Church, the Lutheran Church, the parliaments of Iceland and the Isle of Man, and 62 universities. . . . They have experienced wars, revolutions, depressions, and industrial transformations, and have come out less changed than almost any other segment of their societies. (*Policy Perspectives,* 1994)

Higher education's constancy is truly venerable, but does it stem from innate characteristics of the institution or from the constancy of its underlying technology? A look at history from the modern perspective suggests the latter. Since the Gutenberg Bible was printed in 1456 using movable type, the technology of information storage, retrieval, and transmission—the university's basic technology—has remained essentially constant until the current era. Indeed, the use of written records to supplement oral teaching goes back to the fifth century B.C. Since their inception, universities and colleges have relied upon lectures, discussions, and the written word because these were the only technologies available.

Information technology has opened new and fundamentally different options for teaching and learning. History demonstrates that fundamental technological change ultimately begets significant structural change, regardless of whether the affected participants choose to join or resist the movement. The changes that universities have weathered over the centuries did not upend their basic technology. Information technology does.

Information Technology vs. Teaching-as-Handicraft

This volume's other authors have described how information technology can be used to improve teaching and learning. It seems to me that the benefits can be captured in this brief statement: Information technology permits teachers and students to project themselves across space and time, to locales and circumstances that best meet learner needs, with substantially less degradation than was possible with predecessor technologies.

To put the statement in perspective, consider the classic "gold standard" for education: Mark Hopkins and his student on a log. By delivering education via one-on-one dialog, it is said, the Williams College president could tailor content to his student's needs, interests, and capacities. He could draw the student into an active learning posture, then assess his performance and make corrections in real time. But even the gold standard scenario is not without limitations. It is expensive in terms of student-faculty ratios, and it requires a high degree of synchronization: Mark and the student must balance themselves on the same log at the same time.

Mark Hopkins, the student, and the log provide a quintessential example of a handicraft process. Every output is produced to order using "one-off" methods conducted mainly at a single venue. The process does not involve much capital, aside from the human capital embodied in the participants. The process is regarded as mysterious—even the participants themselves cannot describe it in detail, let alone replicate it through engineering.

The only way to produce the next generation of Mark Hopkinses is through apprenticeship.

Colleges and universities have tried various stratagems for mitigating the difficulties associated with their handicraft methods: offering set-piece lectures to large groups, assigning reading and homework, providing laboratories and internships, and breaking down space barriers via television. But each approach engenders its own difficulties: passive rather than active learning; less access to faculty expertise and insight; and limits imposed by the printed page, the teaching laboratory, and the television screen. Information technology doesn't eliminate all the difficulties. But it does reduce them to the point where colleges and universities can break away from their handicraft traditions for a substantial portion—though probably not all—of their teaching and learning activities.

The process of breaking away won't be quick or easy, but colleges and universities do not stand as unique in this regard. Consider the replacement of steam engines with electric motors in industrial applications, for example. The factory of the early nineteenth century was a multi-storied affair, expensive to build and inefficient in organizational structure and materials handling. One had to live with these constraints because economies of scale dictated a single steam engine which, given the bearing technology of the time, had to be linked to the work stations by vertical rather than horizontal driveshafts. The first electric motors simply replaced central steam engines, leaving other constraints in place. In time, however, it became possible to distribute the motors to individual workstations. This, in turn, led people to restructure the manufacturing enterprise, to flatten the factory and thus eliminate the inefficiencies of the multi-story mills. Colleges and universities have only recently been distributing computing and connectivity to individual workstations on a massive scale. The task of flattening the campus, of restructuring to take full advantage of the new technology, remains before us.

The Post-Handicraft Era

Asking what colleges and universities will be like in the post-handicraft era raises the specter of fear as well as the stirrings of opportunity. Frequently-asked questions include: Will educational quality be improved or undermined? Can and should technology be used to improve institutional productivity—and what is productivity anyway? Those who work in higher education institutions also ask, "How will information technology affect faculty roles and responsibilities? How will it affect professorial numbers and the size of administrative and support units? Will schools pay for technology by reducing labor cost? Will the quality of work life be better or worse?" These are the kinds of questions I will address in this chapter. I will deal mainly with four-year residential institutions, though the benefits of technology will by no means be limited to such schools. One can argue that the benefits of technology are more unequivocal and can be obtained more easily in the nontraditional settings than in the traditional ones—so if anything the questions are more germane in the four-year residential institutions.

Let me begin by going out on a limb and offering some quick answers—answers which I will try to justify later. I believe that the wired four-year residential institution will look about the same as it does today when viewed from outside, but that the view from within will be quite different. That is, the wired institution will still be a campus—populated by faculty, staff, and students—not just a connecting point for dispersed information nodes. However, because equipment, infrastructure, and outsourced course materials will cost more than at present, faculty compensation will represent a smaller fraction of the expenditure base. Support staff in the academic areas will probably grow as a percent of total inputs, though whether the overall percentage of cost represented by non-faculty labor grows or shrinks will depend on the degree of extra efficiency obtainable in central administrative and support areas.

Faculty are quick to ask whether information technology will add to or reduce their numbers. They worry about technological obsolescence: "That's a great lecture you just put on tape, now we don't need to pay you to give it anymore." Or, perhaps more likely, "We can buy Nobel Prize-winner X on laser disk, so we don't need you." However, it seems clear that technology can't replace the human factor in education. It can leverage faculty labor, but it can't replace it. The faculty role will change from being mainly a content expert ("the professor's job is to profess") to a combination of content expert, learning process design expert, and process implementation manager. Faculty also will be motivators and mentors, interpreters (especially of non-codified knowledge), and, as a colleague recently put it, "expert learners"—people who lead the learning process by breaking the trail and setting the right personal example. Technology can leverage faculty time, but it cannot replace most human contact without significant quality losses.

It seems clear that technology will shift higher education's expenditure mix and change faculty roles and responsibilities. But will technology actually reduce cost? The conventional wisdom inside the academy says "no," but a good many outsiders (especially those responsible for providing funds) are increasingly prone to say "yes."

The answer depends less on technology than on society's willingness to pay for educational quality. Bowen's Law states that "Universities (and colleges) will raise all the money they can and spend all the money they raise" (Bowen, 1980). Institutions that can pay for technology *and* sustain faculty-student ratios will surely do so. They will reap the quality-improvement rewards associated with having their cake and eating it too—of becoming *both* capital and labor intensive. Institutions where enrollment increases outstrip funding will sustain faculty numbers while serving more students at lower unit costs and, they hope, with undiminished or perhaps even enhanced quality. Institutions with static enrollments and fiscal constraint will have to reduce faculty numbers to make room in their budgets for technology and support staff. They won't like it, but competition will force them to do so. So the answer to the cost reduction question is, "It depends." Technology will improve productivity as measured by the quality of learning per unit expenditure, but whether the dividend is taken out as more quality at the same cost or lower cost for the same quality will depend on political and market choices.

THREE STAGES OF TRANSFORMATION

One cannot appreciate information technology's capacity for inducing change without parsing its effects on the teaching and learning process. Technology can be brought into the educational process in three ways.

1. ***As productivity aids for individuals.*** Such productivity aids allow teachers and learners to do the kinds of things they now do—plus things yet to be invented—faster and more effectively. Examples include word processing, spreadsheets, graphing programs, and e-mail. These tools should always be available and used as a matter of course, like telephones and pocket calculators.

2. ***As enrichment add-ins.*** Enrichment add-ins inject new materials into the teaching and learning mix without changing the basic mode of instruction. Examples include information acquisition on the Web, and the use of video, multimedia, and simulation to enhance classroom presentations and homework assignments.

3. ***As stimulants and enablers of education process reengineering.*** Reengineering starts by mapping the current process and evaluating it in terms of quality and cost goals. Then the reengineering team designs a new process which optimizes the available technology to better serve the client. The result is a mix of the old and new, each contributing what it can do best.

Education process reengineering means challenging tried and true pedagogical methods, many of which have been in place for decades or even centuries. (Recall how the electric motor eventually flattened the factory.) Examples include the lecture and laboratory, the course as the basic unit of instruction, the academic calendar, and in some cases the role of campus-based instruction itself. Higher education is ripe for reengineering because extant processes have been frozen for a long time, because student needs are changing, and because technology has opened important new possibilities.

Most information technology applications in higher education have been of the first two kinds. Enrichment add-ins improve educational quality, but they do not save either time or money. Productivity aids release faculty and student time for other tasks. Faculty time savings usually are reinvested in research—that is, they fuel the academic ratchet (Massy & Wilger, 1992). Student time savings enhance learning or leisure, but they rarely reduce the time and tuition required for the degree. Hence the individual productivity aids do not save money; indeed, they usually add to the institution's cost base. No wonder, then, that so many pundits question whether information technology can ever save money.

A Reengineering Vision

Imagine how information technology might be used to leverage learning if the bars of convention were dropped. The following vision provides a reference point for the discussion that follows. It builds on Massy and Zemsky (1995), which in turn was inspired by the studio model described by Jack Wilson in Chapter 7 of this volume. Our hypothetical example can go further than Wilson's real case because we are not constrained by the academic calendar or by the availability of facilities and equipment. We have not quite abandoned the course as the unit of instruction—even though, in the fullness of time, all such constraints will have to be rethought.

Consider the teaching of microeconomics: first according to traditional methods and then after reengineering to optimize the use of human and technological resources. The traditional method usually involves a combination of lecture and discussion sessions on a fixed schedule, supplemented with reading and homework assignments. The reengineered method might employ a combination of lectures, interactive studio sessions using simulations and multimedia packages, and small group discussions with faculty about meaning and relevance—discussions rich in personal interaction and mentoring as well as knowledge transmission—all on a flexible schedule geared to student needs.

Figure 13.1 shows how the reengineered method might appear to students as they learn microeconomic theory and its practical applications, and to faculty as they carry out their teaching duties. We do not claim this scenario to be the best that can be achieved, or even that it would work exactly as described. But it does illustrate the kinds of qualitative benefits—for students and for faculty—that can be achieved through reengineering.

FIGURE 13.1

A Reengineered Course

"What is microeconomics and what is it good for?" These natural questions are addressed in a series of three or four lectures at the beginning of the learning process. The department recruits its most charismatic lecturer for this assignment, and the professor gives her all in preparing and delivering the material. Because these lectures are designed to provide one-way communication, each is given only once—to the full group of students taking the course. Convening in a large group provides a sense of excitement, which the professor reinforces by using state-of-the-art multimedia to illustrate and punctuate important points—the students will remember these sessions many years later when much of the detail that comes later will have faded. The lectures also have become major events for the professor. They do not occur so frequently as to become routine; in fact, being chosen for this assignment becomes an important element of recognition by one's colleagues.

Next the student embarks on a series of interactive studio and individual exercises using simulation and multimedia applications (supplemented with the familiar textbook) to develop competence in the course's first content module. Take the economic model of supply and demand, for example. Active learning using simulations, data analysis, and multimedia yields a far better grasp of the content and power of this well-codified theory than could be gained in the conventional setting by passively viewing curves drawn by a professor at the blackboard. Moreover, the courseware's interactive character produces real-time diagnostics about student progress and difficulties as a byproduct of the learning process itself—diagnostics that can be used to design mitigations or control entry to the next learning stage. From the department's standpoint, the fact that much of the intellectual content is built into the materials enables more independent student work and more flexibility in staffing. For example, much of the work needed to bring students to proficiency with the courseware is handled by graduate students or support staff without any loss of effectiveness—or perhaps greater effectiveness than would be delivered by busy faculty.

Once students have mastered the codified knowledge specified for a course module—say after one or two weeks of individual and studio effort—they move into small group discussions with faculty about the non-codified dimensions. "What does the theory say at its deepest level? Why did it develop this way? What objections have been raised and are there competing world-views? How can these concepts help in one's career and life generally?" Because students move into the small group sessions only after they have demonstrated a requisite degree of understanding, the time with the professor is not dominated by elemental questions. Professors will find their students better prepared and more able to engage. The conversations are more fresh and interesting than the typical lecture-discussion format, and they may actually require less faculty preparation than a formal lecture. But regardless of preparation time, these sessions take better advantage of the faculty's unique skills than restating codified wisdom in class after class.

Students advance to the subsequent course module when they have completed the cycle for a given module. This may be gated on an individual basis, as when a student begins the next phase of technology-based independent work, or control may be through completion of the discussion sessions described in the previous paragraph. Either way, student progress will not be bound to a fixed syllabus determined by the average student's ability and motivation. Students needing more time will get it—and still pass the course providing they attain the requisite learning threshold in a reasonable period of time. Better students can move ahead quickly, thus enabling them to gain more education or, at their discretion, reduce the time and cost of attaining the degree.

The scenario also illustrates the other important benefit from reengineering: It relaxes traditional constraints on the economics of the educational process. For example, faculty labor is applied at the times and in the circumstances needed rather than in fixed quanta defined inflexibly as courses per semester (teaching loads). Technology substitutes for some of what has traditionally been viewed as faculty work, but faculty labor is redeployed to tasks that professors can do best. Support staff and graduate student time may be used to a greater extent than in some kinds of institutions currently, but it is concentrated in areas where faculty do not have a comparative advantage—not in places, like small group discussion sections, where a professor's wisdom can confer important benefits.

The basic economic message is that reengineering breaks the widely-perceived linkage between expenditure per student (or the student-faculty ratio) and educational quality. Massy and Zemsky (1995) offer a hypothetical example where total cost after reengineering, including the cost of technology, is equal to cost before reengineering even though educational quality has been improved. Scenarios exist where cost declines are possible (Jack Wilson provides a concrete example in Chapter 7), though even greater benefits can usually be obtained by increasing expenditures.

IMPLICATIONS FOR PRODUCTIVITY

The main impetus for embracing information technology will be to improve the quality of learning. The aforementioned reengineering vision called out some of the ways in which quality can be improved, and more complete accounts are provided by the other contributors to this volume. We shall now turn to a more detailed explanation of technology's implications for college and university productivity. The chapter concludes with a discussion of the quality of the faculty's work life in the post-handicraft era.

At root, the shift from traditional handicraft methods to more capital-intensive ones involves the embodiment of significant educational value in courseware. This requires up-front investments, but it frees faculty from having to recreate these value elements for each new student cohort. The ability to capitalize educational value elements produces three kinds of benefits: economies of scale and scope, more significant institutional learning curves, and better cost trajectories. I noted earlier that such benefits don't drive the unit cost of education—cost per student is determined by what society is willing to pay, not by the technology employed by educators. However, we shall see that technology can provide tangible economic benefits that will be harvested one way or another as improved educational value for money.

Economics of Scale and Scope

Handicraft production processes are not very scalable. That is, production of the nth unit costs nearly as much as production of the first unit. In higher education, the cost of planning and organizing a course usually is small relative to the cost associated with contact hours, office hours, and student evaluation. Variable cost dominates. Even when students can be added to a section with empty seats (in which case the marginal contact cost is zero), the requirements for out-of-class teaching and evaluation grow proportionately. While individual faculty can achieve preparation economies by teaching multiple sections of the same course, teaching-load norms and intellectual fatigue limit the benefits.

Because institutions view unsponsored research as bundled with education, expenditures on faculty tend to increase in proportion to average cost during periods of enrollment expansion (Zemsky & Massy, 1995). Institutions try to maintain their student-faculty ratios when enrollments grow, even though they argue that faculty represent fixed costs when enrollments shrink. Maintaining the student-faculty ratio also protects teaching loads and class sizes. If the student-faculty ratio is forced upward, the result is, first, larger classes and then as a last resort, increased teaching loads (Massy & Wilger, 1995).

Information technology can shift higher education away from the handicraft tradition if it is used to trigger reengineering. In the reengineering example given earlier, more than the traditional amount of faculty time would be allocated to plan the course, to select and perfect the technology, to train those who will assist in its delivery, and to prepare the introductory lectures. These costs are mostly independent of the number of students. There also are fixed costs during the delivery phase, since the time needed to coordinate the course elements does not vary proportionately with enrollment. Because direct faculty-student contact is focused mainly on the small group sessions and associated out of class contact, the overall variable cost per enrollment is lower than with traditional methods. Much of the fact transmission and evaluation burden is carried by the technology and by non-faculty assistants who are paid less than faculty.

If the total cost for a given enrollment level is the same for the traditional and reengineered processes but fixed cost is greater, it follows that the variable cost will be lower using information technology. This means that the reengineered process will enjoy better economies of scale. Additional students can be enrolled with less-than-proportionate cost increases and undiminished quality. The iron linkage between faculty size and student numbers will have been broken. There can be no question that these changes will profoundly affect competition among higher education institutions.

Technology-driven reengineering also can provide economies of scope. Because faculty put more time into course planning and less into the routine aspects of pedagogical delivery, they should be able to adapt educational content and methods to new student groups and new settings more easily than is common with conventional teaching and learning methods. Self-pacing plus closer and more interactive contact with students in the small group sessions should help as well. These scope economies may not result in cost savings, but they may be expected to improve educational quality for nontraditional and disadvantaged students. By freeing faculty from the routine drudgery of teaching, one allows them to direct more of their time and energy to adapting educational strategy to learner needs.

Exploitation of the Learning Curve

Not the least of the advantages conferred by improved focus is the opportunity to build cumulatively and institutionally on experience in pedagogy: in other words, to exploit the learning curve. By learning curve I mean the well-documented tendency for quality to improve and unit cost to decline with the cumulative number of units produced by a given organization. Traditional teaching methods limit such improvements for at least two reasons:

- Because most faculty spend relatively little time thinking about teaching methods (Massy & Wilger, 1995), they tend to repeat the traditional approaches again and again. Individuals get better with experience (for example, they become better lecturers or discussion leaders), but the scope of improvement is bounded by the traditions of working alone and limiting the amount of time thinking about how to do better.
- Because faculty do not work together on teaching to any great extent (Massy, Wilger, & Colbeck, 1994), the experience gained by individuals rarely gets propagated across the department—let alone across the school or institution. Often technology-based enrichment add-ins, on which one professor may have labored mightily, get dropped or diluted when a new professor takes over the course.

Reengineered teaching and learning methods should mitigate some of these difficulties. More conscious effort in the course planning stage offers an opportunity to assess the work of others and see how it might be applied to current tasks. But perhaps even more important, the up-front commitment to use technology-based tools requires the course team to make choices: continue to use the existing tools or adopt new ones; develop materials in-house or use materials developed elsewhere.

Moreover, because subject-matter content and pedagogical strategy must be built into the courseware, and because the courseware will be updated from time to time, the materials available through outsourcing will themselves benefit from cumulative experience. The levels of investment required to build and market successful courseware will induce developers to do research to find out what works and then incorporate the results into their products. (The market will penalize those that fail to do so effectively.) New tools will become available regularly, and they will embody the experience of teachers and learners wherever situated. In other words, the tool developers—whether within or outside the institution—will be exploiting the experience curve. The experience of business school faculty in using materials from the Harvard Case Clearing House demonstrates the power of distributed continuous improvement. Because new materials are shared widely, quality-enhancing innovations flow naturally into courses as a consequence of local faculty choice.

Departments' ability to exploit the learning curve also can be enhanced by consciously adopting continuous quality improvement (CQI) principles along with technology as part of reengineering. These principles include focusing on customer needs, developing feedback systems to track performance and diagnose difficulties, and committing to proactive and continuous improvement efforts. By focusing greater attention on course planning and management, faculty ease the adoption of CQI. In fact, there is a natural synergy between CQI and exploiting the learning curve with technology.

Cost Trajectories

The widespread adoption of information technology almost guarantees an increase in the capital-labor ratio for instruction. Even if faculty size remains constant, increased expenditures on hardware, software, and communications will boost the ratio. In other words, spending on technology means that a smaller fraction of total expenditure will go for salaries and fringe benefits. This will reduce cost-rise pressures even if current expenditures are not reduced.

The "cost disease" argument (Baumol et al., 1989) illustrates why the high labor ratios associated with handicraft production produce regular real cost increases. Consider the classical string quartet playing to a live audience. A thirty-minute piece requires two labor hours, the same is it did centuries ago. Improving productivity by playing faster or dropping the second violin (which some might consider redundant) would diminish quality—which is what many believe happens when college class sizes balloon. Yet the musicians' real wages will escalate due to productivity growth elsewhere in the economy. If musicians did not share in the fruits of such growth (to which they arguably have contributed by improving the quality of life), the supply of new entrants to the field could not be sustained. So the classical string quartet, like traditional education, is what Baumol and his colleagues call a stagnant industry: doomed to become ever more expensive in real terms, all the more so as the economy advances.

Baumol argues that higher education, though a stagnant industry by his definition, can continue to prosper even as it becomes more expensive—by virtue of its value and because an advancing economy makes the cost increases affordable. However, trimming unit costs where possible remains important, and technology offers this possibility. By making its business and support processes more efficient, the string quartet might at least defer some real cost increases.

But technology may do much more than trim expense. For example, by recording its music, the string quartet can reach thousands at low incremental cost. The profits from recordings can cross-subsidize ticket prices for live concerts, thus providing access to many who otherwise would be unable to attend. As long as the real cost of recordings and associated playback equipment continues to drop, the string quartet can hardly be called stagnant. As long as capital is a significant fraction of total cost, and the cost of technology falls in real terms, the quartet will enjoy steady productivity gains. Baumol might argue that, eventually, the cost of technology may fall so much that it becomes a negligible part of the quartet's expenditure mix—at which time the industry would once again be stagnant (Baumol & Blackman, 1983). Perhaps, but it would be operating at a lower cost base and its experience with innovation would alert it to the potential for future technological breakthroughs. Having broken away from handicraft methods, an industry is more likely to take advantages of future innovations when they occur.

We have already argued that one should not expect the adoption of technology to produce immediate cost savings in higher education. Because the old ways must be continued while innovation proceeds, cost may rise during technology's phase-in. Indeed, during the adoption period the university will pay double because it is *both* labor and capital intensive. But eventually the phase-in will end and the university will begin to reap the benefits of a larger capital-labor ratio. Price declines for the technology component of total cost will improve the institution's instructional cost trajectory.

Skeptics may argue that increases in the quality of technology will offset price reductions. For example, today's Pentium computers cost as much as yesterday's 486 machines, which in turn cost the same as their predecessor 386s. But the institution controls the level of technology it acquires, and today's offerings already are powerful enough for many purposes. Hence technology-driven reengineering can be expected to provide at least a partial cure for the cost disease.

Implications for Quality of Faculty Work Life

Many faculty and staff fear that the advent of information technology will change their lives significantly, and not for the better. Certainly no one can claim that technology will not affect them. Doubtless many will have to learn new skills, and some will be better at this than others. Some institutions that operate comfortably in the present environment will fare less well in the new one (the increased competition made possible by technology virtually guarantees that there will be losers as well as gainers), and the discomfort will be shared by the institution's employees. At the same time, however, one can project that the wired campus will confer certain benefits on those who work there—especially the faculty. Therefore, I will conclude my account of life on the wired campus by briefly describing some of these benefits.

First, teaching and learning processes that have been reengineered to take full advantage of information technology also will permit faculty to focus on their highest and best uses. By shifting many of the routine and repetitive aspects of teaching and student evaluation to the technology, faculty will be able to concentrate on the kinds of intellectual questions that represent their comparative advantage. Because the effective use of technology demands that teaching and learning be viewed in systems terms, the new paradigms will invite a more effective division of labor among faculty with respect to educational tasks. Finally, as suggested in the reengineering vision, the new processes may improve research performance by concentrating faculty discretionary time—by leveraging the faculty's work and getting away from the lockstep "*n*-times-per-week" routine of the conventional course structure.

The new methods also may encourage more faculty to focus on teaching. Relieving teachers of repetitive drudgery will contribute to this end, as will the ability to exploit comparative advantage and optimize the use of time. Moreover, the advent of technology will invite faculty to develop projects that map the knowledge base of their discipline to the new educational paradigm. Such work will be considerably more interesting than revising a lecture yet again. It can also generate reviewable outputs that, in the fullness of time, may compete with conventional publications in faculty portfolios and the faculty labor market. Finally, the ability to leverage student as well as faculty time will mean that faculty will be able to engage with more prepared and motivated students. This will boost the intrinsic rewards obtainable from teaching—which, after all, provide the dedicated teacher's most basic impetus.

Conclusion

Information technology allows institutions to improve the quality of the education they provide. As in the case of health care providers, schools will be pressed to do all they can to exploit the new technology. Technology costs money, but whether its use will result in lower or higher unit cost will depend on how much society wants to pay for education and how many people will choose to access its benefits. Technology doesn't impose answers to these questions, but it does open important new alternatives. One should not blame technology if higher education's funders decide to exploit the technology by making tradeoffs among cost, quality, and access rather than simply adding the new costs to the existing budget base.

No matter what happens to unit cost in the short run, information technology will improve colleges' and universities' production processes and economic structure, and the quality of the faculty's work life. The advent of technology also provides a badly needed impetus for reengineering the teaching and learning process. It will allow institutions to break away from handicraft traditions and deepen their use of capital. Schools will improve effectiveness through outsourcing, better exploit the pedagogical learning curve, and mitigate the effects of the cost disease. Technology will shift the professor's role from that of mainly a content expert to a combination of content expert, designer, manager, and mentor. By reducing the repetitive and less interesting aspects of teaching and bringing better-prepared students to the classroom, it will make the faculty's work more rewarding.

Technology will not make obsolete the interaction between student and faculty in a campus setting. Certain important educational and human values cannot be as well promulgated asynchronously or at distance as they can face to face. Technology will reduce the percentage of face-to-face contact in the optimal pedagogical mix, but it will not come close to eliminating it. Cost considerations will limit or perhaps supplant direct contact in some circumstances, but one can expect that the best and the brightest students—regardless of economic status—will continue to enjoy the benefits of campus-based education. Face-to-face interaction will be leveraged, but the optimal educational process will contain many recognizable elements. The wired campus will look different, but it will remain, in its essence, a campus.

[This work was supported by the National Center for Postsecondary Improvement, Stanford University, under contract number R309A6001 with the Office of Education Research and Improvement (OERI), U.S. Department of Education.]

References

Baumol, W. J., & Blackman, S. A. B. (1983). Electronics, the cost disease, and the operation of libraries. *Journal of the American Society for Information Sciences, 34* (3), 181-191.

Baumol, W. J., Blackman, S. A. B., & Wolff, E. N. (1989). *Productivity and American leadership: The long view.* Cambridge, MA: The MIT Press.

Bowen, H. R. (1980). *The costs of higher education: How much do colleges and universities spend per student and how much should they spend?* San Francisco, CA: Jossey-Bass.

Massy, W. F., with collaborators. (1996). *Resource allocation in higher education.* Ann Arbor, MI: The University of Michigan Press.

Massy, W. F., & Wilger, A. K. (1992). Productivity in postsecondary education: A new approach. *Educational Evaluation and Policy Analysis, 14* (4), 361-76.

Massy, W. F., & Wilger, A. K. (1995, July-August). Improving productivity. *Change,* 10-20.

Massy, W. F., Wilger, A. K., & Colbeck, C. (1994, July-August). Overcoming "hollowed collegiality." *Change,* 11-20.

Massy, W. F., & Zemsky, R. (1995). *Using information technology to enhance academic productivity.* Washington, DC: EDUCOM, Occasional paper.

Policy perspectives. (1994). To dance with change. University of Pennsylvania, Pew Higher Education Research Program.

Zemsky, R., & Massy, W. F. (1995, November-December). Expanding perimeters, melting cores, and sticky functions: Toward an understanding of our current predicaments. *Change,* 40-49.

14

Asynchronous Learning Networks: New Possibilities

A. Frank Mayadas

Introduction

Over the past century, we have seen accelerating interest in education for off-campus or nontraditional learners. As technology and infrastructure have progressed, the advances have been modified by educators to package learning resources for these off-campus learners.

The history of serving off-campus learners began a century ago. Correspondence style off-campus education first appeared in the late 1800s and remains popular today. Technology delivery has evolved from print and radio to broadcast television and computer-aided instruction, and now to CD-ROMs and the World Wide Web. These disparate technologies along with some others, are the enabling tools for what is now called distance education. They have had a large—even revolutionary—influence on education. In the process, they have extended educational opportunities to people and places that would otherwise not have been served.

Most of today's distance education techniques can be grouped into two categories: *self-study techniques,* with little or no human interaction (such as books, videotapes, and learning software), and *techniques with limited human interaction* (such as interactive television). While these techniques continue to be important, there is one channel of learning that these techniques fail to address—the channel that goes beyond lectures and reading materials to permit learners to engage in interactive discussion with peers and instructors. A self-study model or a televised classroom, even one advertised as fully interactive, cannot begin to provide the formal and informal person-to-person exchanges that our campuses offer—exchanges that are an important supplement to lecture and textbook instruction.

Today, technologies exist that enable asynchronous interactivity; i.e., a high degree of interactivity among geographically separated learners, independent of time or place. By asynchronous we mean that participants in a discussion need not engage in that discussion at the same time, as they would in a face-to-face or telephone conversation. Rather, as in an e-mail exchange, there is some elapsed time between message exchanges—perhaps minutes, hours, or even days.

Asynchronous interactivity can become the basis for a new and large scale learning model among distance learners. Such interactivity is already the basis for project work in business enterprises, where geographically dispersed teams can develop project goals, share analyses, carry on discussion and debate, and prepare presentations or reports without ever meeting in the same room or even connecting at the same time through a conference call. Such interactions are extraordinarily popular on Internet bulletin boards and associated networks run by organizations such as America Online, CompuServe, and Prodigy, where people who have never met can carry on discussions on a wide variety of topics, all in a time-elapsed, asynchronous fashion.

Asynchronous interactivity is the third major distance education approach. Asynchronous Learning Networks (ALNs) combine self-study techniques with asynchronous interactivity to create environments in which learners can access remote learning resources asynchronously—using relatively inexpensive equipment—to learn at home, at the work place, or at any place of their choosing. Remote learning can enlist dynamic resources such as other students, outside experts, or the instructor, or more static resources such as assignments, course notes, or libraries. Additional digital resources can include databases, spreadsheets, or even software-generated simulations.

In an ALN we can think of every person on the network as both a user and a resource. This concept is crucial to the power of an ALN, making it not just an electronic network but a network of people—an interactive learning community that is not limited by time, place, or the constraints of a classroom.

Rapid asynchronous access to resources is made possible by computer and communications technologies. Group activities or team projects involving discussions, spreadsheet analysis, or report preparation can be carried out through commercial software linked to computer conferencing software or groupware (De Jean & De Jean, 1991). In an ALN, lectures can be transmitted through groupware, videotape, CD-ROM, or the World Wide Web. Books and other printed material continue to have a role. Material may be posted on the World Wide Web or it may be provided through fax or a voice-response unit (Wilson & Stuart, 1996). All represent asynchronously accessed resources. Most of the academic campus activities a student might participate in (Table 14.1) have an asynchronous analog, which allows us to envisage distributed classes, populated with learners we can think of as distributed cohorts, in the same way we think of on-campus classes and cohorts. Participants in these distributed classes, however, access resources and interact asynchronously.

TABLE 14.1

Typical learning-related activities for a student at a traditional institution of higher learning

TRADITIONAL, ON-CAMPUS STUDENT ACADEMIC ACTIVITIES
Attendance at lectures
Recitation sections
Interaction with peers
Self-study, library
Lab work
Interaction with tutors and TAs
Interaction with faculty
Attendance at seminars and colloquia
Enquiries: academic & administrative issues
Exams

The Alfred P. Sloan Foundation has established a program to explore the potential of ALNs to provide learning to anyone who wishes to learn, at a time and place of the learner's choice. Projects at a number of mainstream, campus-based institutions, devoted to exploring the unique possibilities that might emerge from ALNs, are an important element of the Sloan Foundation program. The basic ideas underlying computer network learning pre-date the Sloan projects, having been discussed in the 1970s (Hiltz & Turoff, 1978) with early implementations starting in the 1980s. The number of these implementation projects has grown steadily, so that today, hundreds of courses are listed on the Internet. Some degree programs are available as well.

Although real progress has been made in asynchronous education, this growth is limited. The number of courses available on-line is relatively large, but most are isolated offerings resulting from the zeal and skill of a handful of faculty members. The courses vary widely in approach, quality, and credibility. Some are little more than Web-based reading material; others are advertisements for on-campus continuing education courses. Few are part of a true learning network.

Consider the differences between on-line and classroom-based programs at established colleges and universities. Whether for traditional or continuing education students, classroom programs are more than a skeletal assembly of isolated courses; rather they are a coherent sequence of courses that constitute a curriculum. These programs lead to degrees or certification. They are listed in catalogs and are available at predictable times. Complementing their academic offerings, colleges and universities also provide sophisticated support services including recruitment, orientation, registration, advising, financial aid, grade recording, and report keeping. These support services are quite robust: They handle tens of thousands of students in the largest universities.

By these kinds of measurements, asynchronous learning has much ground to cover. Even self-study and televised classrooms at major institutions are far ahead of ALN-style education in their systematic approach and accompanying services and support (Watkins & Wright, 1991; Blumenstyk, 1996). To distribute education asynchronously in a truly useful way to off-campus learners, educational institutions will have to make a commitment to build organizations that deliver certifications and degrees along with a full array of student services. Society would benefit greatly from the emergence of such organizations serving a community of motivated learners whose life circumstances make it difficult for them to attend scheduled campus classes.

While off-campus learners will benefit the most from ALNs, it is likely that important benefits will also be realized on campuses. ALNs bring with them new kinds of functions that may, in turn, allow new outcomes, particularly in the areas of learning quality and economics of education. For instance, peer-to-peer collaborative learning among students might be greatly enhanced through asynchronous access to each other or to tutors and teaching assistants. Improved communication between all network nodes—in this case students, teaching assistants, and faculty—may favorably impact student motivation and retention. Learning productivity may increase. Self-pacing would also become possible for some students.

Some of the Sloan-supported projects are exploring those and other possibilities by experimenting with new ways to integrate ALNs with traditional on-campus processes. Goals range from an attempt to reduce the overall cost of education with equal or improved learning quality, to increasing flexibility with no additional workload for faculty. We call these on-campus ALNs. Other projects are exploring ALNs for off-campus learners. These can be either near-campus or very-far-from-campus ALNs. For example, a community college that draws students from a radius of 50 or 60 miles might establish a near-campus ALN. Courses might be taken at home or at the workplace through an ALN, but examinations, laboratory work, counseling, and other support activities might require a campus visit. An ALN for learners located at greater distances from the campus requires more function and sophistication.

Some of the Sloan projects are experimenting with one or two courses before making a decision to pursue a more ambitious agenda (Table 14.2). Others are offering, or plan to offer, multiple course sequences leading to certifications or degrees. The focus of these courses is primarily in scientific and technical fields, although other disciplines are represented, as well. Some projects have enrollments in the hundreds. Over the next few years, some course enrollments will exceed a thousand and begin to demonstrate scalability.

It seems quite clear that ALNs offer new possibilities in off-campus as well as on-campus education. However, experience with large-scale implementation and institutional commitment are needed to realize the extent of these possibilities. The remainder of this chapter describes the issues of how well people learn in ALNs, potential outcomes of ALNs, and a possible evolution of this new approach.

Learning in Asynchronous Learning Networks

Do ALNs work? Do people learn in these environments? Will ALN-style learning appeal to a variety of learners across a broad range of disciplines?

These are complex questions, which are embedded with research as well as practical aspects. The research questions will not be resolved quickly, since many variables need to be accounted for and control groups established for comparisons, which is a difficult task in educational environments. Over time, we will learn whether asynchronous learning is more effective in particular discipline areas, and we will learn more about student and faculty characteristics which lead to success in ALNs. At a more practical level, we might apply different kinds of measures. We can ask, for instance, whether the evidence we have supports a conclusion that the learning that takes place

TABLE 14.2

Institutions Participating in Sloan ALN Program		
ON-CAMPUS	NEAR CAMPUS	VERY FAR FROM CAMPUS
Brown University	Augusta Technical College	New York University
Cornell University	Chattanooga State Tech	University of Maryland
Drexel University	Drexel University	Pace University
University of Illinois	Ferris State University	Stanford University
Michigan State University	Gadsden State Community College	University of California–Berkeley
University of California (Irvine)	Miami-Dade Community College	Pennsylvania State University
Virginia Polytechnic & State University	Metropolitan State University	University of Hawaii
	Lesley College	University Of Minnesota
	New Hampshire Tech. College	
	New Jersey Institute of Technology	
	Northern Virginia Community College	
	Rio Salado Community College	
	State University of New York	
	Trident Technical College	
	University of Wisconsin–Stout	
	Vanderbilt University	
	Villa Julie College	
	Westchester Community College	
	Wytheville Community College	

in ALNs is equivalent to traditional classroom learning. We might also try assessing the demand side. Are learners enrolling in properly delivered and properly supported ALN programs? Is a need being fulfilled? To these two practical measures, the answer appears to be affirmative. The majority of institutions in Table 14.2 have now gained valuable learning experience in ALNs, some quite extensive, and in all instances the indicators point to a conclusion of equal or better learning in an ALN compared with traditional methods. Some specific examples follow.

Example 1: Cornell University

In 1993, the Cornell University physics department began a project to rethink and restructure certain physics courses, both at the graduate and undergraduate level, in an attempt to learn more about the possible benefits of extending computer and communications usage and reducing lecture-style pedagogy. A number of ideas were tried; experimentation continues (K. Gottfried, personal communication). The following example is based on Solid State Physics (Physics 545).

Solid State Physics is a four-credit course, with three lecture sessions and one recitation section per week. Typical students are physics undergraduates planning to go on to graduate school or graduate students from engineering and other sciences. In the spring semester of 1995, Professor Robert Silsbee taught the course with no face-to-face sessions. Students were given a course syllabus, along with information about books needed and reading assignments for the semester. They turned in assigned homework problems and took one quiz per week. Learning took place through assigned readings, reviews of a library of 24 computer simulations which illustrated solid-state phenomena created by Silsbee and a coworker (Silsbee & Draeger, 1997), and work on problem sets. Students worked asynchronously. The schedule required that homework problems and quizzes be turned in at prescribed times. Silsbee or a graduate assistant were available through e-mail or a Web-based system, and class participants could get help from each other, either face-to-face or though e-mail.

Silsbee has taught this course using a traditional classroom model many times during the past 30 years. Student learning involves mastering hard-to-visualize topics such as reciprocal lattices and Fermi surfaces. His assessment at the end of the semester was that this asynchronous cohort had learned as much as other classes he had taught. He based his assessment on results from homework sets, quizzes, and post-semester discussions with students on the subject matter. This somewhat unique experiment is an indicator that, at least for this rather specialized group of science and engineering students, an

ALN learning experience was approximately equivalent to that of colleagues in face-to-face classes.

In terms of demonstrating the full capabilities of an ALN, the experiment was only partially successful. Students did access remote resources such as the instructor and a teaching assistant over the network, and there was some networked collaboration among students. However, such collaboration was limited, possibly because the collaboration was optional and not built into the structure of the course. It is also possible that since students met in the computer lab to work on simulations, they needed less in the way of networked communications.

Example 2: Drexel University

Drexel University has converted eight courses in the Information Systems (IS) curriculum to a format suitable for ALN, and has been offering these mainly to their on-campus students over the past two and one-half years. One undergraduate course, System Design and Analysis, has now been taught seven times. A graduate course in Policy and Management has been taught five times. Other courses have been taught from three times to once. Drexel's approach is to put as much of the material needed by students as possible into a Lotus Notes database which is accessed over the computer network. The course materials database contains a course description, a course syllabus, all required reading materials (books, articles, and notes), criteria for grading, as well as photographs and short profiles of students in the class (Andriole & Lytle, 1995).

Unlike physics, the IS discipline is not highly mathematical or quantitative. The System Design and Analysis course, for example, stresses an understanding of the factors (requirements) underpinning the application for which the software is to be designed, how to convert these requirements into a model, and then to convert the model into a prototype. These elements require thought and analysis. However, there is usually no single correct answer. There are likely to be several good designs, as well as mediocre or unsatisfactory designs. Various design approaches can be refined through discussions with experts or by testing them against empirical design principles.

A design course, to be successful, also requires discussion and dialog—among students and between students and the instructor. Discussions are integral to all IS courses, and in the ALN versions they are carried out in the Lotus Notes discussion database. Typically, a discussion is initiated by the instructor; student participation is required for satisfactory performance in the course. In a conventional classroom environment, one opinionated individual can dominate a discussion, in the process excluding the opinions of others. An asynchronous networked version of this phenomenon occurred in one of the Drexel classes when one individual submitted many more messages than other students. However, because of the nature of the medium, this caused no time penalty for anyone else, and the distraction was easily overlooked.

The Drexel courses are all quite structured—readings and assignments are laid out for each week of the term, and one week is devoted to a substantive discussion topic. Students learn new material through assigned readings, then engage in discussions with each other. They turn in homework assignments every week—recorded in a Lotus Notes assignments database—and carry out a system design project for the semester, also recorded in the assignments database. All work, including readings, discussions, and assignments, is carried out asynchronously. Note, however, that the overall course is synchronized. For example, everyone in the class must complete the weekly subject module.

To date, approximately 250 students have completed these courses. Homework and project grades, along with surveys and interviews with students, lead to the conclusion that learning in the ALNs is equivalent to that of face-to-face classes. Particularly striking were results from surveys which showed that virtually all (100%) students felt that seeing the ideas and assignments of others was useful, 67% felt they had more communication with fellow students, 97% felt they had more access to the instructor than in conventional classes, and 91% said they would take another ALN course (Charlton Monsanto, personal communication). We should note, however, that about half of the students also indicated that they missed classroom lectures.

Example 3: Northern Virginia Community College

With five campuses and nearly 40,000 students, Northern Virginia Community College (NVCC) is one of the largest two-year colleges in the country. The Extended Learning Institute (ELI) unit at NVCC is specifically charged with serving home-based, nontraditional learners—who are likely to be working adults—through independent study programs. The average age of the population registering for ELI courses is 28. In 1993, the ELI unit undertook a two-stage program to implement a near-campus ALN that would, when completed, permit off-campus learners to earn a full Associate in Science (AS) degree in Engineering. Fourteen courses will have been converted to a format suitable for an ALN when the project is completed.

The ALN is built around lectures on videotape, books and other instructional materials, recitations, homework help, and other person-to-person communication through networked computers running First Class groupware. Students can register remotely through telephone and computer messaging. This is a typical near-campus ALN in that for services such as financial aid, placement testing, or library books and periodicals, students come to campus. Examinations, when required, are also on campus, as are chemistry laboratories (Sener, 1996).

Chemistry I is a required course in the AS (Engineering) sequence and requires 12 laboratory sessions. NVCC implemented six double sessions on Saturdays and found this arrangement quite satisfactory for students and faculty. While the full suite of courses for the AS (Engineering) degree is still being developed, teaching experience gained so far with approximately 250 students indicates that ELI ALN students are doing as well or better in courses, in terms of grades and retention rates, as NVCC students in the same courses offered in traditional format. Faculty participating in the project are pleased with the results and with their involvement. In addition, students have been very positive in their comments and in survey responses.

Example 4: New Jersey Institute of Technology

The New Jersey Institute of Technology (NJIT) has had a long history of research and experimentation with computer conferencing and education. In 1993, NJIT started a project to develop a suite of courses in a format suitable for ALNs that would lead to two undergraduate degrees—a Bachelor of Arts (BA) in Information Systems and a Bachelor of Science (BS) in Computer Science. A total of 26 courses have been developed and offered, some as many as six or seven times. ALN students view lectures on videotape and participate in class discussions through NJIT's proprietary EIESII computer conferencing system. Homework assignments are received and submitted by students through this system. Because most of the courses in the ALNs were also taught face-to-face, comparisons could be made across a wide range of parameters. The conclusions are somewhat clouded by the fact that students had difficulty accessing the NJIT course server due to an insufficient number of modems at the university. But, in spite of this difficulty, students in ALN sections responded to surveys by indicating that the ALN improved their learning. Distribution of grades are an indicator that students in the ALN performed at least as well, perhaps better, than those in traditional sections (Hiltz, 1996).

The four examples given here all support the conclusion that effective learning takes place in ALNs. Most of the other 34 Sloan supported projects have shown similar results. To be sure, more work on assessment and evaluation is needed. However, we believe that ALN learning can be equivalent to classroom learning and that a steadily increasing number of off-campus learners are willing to enroll in ALNs.

New Outcomes

In this chapter several references have been made to the traditional classroom teaching model, a model that has been dominant for over a century and one that encourages certain accepted practices. For example, learners accept the necessity of coming to a campus center to learn, the idea that a degree requires four years of residence, and the premise that smaller classes and student faculty ratios are preferable to larger ones. One might conjecture that ALNs produce different outcomes, because entirely new capabilities are being brought to bear. Three capabilities—asynchronicity, efficiency, and geographically distributed cohorts—brought together in different ways could create a variety of possibilities with profound implications for education. This section considers examples from a range of institutions where new outcomes are being explored.

One new possibility is widespread availability of high quality, cohort-style education (courses, certifications, and degrees) for anyone, anywhere. Indeed, this possibility is the single most important motivator for developing extensive ALNs that go beyond today's handful of degree programs and isolated courses. Progress is being made by a number of institutions in the near-campus and very-far-from-campus categories, which are developing certifications and degrees. We have already noted that NJIT is offering Bachelor degrees in computer science and information systems. Drexel has used their experience from on-campus ALNs to create a Master of Science (MS) in Information Systems that is initially being offered in the Philadelphia area starting in the fall of 1996. NVCC is offering a two-year Associate in Applied Science degree in engineering. Other institutions are also following this path.

Nonresidency Degrees

The State University of New York (SUNY) now has in place a degree completion program. Learners who finish two years at any of six community colleges in the mid-Hudson Valley can go on to complete bachelor's requirements for either of two degrees without having to leave home and go to a four-year college: liberal studies from SUNY New Paltz, or business from SUNY Empire State. A Lotus Notes network and the Internet are core elements of the SUNY ALN. Stanford, with one of the largest and most successful televised graduate degree programs, has begun to digitize its television lectures and offer them on-demand. Fourteen courses are currently available in asynchronous form, with more to follow.

Nonresidency Certificates

Many certifications are also available. New York University has already graduated two classes with a four-course graduate certification in information technology. They are using a Lotus Notes network and require ISDN connections for learners so that video, animation, and text are all part of the learning materials (DeJesus, 1996). The University of California at Berkeley has enrolled a class for a nine-course certification in hazardous materials management, available over America Online. The University of Wisconsin-Stout offers certification in food handling. Other schools are planning to offer certifications soon: Metropolitan State in purchasing management, Pace University in telecommunications, Pennsylvania State University in acoustics engineering, and Rio Salado Community College in computer usage and applications. The University of California-Berkeley has a major effort underway to have 175 of their extension courses on America Online. A number of other institutions will also be moving forward with degree and certification offerings in the coming years.

At-Risk Populations

The certificate offerings from Rio Salado and Penn State deserve additional discussion, for they illustrate how ALNs can be used to meet the needs of very specific groups of distributed cohorts. Rio Salado's Project Reachout is designed to recruit applicants from an at-risk population—those with physical disabilities, child care issues, and transportation difficulties, factors which may be barriers to a post-secondary education. Members of this group may be the first in their families to have high school credentials. Project Reachout is having surprising course completion rates for this population, currently around 55%. Their near-campus ALN imposes a strict selection process for new applicants, including testing and interviews, to ensure maximum likelihood for success. Once selected, participants are provided counseling and other services, both face-to-face and on-line, to further enhance their chances for success. Participants use the computer network as an added element of support among themselves, since encouragement and support are not always forthcoming from the families.

Low Demand Specialties

The Penn State acoustics engineering certification also aims to demonstrate a new kind of outcome—the special value of an ALN approach in narrow specialties. Acoustics expertise is needed in many industries such as appliances, automobiles and auto parts, office equipment, aircraft, machine tools, and the government sector, where noise control and vibration reduction are important to success. However, many corporations do not have a special acoustics department and may prefer that a mechanical engineer also be a part-time acoustics engineer. Higher education institutions are not likely to offer courses in such narrow specialties because local demand is low. Corporations are also not likely to have on-site classes for the same reason. This does not mean that the specialty is unimportant, only that few individuals at any location require the training. Penn State's plan is to establish cohorts nationally when their acoustics ALN (offered on the Internet and with CD-ROMs) is rolled out, ensuring that classes of 30 to 50 can easily be assembled. Small groups of three to five will work together on engineering projects. Cohort-style education in narrow specialties appears viable on a national scale, even when it is not viable on a local scale in conventional classes.

Efficiency

Access to high quality, cohort-style learning, even for special learner segments and narrow specialties, represents a new outcome that is made possible through the three features of ALN approach: asynchronicity, efficiency, and geographically distributed cohorts. But does asynchronous access to remote resources really introduce new efficiencies? The answer is yes. The rapid increase in use of phone answering machines, digital voice response units, e-mail, and groupware provide the evidence. The reasons for this may have to do with the fact that although the face-to-face method is the most efficient form of communication, in most instances such meetings do not take place very often because of difficulties and costs associated with scheduling and distances. When a group is together in a room, there may be very effective communication. Other than these instances, however, there is little or no communication. Said another way, the communication bandwidth peaks during face-to-face sessions and drops to zero in between. The result is that, averaged over periods of several hours or more, the effective bandwidth for asynchronous communication can be much higher than in face-to-face communication.

The second efficiency has to do with the fact that distribution of documents and other learning materials over the Web and groupware is more efficient than via any other method. These communication and distribution efficiencies make possible the idea of distributed cohorts. If a geographically dispersed group of people were connected only through the mail and synchronous telephony, they would effectively be a self-study group.

On-Campus Outcomes

ALNs may also create new outcomes for on-campus learning. The University of Illinois at Urbana-Champaign has launched an ambitious project through their Sloan Center for Asynchronous Learning Environments (SCALE). SCALE plans to desynchronize elements of more than 100 courses over a three-year period and explore the possible outcomes achievable through on-campus ALNs. So far, asynchronous elements have been integrated into approximately 50 courses ranging across many fields, such as humanities, social sciences, engineering, and physical sciences. Burks Oakley, Associate Director of SCALE and a pioneer in the area of on-campus ALNs, has summarized SCALE projects and activities. He gives one particularly striking example for a high enrollment, lower division electrical engineering course, ECE270 (Oakley, 1996).

Typically, about 500 engineering and physical sciences students enroll in this course each semester. There are usually five sections for this course. Over the past few years, faculty assigned to some sections have opted for the ALN version while others have chosen the traditional version. In the ALN version, students attend lectures but carry out homework drills through a software package called CircuitTutor. Problem sets are also contained in CircuitTutor, which can be submitted for grading anytime through the network to a computer that provides a grade response almost instantly. Problems graded as incorrect can be resubmitted an unlimited number of times. Students may seek assistance at any time from fellow students or from on-line undergraduate tutors between 8 a.m. and 12 midnight on weekdays, or from the instructor. With these features in mind, it is easy to imagine the following scenario: A student completes the four assigned homework problems late at night and submits them for grading. The computer marks three correct and one incorrect. The student tries two more times but still does not get the assignment right. Of course, this situation is not uncommon in a quantitative field where problem solutions depend on a series of intermediate steps, some of which may involve computations or assumptions. A wrong answer is usually traceable to some incorrectly performed intermediate step; however, the person working on the problem may be unable to find the error—the person is stuck. Often a few hints from someone else can unstick the thought process. Late at night that other person may be hard to find; an appointment with the instructor may delay the process a day or more. The solution is to turn to the learning network and ask for help—from anyone. And help is usually swift in coming.

Not surprisingly, the students in ALN sections achieved better results than those who submitted paper and pencil homework problems and received help in traditional face-to-face fashion. Students in the ECE270 ALN sections also demonstrated reduced dropout rates. Somewhat more surprising was the fact that the superior results achieved by the ALN students were unchanged even when the student/faculty ratio for these sections was increased by 50%.

It has long been assumed that learning outcomes deteriorate as student-to-faculty ratios increase in traditional classrooms. There is, however, no data to tell us how learning networks scale—what the relationship is between learning quality and the number of people on a network. Classrooms with 10 to 20 students are quite viable, in fact, very effective. Asynchronous learning networks of this size are viable, as the Drexel experience shows, but the work at Illinois shows that networks of 50 or more students are also viable and effective. As this work indicates, if the users within a network serve as resources to other users, a properly structured learning network may scale very differently from a classroom. Economic benefits could follow.

Laboratories

ALNs might produce other kinds of outcomes. Weekly laboratory sessions taking several hours are required in many science and engineering courses—sometimes with a partner. Could the bulk of a laboratory course be moved onto an ALN so that lab participants (and partners, if appropriate) would need to spend fewer, shorter, and more intensive sessions in a real laboratory? Answers to this question would clearly have implications for off-campus learners as well for those on the campus.

At Vanderbilt University, John Bourne of the electrical engineering department and co-workers have developed a software simulator for a junior level electrical engineering laboratory (Bourne & Brodersen, 1993). This simulator features state-of-the-art commercial laboratory equipment, electric circuit components, wires, and a board on which circuits can be constructed. Part of the simulation software has exercises which direct students to familiarize themselves with the instruments and build assigned circuits. Once a circuit is built it can be tested on the simulated instruments. Recently, the Vanderbilt group carried out controlled assessments to determine the extent to which a simulated laboratory can replace a real laboratory. Students were given comprehensive exams before starting the laboratory course, either the simulated version or the traditional one. Students in the simulated laboratory then took three real laboratory sessions, versus the

12 taken by traditional lab students. The result of the assessment was that students in the simulated laboratory, with only three real sessions, outperformed the students in the traditional laboratory with 12 real sessions, based on pre- and post-test comparisons of the two groups (Campbell, 1995). The conclusion is that ALNs involving laboratory simulations hold some promise for producing positive economic outcomes and may permit students to pursue large parts of a laboratory course away from a physical laboratory in a self-paced mode.

Self-Pacing

Self-pacing is an attractive option for some on-campus students who wish to accelerate their progress or for others who are intellectually capable but lack the background to keep up in a regular class, and thus face the prospect of having to drop the course. A self-pacing capability may affect only a few students, and it does take away the cohort concept, but it is worth exploring. The chemistry department at Brown University has begun an exploration aimed at understanding the extent to which material on the World Wide Web and networked communications can enable self-paced learning. Very early indications are that some students can self-pace successfully, but considerable care is needed to select only highly motivated individuals in such a program.

There are a number of possible outcomes that could result from ALNs. Some, such as multiple courses leading to certification for off-campus learners in a wide variety of fields, analogous to a university, are likely to become a reality. Others remain attractive possibilities but are not yet fully proven.

ALN: Institutional Adoption

Progress is being made toward the goal of providing anyone who wishes to learn with the opportunity to study in a time, a place, and a field of their choice. Can this progress be sustained or accelerated? The self-study and interactive televised classroom models, with occasional augmentation by e-mail communications, are well-established. It would seem that a multiplicity of approaches are likely to co-exist in the future. Asynchronous Learning Networks can grow to become an important, even dominant, presence in off-campus education. Existing organizations, which specialize in networked education, and newly formed organizations such as fledgling Internet universities, are likely to contribute to this growth. The Western Governors University, for example, will most likely feature a computer network component.

The highest potential for large-scale ALNs will, however, come from mainstream, campus-based institutions because of their sheer numbers and overall presence. Not all will participate, but many will see ALNs as an excellent opportunity and will take steps to move beyond the small-scale experiments with Web-based education that are so common today. These institutions are the ones who recognize that there are no technology limitations today for implementing ALNs. Rather, the limitations come from uncertain institutional commitment.

The need is to build a consensus for reaching beyond campus boundaries to develop near-campus or very-far-from-campus ALNs, or both. Institutions will face two prominent obstacles. One is to make time available for faculty to rethink their lecture style—to turn face-to-face courses into asynchronous ones. This may require the commitment of discretionary funds, since on-campus classes still need to be taught. The second is student recruitment. Explaining an ALN to off-campus learners is often a challenge. The standard expressions of "learn by computer, anytime, anyplace" lead to a perception that the requisite knowledge is in the computer, and the learner's task is to somehow coax it out—a self-study mode. Attention to effective student recruitment will be a necessity for ensuring reasonably large class sizes and economic viability. Recruiting is only the beginning. Sustaining a significant activity built around ALNs will also require robust and responsive student services. All this requires attention to detail and new budget priorities at the institutional level.

Within institutions participating in Sloan Foundation projects, we see evidence of meaningful institutional commitment. To be more specific, we can assess the degree of institutional commitment by noting answers to four questions: 1) Are more than a few faculty involved? 2) Is the institution contributing a significant amount of its own resources to the ALN effort? 3) Does the institution have a strategic vision for a complete suite of student services? and 4) Does the institution have a strategic vision for making ALN a core, financially viable activity?

Most of the colleges and universities with near-campus and very-far-from-campus ALNs, whose ALN experiences were discussed in the previous sections, score very well in terms of these criteria. Their ALN programs will grow over the coming years; a few could grow to large-scale implementations. In summary, we see that a committed, core ALN group is in place and a start has been made towards the goal of making anytime, anyplace learning available.

Making quality education available to off-campus learners through ALNs is a primary goal, but other possible outcomes arising from asynchronicity, efficiency, and distributed cohorts were also highlighted earlier. We can be quite confident that these outcomes will be explored and exploited by the activities of institutions committed to off-campus education, but serious exploration in the on-campus environment is at a very low level. Most major institutions have wired campuses with high-speed Internet connections carrying a large amount of traffic. However, exploration of new outcomes, as we have used the term in this chapter, is largely absent, partly because there appears to be little motivation to explore outcomes which could impact costs through larger class sizes, improved student retention, and self-pacing while at the same time improving learning quality.

More exploration in on-campus environments is necessary so we can gain new insights about proper balance between ALNs, lectures, recitations, laboratories and other on-campus process. Universities such as Illinois, Michigan State, Virginia Polytechnic, and Brown are already exploring these issues but are still at an early stage. Explorations at many other institutions are also needed. Even the small number of on-campus explorations presently underway are yielding important information about new outcomes and validation of some of the early indicators is likely soon.

CONCLUSION

Asynchronous Learning Networks are a relatively new kind of entry into the milieu of technical possibilities that make up the area broadly known as distance education. They combine elements of self-study techniques and asynchronous interactivity, which along with synchronous interactive television, are the building blocks for most distance education implementations. The appeal of ALNs lies in their ability to enable anytime, anyplace education with high human interactivity for geographically distributed cohorts—and these characteristics could make ALNs the largest contributor to distance education.

Although ALNs do not depend on courseware of any kind, available courseware or commercial application software can be used effectively. We have seen where specialized, faculty-developed learning software played an important role in the Cornell and Illinois examples. However, SUNY, NVCC, and Drexel, among others, use only commercial software. ALNs do require asynchronous communication software which can range from e-mail to bulletin boards to sophisticated groupware, and other asynchronous communications methods such as voice response units, all available as standard commercial products. ALNs need large-scale implementations, and current work is creating an experience base for future large-scale activities.

While near-campus and very-far-from-campus ALNs are likely to be important in distance education, the attributes of asynchronicity, increased efficiency, and distributed cohort groups open up new options for on-campus education as well. These options, now being investigated at a number of institutions, aim to discover new balance points between traditional on-campus processes and ALN-style learning with a view to improving learning quality and reducing costs.

A number of mainstream institutions are offering degree and certification programs through ALNs. More are preparing to follow. There is evidence of serious institutional commitment to sustain and grow these programs, and we will see large-scale implementations within the next few years. Asynchronous Learning Networks will be an important element of the options offered by many mainstream institutions, best known today for their campus programs.

References

Andriole, S.J., & Lytle, R.H. (1995, October). Asynchronous learning networks: Drexel's experience. *T.H.E. Journal*, 97-101.

Blumenstyk, G. (1996, May 31). Maine's large distance education network gets mixed reviews. *The Chronicle of Higher Education,* A15.

Bourne, J.R, & Brodersen, A.J. (1993). *Anchored instruction in engineering education.* Proceedings of New Approaches to Undergraduate Engineering V. Conference.

Campbell, J.O. (1995). Interactive distance learning: Issues and current work. *Journal of Instruction Delivery Systems, 9* (3), 32-35.

De Jean, D., & De Jean, S. B. (1991). *Lotus Notes at work.* New York, NY: Brady.

DeJesus, E.X. (1996, February). How the Internet will replace broadcasting. *Byte*, 51-64.

Gottfried, K. (Personal communication).

Hiltz, S.R. (1996). Personal communication. Newark, NJ: New Jersey Institute of Technology.

Hiltz, S.R., & Turoff, M. (1978). *The network nation: Human communication via computer.* Reading, MA: Addison-Wesley.

Monsanto, C. (Personal communication).

Oakley, B. II, (1996). A virtual classroom approach to learning circuit analysis. *IEEE Transactions on Education.*

Sener, J. (1996, Winter). Developing a distance education engineering program for home-based learners: Lessons learned. *Journal of Instruction Delivery Systems, 10* (1), 41-45.

Sener, J. (1996). ERIC Clearinghouse for Community Colleges. Los Angeles, CA: University of California

Sener, J. (1996, June). *Proceedings.* Association for Advancement of Computing Education (AACE) ED-MEDIA Conference.

Silsbee, R. H., & Draeger, J. (1997). *Exploring the solid state: Guided simulations for teaching.* Cambridge, U.K.: Cambridge University Press.

Watkins, B. L., & Wright, S. J. (Eds.). (1991). *The foundations of American distance education.* Dubuque, IA: Kendall/Hunt.

Wilson, F. S., & Stuart, A. D. (1996). Engineering courses for home-based learners: Distance education using multiple media. *Journal of Instruction Delivery Systems,* Society for Applied Learning Technologies.

ACKNOWLEDGMENTS

The author is indebted to Ralph E. Gomory, President of the Sloan Foundation, for his support of this program and for his ideas. He is equally indebted to members of the Sloan projects without whose contributions this chapter would not have been written.

15

CHALLENGES OF THE LEARNING REVOLUTION

Diana G. Oblinger and Sean C. Rush

Historically, there have been many changes in how education is delivered. The one-room schoolhouse served the needs of an agrarian society to provide literacy and a sense of community. As we industrialized and moved to larger population centers, educational institutions became larger and were organized around grades and classes. In higher education, we began as church sponsored institutions. The Morrill Act created our land grant colleges and universities. In the 1960s, the community college movement established colleges that were community based and designed to support business and industry in the region.

The needs of our society have continued to evolve. The Information Age or the Knowledge Society are terms we use to describe our society's dependence on the rapid exchange of information. Since the early 1980s, the mobility of information has increased due to technology and the Internet. Rio de Janeiro or Seoul can be as close as New York or Boston. Shouldn't education be as mobile as information?

Carried to their ultimate extension, the central issues of this book might be encapsulated in the contrast between the phrases "the campus of the future" or "the future of the campus." Without changes that accommodate the learning revolution, will our campuses have a future?

There are a number of challenges inherent in the learning revolution, either due to higher education traditions or organizational structures. Each institution will need to find its own adaptation of tradition and organization. Our purpose is to highlight some of the issues.

RESISTANCE TO CHANGE

"Resistance to change is a hallmark of higher education. It has been said that changing a college is a lot like moving a cemetery—you don't get a lot of help from the residents. In this case the residents include the education bureaucrats, the faculty, the administrators, the students, and the parents—all stakeholders in the status quo" (O'Banion, 1997).

In O'Banion's book, *A Learning College for the 21st Century*, he describes many of the sources of resistance to change in education. "The bureaucracy of education is what keeps in place the time-bound, place-bound, efficiency-bound, and role-bound architecture. If learning is to become the primary focus of restructuring educational systems, the educational personnel who maintain the bureaucracy will have to be enlisted or they will have to be bypassed or eliminated." But the numbers involved are huge. There are tens of thousands of specialized educational personnel at the federal, regional, state, and county level managing and coordinating educational programs and practices. Each specialist has a vested interest in maintaining his or her territory, and any suggestion of change is a threat to the established order.

Consider one specific group: administrators. Administrators have territories to protect. Because they are almost always directly involved in creating the structures, the rules, and procedures related to their span of control, they may not be comfortable changing their architecture. Moreover, suggested changes hint at something wrong with how business has been conducted. Administrators are not particularly well-equipped to become risk takers: Most want to be loved by the faculty and administrative survival is fragile compared to that of faculty.

College and university presidents face similar challenges in stimulating change. Many presidents are selected for their leadership abilities to secure funds, work with the legislature, or represent the institution to the community. Creating a learning revolution on campus is a challenge which not all presidents are prepared to take on. Often they do not sense support either from within or from outside the institution. There is also an acknowledgement that change will be difficult and time consuming. Many question whether the pain will be worth the gain.

As O'Banion notes, those who are most likely to benefit from the changes of the learning revolution may be among those most resistant to change. "The greatest resistance to placing learning first may come from students and their parents. Students who have figured out the system of schooling and who excel in this system certainly do not want the system changed. Parents often indulge in a nostalgic yearning for the "good old days." The current system has created a nation of passive learners who will resist change, and they will be supported by vocal parents."

FINANCIAL STRUCTURE

Problems arise from the existing financial structure of higher education, as well. First, the funding patterns of higher education are archaic, when considering the need to change. Institutions each raise all the money they can, spend all they get, and spend it in ways that relate closely to the way they spent the money the previous year. There is little relationship in patterns of spending even among institutions that appear on the surface to be quite similar. The institutions spend different amounts per student, and they spend the dollars differently. Apparently, there is no way to state rationally what it ought to cost to educate a student properly (Ehrmann, 1995).

A second source of resistance to changing the status quo is a funding strategy based on inputs rather than results achieved. "The higher education system as currently financed is not adequately serving the public interest. As long as payments are made to colleges and universities on the basis of intent and not results (for example, graduation rates or the demonstrated competence of graduates), inefficiency is built into the financial structure. As long as the higher education financial structure also includes a faculty reward system that encourages them to pay less attention to public need and more to professional demands, research will continue to be valued over teaching and teaching less over teaching more" (Eaton, 1993).

Funding is contingent on student credit hours generated, not learning achieved. "One of the absurdities of current funding formulas is that an institution could utterly fail its educational mission and yet its revenue would remain unaffected. Nothing could facilitate a shift to the learning paradigm more swiftly than funding learning and learning-related institutional outcomes rather than hours of instruction" (Barr & Tagg, 1995).

GOVERNANCE

Cohen and March's classic study of presidential decision-making led them to coin the term "organized anarchy" to describe how higher education institutions function (Cohen & March, 1974). There is a powerful tradition of local control over most of the things that matter: Departments, where the institution's strategy for academic development is formulated in practice, are managed by consensus. Their chairs are temporary stewards who are likely to maintain the status quo. University leaders have become hesitant about attempting major initiatives. The politics of academic life make faculty support critical, and efforts to create major shifts in direction are always risky (Kennedy, 1995).

Institutions tend to operate as systems with fixed relations between inputs and outputs. Economists would describe their core production processes—those that deliver instruction and research—as "sticky." They do not adapt readily to change. Colleges and universities—run for the most part by faculty—have tended to value inputs almost as much as outputs. Not surprisingly, faculty particularly try to maximize the number of inputs in the form of faculty members from their own departments. The stalwart belief that maintaining or increasing faculty numbers is inherently good regardless of market conditions or specific tasks to be performed leads to an environment where restructuring is resisted (Massy, 1995).

Culture

"The traditions of the academy strongly favor individuality, creativity, even heterodoxy. Freedom of action is highly valued. Accountability is viewed as much less important than independence" (Kennedy, 1995). The dilemma is that "the university is a place in which people do exactly what they want to do. Academic freedom means a great deal, but it should not mean freedom from responsibility to students."

Some faculty are reluctant to fully embrace opportunities presented by information technology. This happens not so much because faculty don't understand technology, but rather they fear the loss of control inherent in the student-centered learning environment that technology enables. The faculty credo at many colleges and universities is "our place, our time, our way" not "your place, your time, your way" (Massy, 1995).

Some faculty may resist technology in the classroom because, never having had instruction in how to teach, they teach only as they themselves were taught, which for many means exclusively lecturing (Rutherford & Grana, 1995). Yet many faculty are either leading or enabling the transformation of higher education. They do so by curricular innovation, through network scholarship and research, by engineering highly effective learning applications and modules, and by dedicating themselves to the education of individual students under their guidance. Some faculty are highly resistant to change—but by no means all. The major impediment to faculty embracing new roles and responsibilities is the absence of an effective articulation of these roles and their place in a transformed learning vision for the 21st century (Dolence & Norris, 1995).

The risk is that the technological revolution in the academy will be stalled unless the faculty's immense intellectual resources are brought to bear on realizing the promise of technology. That willingness depends primarily on the faculty's capacity to be deeply self-reflective, to master its anxiety that these changes threaten the professor's traditional role and status (Miller, 1995).

CURRICULAR CHANGES

In contrast to the rapid changes in the workplace and the explosion of information, higher education's degree programs are relatively stable; some would say inflexible as well. On many campuses, curriculum design is essentially a process of adding new courses to a historical base. True reassessment of needs, determination of competencies, and reevaluation of objectives is the exception. Skill requirements on the job changed at a rate four to five times faster than curriculum and organizational changes in our schools, leaving a gap between what students learn in the classroom and what is expected of them in the workplace (Daggett, 1992).

FEARS ABOUT TECHNOLOGY

Technology Will Replace the Professor

There is an anxiety that technology will supplant the faculty. It may indeed supplant certain professorial functions, like simple information transmittal. But the professor becomes indispensable in other functions, such as providing students with a sense of the whole, with a rubric of essential questions and possible paths to follow in seeking their answers (Miller, 1995). Rather than standing at the front of the class as the complete, perfected knower, the professor surfs alongside students, sharing curiosity, delight, and tumbles—not a repository of answers but a model questioner and problem solver.

Technology Will Dehumanize Instruction

One concern often expressed about technology is that students will, by using machines, somehow become machine-like. Nothing is actually more likely to turn most students into automatons than the typical 250-person lecture (Miller, 1995).

In fact, students often find technology both liberating and more personal than traditional instruction. In studies of asynchronous learning environments, one consistent finding is that students feel they have more access to the professor than they did in traditional lecture courses. In addition, they feel they have more interaction with other students. Results from computer-mediated conferencing studies show

- On-line courses are distinguished by active peer-to-peer discussion and exchange.
- Messaging is fairly evenly distributed among students. On-line interaction displays fewer extremes such as dominant input by a few individuals and little or no participation by anyone else in class.
- There are increased opportunities for access offered by the asynchronous, place-independent environment.
- Asynchronicity provides learners with time to formulate ideas and contribute responses. Students report that asynchronicity enables them to participate more actively and effectively.
- Group interaction motivates students and exposes them to a diverse range of perspectives. Students read input from all other students, rather than only the ideas of the instructor and a few students (Harasim, 1993).

Students do not necessarily require the kind of socializing that goes on in most classrooms (Jaeger, 1991). "Teaching on-line can and does foster a sense of closeness between student and instructor."

Use of Technology Will Lead to a Decline in Literacy

Many are concerned that the use of technology, particularly multimedia, will result in declining reading skills and critical thinking. The fear is that entertainment will be substituted for substance.

It is revealing to consider the last great shift in information processing—the one from orality to literacy as mediated by the technology of the alphabet. Socrates lamented the destruction of memory by writing. Plato predicted, correctly, the loss of the capacity to memorize large bodies of acoustical material (Miller, 1995).

The use of written records for teaching—a practice well-established by the fifth century B.C.—was one of education's great technological innovations. As Plato recounts in *Phaedrus*, however, many thought written materials made learning impersonal and destroyed the intimate relationship between student and tutor (Massy, 1995). However, printed information has become an accepted part of our society. Books are a labor-saving technology that has been rendered invisible by its very omnipresence (Miller, 1995).

Although books may have become an accepted technology, the computer and communications technologies are being questioned. The justification must be that they yield learning benefits. Even in young children, the use of technology is showing benefits. Many children use the Internet. "Kids learn to ask better questions, to make better arguments, and to present themselves more positively over the net. Beginning with e-mail, children concentrate harder to express themselves when sending a message to another country or state. They work on vocabulary and clarity as never before. When they know a student in Stockholm, or an engineer at NASA will be writing back, children recognize the difference between slang and formal language" (Ellsworth, 1994).

In higher education, there is an increasing use of learning networks. Learning networks are designed to encourage active participation in group learning and knowledge building. Knowledge building implies that understanding grows out of interacting with information and ideas such as reconstructing ideas, setting ideas within frameworks, viewing multiple perspectives on ideas, questions, and posing theories or hypotheses about ideas. This contrasts with the more passive learning strategies in which knowledge is transmitted from expert or teacher to the learner. In the passive model, the learner reproduces information and tells what she or he has learned without having transformed the knowledge.

As individuals bring different background knowledge, experience, and interests to the learning situation, they make unique connections in building their knowledge. Students and teachers both play a role in facilitating and generating knowledge. Students are encouraged to question each other's understanding and explain their own perspectives. These opportunities help hand over responsibility for knowledge generation to the learners (Maxwell, 1995).

Early experiences with learning networks have demonstrated the potential for significant educational gains. Networks offer learners and teachers access to new ideas, perspectives, cultures, and information—enriching locally available resources (Harasim et al., 1995). Students can easily interact with their fellow classmates, regardless of the fact that they may be spread across the country. This capability to engage in substantive discussion with other students about course content is another dimension that seems to be missing from many traditional university classes today. Another element that is different for students in on-line classes is the opportunity to see the work of others and to compare their ideas with those of their classmates. People can not only learn from their own work, but they also can learn from everyone else. By its very nature, this kind of on-line environment encourages collaboration and group interaction (Kearsley et al., 1995).

Ensuring Equity

As we increasingly face the prospect of a two-tiered society, it is important to seek mechanisms that will ensure equity among all. More and more people are turning to higher education in hopes of improving their economic well-being. The difference in earning potential between a college graduate and a worker without a degree has never been greater. As many scholars have documented, the quality of life for those who have participated in higher education is typically greater.

Two major factors make higher education inaccessible to those who may need it most: temporal constraints of time and location and cost. Networked delivery of education has the potential to reduce both of these barriers.

Network-based learning can promote diversity by significantly improving access to affordable, high quality college learning for traditionally under-represented students such as the economically disadvantaged, the disabled, those who are geographically isolated, as well as workers and students with different learning styles. The need for human capital in our society is immense. We cannot afford to miss the opportunity to maximize human potential by allowing some learners to remain disenfranchised.

The Potential of Technology

Access to information technology can enhance learning in several ways. One of the challenges of the learning revolution is for the stakeholders in education to believe there is greater potential benefit to using information technology than maintaining the status quo. Another challenge is to expose stakeholders to the potential of technology. Many resist change because they are uninformed.

Access to information technology can enhance learning in several ways. When compared to traditional classes, student satisfaction with on-line courses is higher; GPA and other measures of student achievement are the same or better; a higher level of critical thinking and problem solving is reported; and there is often more discussion among students and instructors in a course. Instructors are able to track the progress of their students in a detailed way and have a better understanding of what students are/are not learning. Finally, computer networking provides a more authentic learning environment in the sense that students can easily communicate with other educational professionals outside of the class if they desire (Kearsley et al., 1995). More specifically:

- *Achievement.* Educational technology has demonstrated a significant positive effect on achievement. Positive effects have been found for all major subject areas, in preschool through higher education, and for both regular education and special needs students (Sivin-Kachala & Bialo, 1995).
- *Attitude.* Education technology has been found to have positive effects on student attitudes toward learning and on student self-concept. Students felt more successful, were more motivated to learn, and had increased self-confidence and self-esteem when using technology. This is particularly true when technology allows learners to control their own learning (Sivin-Kachala & Bialo, 1995).
- *Learner-centered.* Introducing technology into the learning environment has been shown to make learning more student-centered, to encourage cooperative learning, and to stimulate increased instructor/student interaction (Sivin-Kachala & Bialo, 1995).
- *Interaction.* Courses for which computer-based networks were used increased student-student and student-instructor interaction, increased student-instructor interaction with lower-performing students, and did not decrease the traditional forms of communication used (Sivin-Kachala & Bialo, 1995).
- *Pacing.* "The computer makes it possible for the learner to make choices that determine both the kind of material presented and the rate of information flow. Hypertext or hypermedia documents open up the ability to follow relationships among ideas. The timely access to relevant information is intellectually arousing for the student and assists in discovery learning. The interactive format makes it possible for the presentation of information to occur under natural conditions of inquiry, that is, when the learner has framed a question and is receptive to the answer" (Noblitt, 1995).
- *Retention.* "Many have noticed improved retention from interactive instruction. Students seem to remember when they are actively involved in absorbing data, and it appears that a combination of

media, including visual and audio cues, tends to make a stronger impression" (Tynan, 1993).

THE CAMPUS OF THE FUTURE

We see an immense opportunity to establish forms of electronic-based collaboration—from the student level to the institutional level—that can bring about major improvements in both access and learning, while meeting the legitimate public and institutional concerns about cost and quality. This is not to suggest that technology-based learning should replace traditional pedagogy; this is not an either/or proposition. Computer-assisted, self-directed, electronically-mediated learning will work for some institutions but not for others, for students in some fields, but not for all students in all fields (Mingle, 1995). As institutions move toward the creation of their campus of the future it will be important to understand the nuances of where networked learning is the most appropriate alternative or supplement to traditional residential education, and how it can best be implemented.

In fact, there is an opportunity for a new level of multi-state, multi-institutional, multi-national collaboration to provide postsecondary education and training through existing and emerging global networks. Collaborating institutions would deliver modules, courses, and degrees to individuals and groups of learners who interact with faculty and with organized learning materials, both in real-time and delayed-time (asynchronous) mode. Their audience would consist of both the distant learner who is not able to be physically present on campus, the on-campus student who wishes a more individualized, self-paced, self-directed learning experience, and the student who finds real value in combining both approaches to learning.

As Farrington states, the most likely future is one which accommodates more options for learners. Residential colleges and universities will still be in demand for many learners. However, technology expands the reach and range of these traditional settings. Hybrid organizations may be formed where students can synthesize on-campus with on-line experiences. Other students, particularly working adults, may opt for on-line educational experiences that provide them with the education and flexibility they need.

The Residential Experience

Communication, computing, and networking technologies have a potentially significant role in enhancing the residential college or university experience. For example, the on-campus student who wishes a more individualized, self-paced, self-directed learning experience may find that technology helps achieve that desire. The network can expand options for interaction among faculty and students. External experts are more easily accessed. The opportunity for faculty to individualize and personalize contact with students is increased.

The Hybrid Experience

Some learners will seek a mixture of face-to-face experiences and network-based education. With a goal of reducing the time to degree, some students may choose to complete courses in residence while simultaneously fulfilling other graduation requirements on-line. The flexibility of this hybrid experience most likely will be suited to more mature students who merge their education with job and family responsibilities.

The On-Line Experience

The on-line experience will allow colleges and universities to project themselves far beyond their physical locations. Already, hundreds of institutions offer courses on-line. Perhaps more appropriate for adult learners than the 18-year old freshman, on-line experiences offer educational opportunities to millions of learners. Unconstrained by time, location, or other factors, the on-line experience is well-suited to learners who cannot access education through traditional means. The on-line format can significantly expand the availability of continuing education programs and offerings for recreational learners as well.

SUMMARY

What should be done to make the learning revolution a reality? Some theorize that a crisis must precede major change. Crises have been predicted since the 1980s, yet there has not been widespread change. Others advocate wresting control from higher education. Whatever the answer, it will not be simple.

The learning revolution is about human potential. Although there are many challenges to implementing the learning revolution, there is too much at stake to not take the risks that will be necessary for success. Certainly, the inhibitors are more social than technological.

More than anything, the learning revolution is a call to action. We hope higher education will accept the challenge.

REFERENCES

Barr, R., & Tagg, J. (1995, November/December). From teaching to learning: A new paradigm for undergraduate education. *Change*, 12-25.

Campbell, O. (1995). Interactive distance learning: Issues and current work. *Journal of Instruction Delivery Systems, 9* (3), 32-25.

Cohen, M. D., & March, J. G. (1974). *Leadership and ambiguity: The American college president.* New York, NY: McGraw-Hill.

Daggett, W. R. (1992). *Preparing students for the 1990s and beyond.* Unpublished.

Dolence, M. G., & Norris, D. M. (1995). *Transforming higher education: A vision for learning in the 21st century.* Society for College and University Planning.

Eaton, J. S. (1993). *The case for restructuring higher education finance.* Council for Aid to Education.

Ehrmann, S. C. (1995). Asking the right questions: What does research tell us about technology and higher learning? *Change, 27* (2), 20-28.

Ellsworth, J. H. (1994). *Education on the Internet.* Indianapolis, IN: Sams Publishing.

Harasim, L. (1993). Collaborating in cyberspace: Using computer conferences as a group learning environment. *Interactive Learning Environments, 3* (2), 119-130.

Harasim, L., Hiltz, S., Teles, L., & Turoff, M. (1995). *Learning networks: A field guide to teaching and learning on-line.* Cambridge, MA: MIT Press.

Jaeger, G. (1991, April). Description of a freshman computer class taught completely on-line by computer and modem hosted on a BBS Spring/Fall 1990. *Ed, 5* (4), 8-13.

Kearsley, G., Lynch, W., & Wizer, D. (1995). The effectiveness and impact of on-line learning in graduate education. *Educational Technology, 35* (6), 37-42.

Kennedy, D. (1995, May/June). Another century's end, another revolution for higher education. *Change, 27* (3), 8-15.

Massy, W. F. (1995). *Leveraged learning: Technology's role in restructuring higher education.* Stanford Forum for Higher Education Futures.

Maxwell, L. (1995). Integrating open learning and distance education. *Educational Technology, 35* (6), 43-48.

Miller, M. A. (1995). Technoliteracy and the new professor. *New Literary History, 26* (3), 601-612.

Mingle, J. R. (1995, October). *A proposal for a multistate or multiinstitutional consortium (charter university) for developing and certifying electronically-delivered curriculum.* Unpublished.

Noblitt, J. S. (1995). Redefining the boundaries of language study. In C. Kramsch (Ed.), *Issues in language program direction.* Boston, MA: Heinle and Heinle.

O'Banion, T. (1997). *A learning college for the 21st century..* Washington, DC: ACE/American Association of Community Colleges.

Rutherford, L. H., & Grana, S. J. (1995). Retrofitting academe: Adapting faculty attitudes and practices to technology. *THE Journal, 23* (2), 82-86.

Sivin-Kachala, J., & Bialo, E. R. (1995). *Report on the effectiveness of technology in schools, 1990–1994.* Washington, DC: Software Pulishers Association.

Tynan, D. (1993). Multimedia goes on the job—just in time. *New Media, 3,* 38-46.

INDEX